Presidents from
Hayes through McKinley,
1877–1901

Recent Titles in
The President's Position: Debating the Issues

PRESIDENTS FROM HAYES THROUGH McKINLEY, 1877–1901

Debating the Issues in Pro and Con Primary Documents

AMY H. STURGIS

The President's Position: Debating the Issues
Mark Byrnes, Series Editor

GREENWOOD PRESS
Westport, Connecticut • London

Library of Congress Cataloging-in-Publication Data

Presidents from Hayes through McKinley : debating the issues in pro and
    con primary documents / [compiled by] Amy H. Sturgis.
        p.   cm.—(The president's position)
    Includes bibliographical references and index.
        ISBN 0–313–31712–7 (alk. paper)
        1. United States—Politics and government—1865–1900—Sources.
        2. United States—Foreign relations—1865–1921—Sources.
        3. Presidents—United States—History—19th century—Sources.   I. Sturgis,
    Amy H., 1971–   II. Series.
    E661.P745   2003
    973.8'092'2—dc21   2003048523

British Library Cataloguing in Publication Data is available.

Library of Congress Catalog Card Number: 2003048523
ISBN: 0–313–31712–7

First published in 2003

Greenwood Press, 88 Post Road West, Westport, CT 06881
An imprint of Greenwood Publishing Group, Inc.
www.greenwood.com

Printed in the United States of America

The paper used in this book complies with the
Permanent Paper Standard issued by the National
Information Standards Organization (Z39.48–1984).

10 9 8 7 6 5 4 3 2 1

For Larry,
with love
in the grand way

CONTENTS

SERIES FOREWORD

When he was running for president in 1932, Franklin D. Roosevelt declared that America needed "bold, persistent experimentation" in its public policy. "It is common sense to take a method and try it," FDR said. "If it fails, admit it frankly and try another. But above all, try something." At President Roosevelt's instigation, the nation did indeed take a number of steps to combat the Great Depression. In the process, the president emerged as the clear leader of American public policy. Most scholars see FDR's administration as the birth of the "modern presidency," in which the president dominates both domestic and foreign policy.

Even before FDR, however, presidents played a vital role in the making of public policy. Policy changes advocated by the presidents—often great changes—have always influenced the course of events, and have always sparked debate from the presidents' opponents. The outcomes of this process have had tremendous effects on the lives of Americans. The President's Position: Debating the Issues examines the stands the presidents have taken on the major political, social, and economic issues of their times as well as the stands taken by their opponents. The series combines description and analysis of those issues with excerpts from primary documents that illustrate the position of the presidents and their opponents. The result is an informative, accessible, and comprehensive look at the crucial connection between presidents and policy. These volumes will assist students doing historical research, preparing for debates, or fulfilling critical thinking assignments. The general reader interested in American history and politics will also find the series interesting and helpful.

Several important themes about the president's role in policy making emerge from the series. First, and perhaps most important, is how greatly the president's involvement in policy has expanded over the years. This has happened because the range of areas in which the national government acts has grown dramatically and because modern presidents—unlike most of their predecessors—see taking the lead in policy making as part of their job. Second, certain issues have confronted most presidents over history; tax and tariff policy, for example, was important for both George Washington and Bill Clinton, and for most of the presidents in between. Third, the emergence of the United States as a world power around the beginning of the twentieth century made foreign policy issues more numerous and more pressing. Finally, in the American system, presidents cannot form policy through decrees; they must persuade members of Congress, other politicians, and the general public to follow their lead. This key fact makes the policy debates between presidents and their opponents vitally important.

This series comprises nine volumes, organized chronologically, each of which covers the presidents who governed during that particular time period. Volume one looks at the presidents from George Washington through James Monroe; volume two, John Quincy Adams through James K. Polk; volume three, Zachary Taylor through Ulysses S. Grant; volume four, Rutherford B. Hayes through William McKinley; volume five, Theodore Roosevelt through Calvin Coolidge; volume six, Herbert Hoover through Harry Truman; volume seven, Dwight D. Eisenhower through Lyndon Johnson; volume eight, Richard Nixon through Jimmy Carter; and volume nine, Ronald Reagan through Bill Clinton. Each president from Washington through Clinton is covered, although the number of issues discussed under each president varies according to how long they served in office and how actively they pursued policy goals. Volumes six through nine—which cover the modern presidency—examine three presidencies each, while the earlier volumes include between five and seven presidencies each.

Every volume begins with a general introduction to the period it covers, providing an overview of the presidents who served and the issues they confronted. The section on each president opens with a detailed overview of the president's position on the relevant issues he confronted and the initiatives he took, and closes with a list of recommended readings. Up to fifteen issues are covered per presidency. The discussion of each issue features an introduction, the positions taken by the president and his opponents, how the issue was resolved, and the long-term effects of the issue. This is followed by excerpts from two primary documents, one representing the president's position and the other representing his opponents' position. Also included in each volume is a timeline of significant events of the era and a bibliography of sources for students and others interested in further research.

As the most prominent individual in American politics, the president receives enormous attention from the media and the public. The statements, actions, travels, and even the personal lives of presidents are constantly scrutinized. Yet it is the presidents' work on public policy that most directly affects American citizens—a fact that is sometimes overlooked. This series is presented, in part, as a reminder of the importance of the president's position.

Mark Byrnes

ACKNOWLEDGMENTS

My thanks go to Mark Byrnes for inviting me to contribute another volume in this series and Kevin Ohe for guiding this project. I am indebted to the staffs of the Belmont University and Vanderbilt University libraries for their tireless assistance, in particular Belmont's Paige Carter. Professor Susan Hoffman offered much-appreciated insights regarding the organization of the volume. The Shire's Virginia Lórien has my gratitude for her enthusiastic editorial involvement. I am grateful for the ongoing encouragement and support I receive from my sister, parents, grandparents, friends, and colleagues. Most importantly, I thank Dr. Larry M. Hall for kindnesses far too numerous to count. Any errors remaining in this work are my own.

TIMELINE

1876

November 7   The presidential election is held but its outcome remains contested.

1877

January 29   The U.S. Congress creates the Election Commission to investigate the Tilden-Hayes Affair and determine the outcome of the presidential election.

March 2   The Election Commission created by the U.S. Congress votes along party lines to recognize Rutherford B. Hayes as president.

March 5   Rutherford B. Hayes is inaugurated as president.

May   Hayes begins withdrawing troops from the Southern states.

July 21   Hayes issues a proclamation denouncing the strikes against the railroads that began in Baltimore and soon spread.

October 5   Chief Joseph surrenders to U.S. forces in the Bear Paw Mountains.

1878

February 28   Hayes vetoes the Bland-Allison Act, which Congress then passes over his veto.

November 2   James A. Garfield is elected president.

1881

March 4   James A. Garfield is inaugurated as president.

July 2   James A. Garfield is shot in the back by Charles J. Guiteau in
               Washington, D.C.

September 19   James A. Garfield dies. Chester A. Arthur is sworn in as presi-
               dent.

1882

April 4   Arthur vetoes the Chinese Exclusion Act and its twenty-year ban
               on immigration.

August 1   Arthur vetoes an internal improvements bill for rivers and har-
               bors.

1883

January 16   The Pendleton Civil Service Act becomes law, fulfilling Garfield's
               wishes for civil service reform.

November 4   Grover Cleveland is elected president.

1885

March 4   Grover Cleveland is inaugurated as president.

1886

November 18   Chester A. Arthur dies.

1887

February 8   The Dawes Severalty Act becomes law and institutes allotment.

February 11   Cleveland vetoes the Civil War Pensions Bill.

1888

November 6   Benjamin Harrison is elected president.

1889

March 4   Benjamin Harrison is inaugurated as president.

1890

July 2   Harrison signs the Sherman Anti-Trust Act into law.

July 14   Harrison signs the Sherman Silver Purchase Act into law.

1892

November 8   Grover Cleveland is elected president.

1893

January 17   Rutherford B. Hayes dies.

March 4   Grover Cleveland is inaugurated for his second term as president.

1894

May 11   The Pullman Strike begins.

1895

December 17   While discussing Venezuela, Cleveland adds the Olney Corollary to the Monroe Doctrine.

1896

July 9   William Jennings Bryan delivers his "Cross of Gold" speech.

November 3   William McKinley is elected president.

1897

March 4   William McKinley is inaugurated as president.

1898

February 9   The Spanish Minister to Washington's intercepted letter is published.

February 15   The U.S. battleship *Maine* explodes and sinks in Havana harbor.

April 20   Congress grants McKinley the right to use force in securing the independence of Cuba.

April 25   Congress passes an official (and retroactive) declaration of war against Spain.

December 10   The Treaty of Paris is signed, ending the Spanish-American War.

1899

September 6   Notes explaining the Open Door Policy are sent to U.S. diplomats overseas to be circulated.

1900

November 6   William McKinley is reelected president.

1901

March 4   William McKinley is inaugurated for his second term as president.

March 13   Benjamin Harrison dies.

September 6   William McKinley is shot in the stomach by Leon Czolgosz in Buffalo, New York.

September 14   William McKinley dies.

               Theodore Roosevelt is sworn in as president.

1908

June 24   Grover Cleveland dies.

INTRODUCTION

The period from 1877 to 1901 marked the end of one United States—a country on which the Civil War still hung heavily, the divided nation of Reconstruction, a land of economic depression, sectional hostility, and governmental corruption—and the beginning of another—an empire, an international power that both negotiated with and fought against European nations successfully, a country with a rebounding economy, vigorous industry, and restored faith. The path that led from one United States to the other was fraught with controversies, some violent, and lessons learned by dramatic and costly mistakes. At least one arguably great president emerged from the era. Two more did not survive it.

During the era, which is often known as the Gilded Age, the nation expanded as settlers moved west, displacing native nations. Immigrants entered at the highest rate in the country's history and industrialism brought the growth of cities and urban areas while economic difficulties brought hardships to rural countrysides. With this geographic expansion came the railroads, and with industrial expansion came corporations, company towns, and monopolies. Labor became organized, as did agrarian interests.

Most notably, two "isms" became players on the national scene. Populism served as a reaction against change. Drawing its ranks from the lower agrarian and working classes—the so-called "common men"—populism criticized technological, political, economic, and intellectual innovation. In particular, populism of this era united the agrarian backlash against industrialism and the labor backlash against existing power structures. Populism played a key role in the debates over monetary policy, as many populists supported free silver coinage and inflationary policies to help debtors and the poor.

Anarchism also enjoyed a resurgence at this time. Based on the ideal of noncoercion, anarchism divided into multiple subgroups. Two in particular influenced the era: anarcho-capitalism, or anarcho-individualism, which held the individual as the building block of the world before any society or government, and revolved around a theory of individual, or natural, rights; and anarcho-communism, which held to collectivism instead of individualism, and sought a redistribution of wealth and resources. Anarcho-individualism offered critiques of the government's legitimacy and monopoly over money. Anarcho-communism played a small role in the assassination of a president.

Perhaps the most telling change over the period from 1877 to 1901 was the shift in the U.S. gaze from itself, through domestic policy, to the world, from the Western Hemisphere with the Monroe Doctrine to the far reaches of the planet with the Open Door Policy. The nation came into its own as a figure on the world stage, a significant step considering it was nearly two separate nations under Reconstruction a few years earlier.

As the United States became a greater world power, so too did the presidents seek to become more assertive leaders. With the exception of Benjamin Harrison, who relinquished a great deal of control to Congress and party leaders, the presidents of the era were driven leaders who actively campaigned for office, advocated legislation, and made policy. Grover Cleveland, for example, used the veto as it had never been used before (and more often, as well, vetoing more measures than all previous twenty-one executives combined), and William McKinley not only dominated foreign policy decisions but also personally choreographed the Spanish-American War.

If the shift from domestic to international concerns was the most obvious policy shift during the era, and the rise of presidential power a corresponding new development, then the most dramatic continuity across the years was a thread of tragedy unparalleled in the following century. In 1877 the memory of President Abraham Lincoln's 1865 assassination was still fresh. The Gilded Age added two more horrific deaths to his. President James Garfield's assassination, like Lincoln's, was personal; in Garfield's case, a frustrated office seeker sought to replace Garfield with his vice president, who belonged to the same party faction as the assassin. William McKinley died not for his policies or personality, but simply because he was the president at the time, and a deeply troubled young man took exception to presidential power and prestige in general. Several assassination attempts followed—including McKinley's succeeding vice president, Teddy Roosevelt—but none were successful until John Kennedy was killed in 1963. To add to the cycle of tragedy, Chester Arthur inherited office a dying man, and suffered with disease throughout his administration only to die shortly thereafter.

Issues, as well as tragedy, united the presidents during the era. The entire period encountered economic depression, which peaked with the Panic of 1893. Only by McKinley's administration did the economy feel the first signs of rebound. Almost all of the executives, then, wrestled with economic policy, especially the questions of currency (the gold standard versus bimetallism) and the tariff (protectionism versus free trade). Likewise, western expansion kept the question of native American policy relevant across the years. Labor strikes and their effects challenged more than one president, as did the question of Hawaii's relationship to the United States. Each administration had its own flavor and priorities, yet many of the same debates resurfaced time and again.

The era began with tremendous controversy over the election of 1876. The so-called Tilden-Hayes Affair, with its confusion of election returns and competing reports from key states, led Congress to create a special Election Commission to determine whether Republican Rutherford B. Hayes or Democrat Samuel J. Tilden was president. The commission voted on party lines for Hayes, thus giving him the White House but also robbing him of some of the legitimacy a straightforward election, or even a nonpartisan decision, would have earned. This opening twist to the Hayes administration story was particularly ironic since Hayes, unlike his predecessor Ulysses S. Grant, had built a career above reproach and supported the cause of civil service reform, or the improvement of the administrative structures and processes of government.

Hayes ended Reconstruction with his New Departure policy, which withdrew the occupying U.S. troops from the former Confederate states of the South and emphasized a return to local and state self-rule. Hayes also, like many presidents after him, advocated the gold standard, or hard money, over the inflationary policies of greenback and silver advocates, who believed that increased currency helped debtors. Hayes both won and lost on economic questions: he succeeded in executing the Resumption Act despite protest from populist factions, but Congress overrode his veto of the Bland-Allison Act, and so the silver dollar was restored as legal tender. On two issues, labor strikes and Amerindians,

Hayes maintained a pattern of force that offered stopgap if not satisfactory short-term resolutions and prolonged the problems for later presidents to encounter. Hayes left office by his own choice, preferring not to run again, and turned the White House over to his fellow party member and Ohio native, James Garfield.

Garfield, a dark horse candidate, initially wished to decline the Republican nomination, but eventually changed his mind and campaigned for the White House. His positions for the most part matched those of Hayes, though he seemed to articulate them with more fervor. Like Hayes, Garfield advocated hard money on questions of economic policy and, also like Hayes, appreciated the remaining problems in the U.S. South. Garfield stressed the importance of education—for African Americans in particular—as a means of creating knowledgeable voters who could protect their own rights and help re-create the South as a viable and progressive political region.

Most importantly, Garfield advocated civil service reform. As Hayes did, Garfield encountered conflict with Republican Senator Roscoe Conkling, who ran the New York patronage machine. Garfield fought against the spoils system and, practicing what he preached, tried to unite every faction of his party by representing each in his cabinet. The fact that his vice president was a Stalwart and a conservative follower of Conkling's proved especially important. The nation as a whole saw the need for civil service reform when Garfield was shot and killed only months into his term by a frustrated office seeker who wished Stalwart vice president Chester Arthur to become chief executive. The assassination not only ended Garfield's life but also changed Arthur's forever.

Inheriting the White House from his assassinated predecessor was doubly hard for Arthur, who, as a past participant in the New York patronage machine, seemed to embody what Garfield had fought against and, in a sense, the issue for which he had died. Rather than using his executive authority to take policy in a different direction, Arthur, now convinced of the need for civil service reform, used his office to champion Garfield's cause. The resulting Pendleton Civil Service Act created a national civil service based on merit instead of politics or partisan affiliation (or, for that matter, race or creed or national origin). Arthur also tackled ongoing issues such as Amerindian affairs, for which he devised the idea of allotting government-sanctioned land to individual native Americans, and internal improvements, on which Arthur upheld the example provided by former president James Monroe of insisting that national funds be spent on national, not regional, projects.

Arthur also weighed in on questions dealing with minorities in the United States. He criticized the practice of Mormon polygamy in the Utah territory and called for a vigorous enforcement of the law against it, leading to the Mormon abandonment of that article of faith and eventual statehood for Utah. He also vetoed a Chinese Exclusion Act calling for a twenty-year ban on Chinese immigrants of the laboring class on the basis that it violated U.S. treaty agreements with China. This led to a weaker ten-year ban on such immigration. Arthur's strong positions, most notably on civil service reform, led to the public's reevaluation of a man it had first mistrusted. His kidney disease, more than any political opponent, ended his political career.

Grover Cleveland first took the White House in 1885, and went on to become the only president to serve two terms nonconsecutively. His plainspoken, defiant, stubborn, and achingly honest disposition (even about his own failings, such as his past affair and illegitimate child) set him apart from his more polished and politically savvy predecessors. Few had wielded such power, however; Cleveland used and enjoyed the executive's veto power and sought to end waste and corruption when possible. Though the anarcho-individualist critique of the U.S. government claimed the system was illegitimate, Cleveland believed that the peaceful transfer of power, such as that from the Republican party with Arthur to the Democratic party with his own election, proved that the U.S. Constitution really did capture the will and consent of the people.

Though Cleveland belonged to the party opposite his immediate predecessors, he shared the conservative economic policy of Hayes, Garfield, and Arthur and defended the gold standard. He challenged waste when he saw it—even daring to take unpopular stands, as when he vetoed the Civil War Pensions Bill as unnecessary and expensive despite sentimental rhetoric in favor of providing for all who fought to preserve the union. Cleveland also fought against protectionism, citing the unfairness of using public power to promote private gain by raising tariffs to benefit some domestic industries. In this latter battle, he chose to make his stand near the end of his term, thus causing the following election to revolve around the tariff issue. Republican Benjamin Harrison secured pro-business funds in support of the tariff and managed to pull out a win in the electoral college, even though Cleveland won the popular vote. The protectionism issue cost Cleveland in the short term, but it eventually cost Harrison in the long term.

In effect, in 1889 Harrison moved into the White House that Protectionism Built, creating an administration anchored almost solely to one issue. Unlike the risk-taking, veto-wielding, bold-speaking Cleveland, Harrison was not a leader and he allowed Congress and Republican party officials to take the initiative. Congress happily spent in the absence of close supervision, making quick work of depleting the surplus Cleveland had gathered in the U.S. Treasury. Three important measures passed during Harrison's term: the Sherman Anti-Trust Act, the Sherman Silver Purchase Act, and the McKinley Tariff Act. The Sherman Anti-Trust Act responded to public fears about monopolies and the concentration of industrial power in the hands of the few who colluded and manipulated the market. It outlawed any conspiracy that hindered trade. The Sherman Silver Purchase Act required the government to buy even more silver bullion than did the Bland-Allison Act. It was a victory for soft money advocates, tolerated by the ambivalent Harrison in order to gain support for the tariff.

The McKinley Tariff Act raised the highest duties in the nation's history on imports, thus encouraging consumers to buy domestic rather than international goods. Despite several measures to placate agrarian interests, however, the protectionist measure backfired. Farmers saw their prices continue to fall while the cost for necessary items rose. Western and Southern interests turned against the tariff and therefore against Harrison. He lost his bid for reelection to none other than Grover Cleveland. Cleveland not only defeated Harrison but also blocked Harrison's proposed annexation of Hawaii on the basis that the United States had wrongly intervened in Hawaiian affairs and thus come by the land through unconscionable means.

Cleveland's 1893 return to the presidency coincided with a national financial panic resulting in a severe depression. Cleveland chose to use federal force against a Chicago-based railroad strike despite the wishes of the governor of Illinois, a move that terminated any labor support he had enjoyed. He further alienated populists through his necessary but unpopular moves to stabilize the economy, namely working with banking leaders to secure more gold for the U.S. Treasury and repealing the Sherman Silver Purchase Act. In international affairs, Cleveland won a victory by successfully forcing Great Britain to accept arbitration in its boundary dispute with Venezuela about that country's boundary with British Guiana, but his expansion of the Monroe Doctrine was neither glamorous nor climactic, and public enthusiasm was limited. A rebellion in Cuba against Spanish colonial forces proved much more important to mainstream U.S. citizens. Cleveland, however, chose not to intervene on behalf of those many saw as freedom fighters, and instead sent mixed messages to Spain that brought no resolution to the violence.

Though considered in retrospect by many to be the greatest president of the era thanks to his honesty and initiative, Cleveland lost not only the next election but even his party's nomination, becoming the only president repudiated by his party. Populist orator William Jennings Bryan received the Democratic presidential nomination in Cleveland's place. The non-interventionist Bryan lost, however, to Republican William McKinley, who made the United States into an empire. Cleveland's political defeat marked the last time a pro-business, conservative Democrat would serve as chief executive.

When William McKinley entered office in 1897, he inherited both positive and negative situations from the second Cleveland administration. On the one hand, the economy that Cleveland had worked so hard to heal began to rebound, and McKinley accepted much of the credit. He was thus able to see his own policies, such as a protective tariff even higher than the one passed during Harrison's term, realized. Like Cleveland, McKinley championed the gold standard against advocates of inflationary, soft-money measures.

On the other hand, Cleveland left a war between Cuban revolutionaries and Spanish colonialists raging scant miles from the U.S. coast, wreaking havoc with U.S. trade and commerce and endangering U.S. citizens on the Caribbean island. At first McKinley tried to negotiate with Spain, but events—including the publication of an intercepted letter by the Spanish minister to the United States and the sinking of a U.S. battleship harbored in Cuba—conspired to force McKinley's hand. Then, against the protests of anti-imperialists, McKinley led the nation in a successful war against Spain and in return received Guam, Puerto Rico, and the Philippines from the Spanish. McKinley held tightly to control over these lands, even fighting Filipinos who struggled for their own independence, and earned the criticism that a democracy like the United States could not reconcile its political principles and imperialistic, dominating behavior. Some said that, in fighting Spain, the United States became the very thing that it had struggled against. McKinley moved the United States a step closer to empire, then, by annexing Hawaii and proposing the Open Door Policy, allowing economic access to China. McKinley moved U.S. foreign policy far beyond the Monroe Doctrine to make the nation a player, not only in the Western Hemisphere but also on the world stage.

When he was assassinated in 1901, McKinley left the presidency to his new vice president, Teddy Roosevelt. The former leader of the "Rough Riders" 1st Volunteer Cavalry in Cuba, Roosevelt followed McKinley's policy of making the United States an imperial world power. In just a few short years, the country had developed from a divided and still war-torn child of Reconstruction to a dominating presence that could challenge the powers of Europe and their policies in both hemispheres.

The transition from a Reconstruction nation to a world power cost many lives—not the least of which were those of two presidents—and left unresolved issues that later presidents would revisit with only varied success, such as the "problems" of labor strikes, African-American opportunity, Amerindian rights, and imperialism. The gold standard advocated by so many of the era's leaders would not survive the Great Depression of the 1930s, and the limited-government sensibility of national funds only for national projects would crumble as the state government–national government balance failed under the New Deal. Concerns about corruption in the nation's highest offices would recur repeatedly with presidents such as Nixon and Clinton, and the 2000 election would underscore the same kind of national anxieties that surrounded the election of 1876. What is clear, however, is that the presidents from Hayes through McKinley shaped a nineteenth-century nation and prepared it for the world of the twentieth century—a world that would recognize the United States first as a significant power, then as one of two superpowers, and finally as the sole superpower of the world.

1

RUTHERFORD B. HAYES

(1877–1881)

Rutherford B. Hayes's inauguration in effect closed the Civil War era in the United States and ushered in a new one. Hayes succeeded three presidents intimately tied to the recent war: Abraham Lincoln, who served as chief executive from 1861 to 1865, during the conflict; Andrew Johnson, the controversial and ultimately impeached former vice president who assumed the presidency from 1865 to 1869, after Lincoln's assassination; and Ulysses S. Grant, the victorious leader of the Northern forces in the war, who rode his military success to the White House from 1869 to 1877. The focus of all three men—the fallen hero, the suspect Southerner, and the lauded general—remained on the conflict, whether it be executing the war or managing its aftermath. Administering the war-torn nation, rebuilding the economy, and occupying the former Confederate states required the attention and resources of the nation. Hayes, as president, entered the political landscape with a new message, in ways both intentional and unintentional: other subjects required the focus of the country; it was time for U.S. citizens to put the Civil War behind them and consider the future.

Hayes brought an impressive pedigree with him to the White House. Born the son of an Ohio farmer on October 4, 1822, Hayes graduated at the head of his class from Kenyon College and then earned a law degree from Harvard University. He established a successful legal practice in Cincinnati, where he represented defendants in several fugitive-slave cases and became active in the fledgling Republican party. His wife, the former Lucy Ware Webb, was herself very well educated, and her cultured background complemented his professional lifestyle. After serving with the Union army during the Civil War, Hayes was elected first to Congress (1865) and then to the governorship of his home state of Ohio (1868–1876). Hayes's commitment to a sound currency backed by gold brought him widespread attention, especially during his third gubernatorial campaign, as the money issue assumed national importance, and in 1876 the national Republican nominating convention named Hayes the party's presidential candidate.

If Hayes possessed leadership skills, proven experience, and Republican stands on the issues (especially the currency question), he was most attractive to his party for what he did not have: namely, skeletons in the closet. Johnson's impeachment and near removal, followed by Grant's scandal-ridden administration, left the nation weary of allegations of corruption in the nation's highest office. Hayes came to the election with an unblemished record of public service and a devout—some would say dour—dedication to moral standards. In fact, the serious Hayes took the subject so far that he forbid dances or card parties in his residence, and Mrs. Hayes, known as "Lemonade Lucy," refused to serve alcohol in the home. When they moved into the White House, they showed their disapproval of gaming by moving the presidential billiard table to the attic, where it served as a makeshift bed for their son when the residence was overrun with visiting guests.

Despite his straight-laced, high moral tone, however, Hayes's election to the presidency in 1876 was plagued by nearly disastrous controversy. The so-called Tilden-Hayes Affair erupted when the Democratic presidential candidate, Samuel J. Tilden, won a popular majority of the vote and appeared perhaps to have won the electoral college vote, as well. Hayes's campaign managers challenged suspicious vote returns in several states, however, and the irregularities uncovered there ignited a firestorm of debate. At last, Congress created a special Electoral Commission composed of appointed congressmen and Supreme Court justices to determine the election's outcome, making Hayes the first and only president to have gained the White House by the decision of such an extraordinary body.

Though the sectional conflict underscored by the Tilden-Hayes Affair suggested that the wounds of the Civil War were far from healed, Hayes entered office with the goal of escaping the trap of the past. He ended Reconstruction by withdrawing the troops occupying the Southern region and instead challenging the state and local governments to rise to the challenge of self-rule. In truth, removing the troops fulfilled covert promises Hayes had made to some Southern factions during the election dispute in return for political support. This "New Departure" allowed the South to escape its Reconstruction-era political, economic, and social state of limbo, while also ending a significant drain on national resources. The move left unanswered questions with regard to the protection of African Americans and their rights in the South; though Hayes recognized the problem, he did not follow up his concerns with active policy to address them.

Hayes's position for hard money, or gold, may have helped him earn the presidential nomination, but he did not meet complete success on economic questions during his term. He did succeed in executing the Resumption Act, despite protests from factions who favored a policy promising inflation, but Congress overrode his veto of the Bland-Allison Act, which provided for the restoration of the silver dollar as legal tender. Hayes maintained throughout his presidency that such fiscal questions were moral issues inevitably bound with the questions of manipulating the economy for the benefit of the few, changing the substance of agreed upon contracts, and undercutting the U.S. position on the world economic stage, all of which he considered wrong. His opponents continued to paint his positions in terms of class, condition, and region—this was ironic since Hayes, like many of his political opponents, was himself a debtor with little to gain personally from the policy he advocated.

Old and new problems assailed the nation during the Hayes administration, both of which brought violence to the country once again. The so-called "Indian problem" and the pattern of force that in some ways maintained it—whether that force was used for the coercive removal of native nations from their homelands or the control of those already on reservations—did not change during Hayes's term. The growing discontent of labor exploded in bloody riots centered around the railroad industry, and Hayes's forceful response offered only a temporary solution to a problem that would grow into the next century.

Perhaps more ominous still than these eruptions of violence was the seed of a most contentious issue, the need for civil service reform. Hayes was consistently interested in reform of all kinds—as reflected in his life-long commitment to progress that was evident in his personal work with schools, hospitals, and prisons—but the specific desires of decreasing the opportunity for corruption and increasing efficiency, as well as reclaiming public faith in government and its officials, weighed on him. It defined his most important political relationship, that of his overt and ugly struggle with New York Senator and fellow Republican Roscoe Conkling, who championed the aggressive use of the spoils system to reward supports with official positions. The Hayes-Conkling battle stalled Hayes's reform agenda, and eventually ended Conkling's career. The unchecked office-seeking mentality borne of the civil service problem would claim the life of Hayes's successor in an almost unthinkably bloody and gruesome way.

With his stalemates, success, and failures, and in some cases his embrace of the status quo, Hayes emerged as a transitional figure, a man who brought closure to the Civil War era by ending its most significant Reconstruction policy, and a man who held office before the shocking era of presidential assassination began. He ended his life quietly, refusing his party's nomination for a second term and instead contenting himself with humanitarian causes in both the North and South. As a private citizen he put his efforts where his presidential rhetoric had been, even campaigning for educational opportunities for Southern black youth, and observing the standards of personal morality that neither the sordid Tilden-Hayes Affair nor the wearying battle with Roscoe Conkling had managed to shake.

THE ISSUE: THE ELECTION OF 1876

Many presidents had entered the executive office facing challenging political issues, but none before Rutherford B. Hayes had entered the White House with one pressing goal dwarfing all others: defending his very right to be there. For Hayes, his first and most important battle was convincing the U.S. public in general, and his vocal opponents in particular, that he was the legitimate president of the United States.

The presidential election of 1876, in which Republican Rutherford B. Hayes ran against Democrat Samuel J. Tilden, was a complicated one. At first, the outcome seemed clear. For the first time since before the Civil War, the Democratic party polled a majority of the popular vote and reported Tilden with 184 electoral votes to Hayes's 165. Since only 185 votes were needed to secure the victory, Hayes and many of his supporters prepared to concede the election and congratulate the new president-elect Tilden.

New Hampshire Republican leader William E. Chandler, however, cautioned against easily accepting defeat. He noted that if all of the remaining states left in doubt—namely Florida, Louisiana, and South Carolina—and the uncertain vote of one of Oregon's electors all went to

Hayes, then Hayes would win. Eager to secure leadership, both parties then claimed wins in the three remaining states and sent staff and lawyers to oversee the vote count. An already complex process was further complicated with the addition of the partisan observers, some of whom sought to be more involved than the law allowed.

When Congress met on December 7, its members received conflicting reports from the states in question, leaving the outcome of the election unclear. The almost even balance between the political parties in Congress simply transplanted the stalemate from the states to the national legislature; moreover, Congressmen were uncertain what, exactly, they could do to remedy the situation. Although the U.S. Constitution provided that the Senate and House of Representatives witness the opening and counting of the electoral vote certificates, it did not explain if Congress had the authority to investigate how the votes came to be placed within the states or how the electors came to be chosen. Clearly something had to be done in order to untangle the mess at the state level and thereby determine who had won the election, but what? For well over a month Congress debated the question, and the threat of a second Civil War increased.

At last, Congress created an Electoral Commission on January 29, 1877, to determine the winner of the election. Its decision would be law unless both houses of Congress rejected it. The precedent-setting commission consisted of fifteen officials representing the U.S. Senate, House of Representatives, and Supreme Court. Perhaps unsurprisingly, its votes followed the 8-7 strict party lines of its members, thus determining the election in favor of Rutherford B. Hayes. Who truly won the election remains uncertain: though Hayes's claims to Oregon seemed legitimate, he almost certainly lost the Florida vote, and irregularities in Louisiana and South Carolina made any decision about the true and fair outcome almost impossible.

Congress counted the final vote as reported by the Electoral Commission on March 2, and Hayes was sworn in as president in private one day later; his inaugural address reflected his position that his presidency was legitimate. Democrats from the North, such as Ohio Representative A.T. Walling, who spoke against Hayes in the House of Representatives, protested bitterly, despite Tilden's attempt to quiet his supporters. The controversy followed Hayes to the White House; in his inaugural speech, his praise of the peaceful process provided by Congress and the Electoral Commission served as his first official defense of his legitimacy. Many of his detractors, however, remained unconvinced.

Interestingly, Southern Democrats received Hayes's victory more calmly than their Northern counterparts. Hayes and his allies had promised them that, should Hayes become president, he would follow a "New Departure" policy including the removal of federal troops from their Reconstruction-era occupation of the former Confederate states. This promise eased the sting of Tilden's loss, and Hayes quickly fulfilled it. His prompt action on behalf of Southern Democrats, coupled with Tilden's acceptance of the Electoral Commission's verdict, helped to avert the violence that seemed almost inevitable in the wake of the contentious decision. Hayes never possessed the same legitimacy previous executives had enjoyed, however, because his administration began on such a controversial and uncertain note. In fact, some Northern Democrats continued to call him "His Fraudulency" throughout his term.

The President's Position: Legitimate Process

FROM HAYES'S INAUGURAL SPEECH
MARCH 5, 1877

Fellow-citizens, we have reached the close of a political contest marked by the excitement which usually attends the contests between great political parties whose members espouse and advocate with earnest faith their respective creeds. The circumstances were, perhaps, in no respect extraordinary save in the closeness and the consequent uncertainty of the result.

For the first time in the history of the country it has been deemed best, in view of the peculiar circumstances of the case, that the objections and questions in dispute with reference to the counting of the electoral votes should be referred to the decision of a tribunal appointed for this purpose.

That tribunal—established by law for this sole purpose; its members, all of them, men of long-established reputation for integrity and intelligence, and, with the exception of those who are also members of the supreme judiciary, chosen equally from both political parties; its deliberations enlightened by the research and the arguments of able counsel— was entitled to the fullest confidence of the American people. Its decisions have been patiently waited for, and accepted as legally conclusive by the general judgment of the public. For the present, opinion will widely vary as to the wisdom of the several conclusions announced by that tribunal. This is to be anticipated in every instance where matters of dispute are made the subject of arbitration under the forms of law. Human judgment is never unerring, and is rarely regarded as otherwise than wrong by the unsuccessful party in the contest.

The fact that two great political parties have in this way settled a dispute in regard to which good men differ as to the facts and the law no less than as to the proper course to be pursued in solving the question in controversy is an occasion for general rejoicing.

Upon one point there is entire unanimity in public sentiment—that conflicting claims to the Presidency must be amicably and peaceably adjusted, and that when so adjusted the general acquiescence of the nation ought surely to follow.

It has been reserved for a government of the people, where the right of suffrage is universal, to give to the world the first example in history of a great nation, in the midst of the struggle of opposing parties for power, hushing its party tumults to yield the issue of the contest to adjustment according to the forms of law.

Looking for the guidance of that Divine Hand by which the destinies of nations and individuals are shaped, I call upon you, Senators, Representatives, judges, fellow-citizens, here and everywhere, to unite with me in an earnest effort to secure to our country the blessings, not only of material prosperity, but of justice, peace, and union—a union depending not upon the constraint of force, but upon the loving devotion of a free people; "and that all things may be so ordered and settled upon the best and surest foundations that peace and happiness, truth and justice, religion and piety, may be established among us for all generations."[1]

Against the President's Position: Illegitimate Process

REPRESENTATIVE A. T. WALLING OF OHIO
SPEECH IN HOUSE OF REPRESENTATIVES
MARCH 1, 1877

Mr. Speaker: In the ten minutes allotted to me to close the debate on the last State to which objections can be made, I do not intend to discuss the proposition contained in the resolution of the gentleman from Wisconsin [Mr. Lynde], as that has been fully done by the honorable gentleman himself, but I desire first to send to the Clerk's desk to be read a communication I have received from the city of New York since the gentleman from that city [Mr. Wood] has become the leader of the republican party on this floor, [laughter,] to show that not all, at least, of the business men of that city, the men who are interested in this contest, have agreed to this transfer of the democracy to the other party to save their ducats.

The Clerk read as follows:

New York, February 26, 1877

Dear Sir

We wish to indorse the request made by Peter Duffy, of Perry County, Ohio, that you "Thwart the thieves at all hazards," and prevent the outrageous counting of a usurper as President. We consider it the duty of every American citizen to himself, and above all to his country, to use every effort to prevent such a result.

With great respect, yours, &c.,
Elton Jordan, 285 Broadway, New York . . .

To Gen. W. T. Sherman,
Washington, D.C.:

Instruct General Augur in Louisiana and General Ruger in Florida to be vigilant with the force at their command, to preserve peace and good order, and to see that the proper and legal boards of canvassers are unmolested in the performance of their duties. Should there be any grounds of suspicion of fraudulent counting on either side, it should be reported and denounced at once. No man worthy of the office of President would be willing to hold the office if counted in, placed there by fraud. Either party can afford to be disappointed in the result, but the country cannot afford to have the result tainted by the suspicion of illegal or false returns.

U.S. Grant . . .

I present those telegrams for the purpose of extending the assurance they convey to our southern brethren, who seem to have abandoned the northern and western democracy on this occasion, that all their expectations, all their hopes will be fulfilled. There cannot be a possibility of doubt that if Nicholls is governor of Louisiana, Tilden is President of the United States. Packard received several hundred more votes for governor than did Hayes for President. He was counted in by the same returning board that counted the State for the Hayes electors. If Hayes be President, how much more certain is Packard governor. To suppose otherwise—to suppose that Hayes can recognize the Nicholls government—is to assume that the President about to be counted in will act as absurdly as a man who having purchased an estate should burn his deed, the only muniments of his title, before the same was recorded.

As for myself I can only say, that I have done all I could: have as I think performed my whole duty in trying to prevent the consummation of what I believe to be a fraud upon the solemnly declared verdict of the American people, committed by a commission appointed under a law of this House, with three judges at its head, who, forgetting the high duty they owed to themselves and to their country and to right and justice, permitted themselves to be made partisans of, and voted in that condition as they would vote at the polls for the election of a constable. I can only say that I disclaim their acts. . . .

Yes, sir, this great wrong will be consummated. A man repudiated by the people will be elevated to the most enviable position on this earth by a national returning board. It may be deemed offensive to speak of the electoral commission as a returning board. I concede that the infamies perpetrated in Louisiana, South Carolina, and Florida by the men who composed the returning boards in those States have brought the term into merited ill-repute. It has become offensive to all honest men, and is used in ridicule of justice. It is synonymous with mockery. With a full appreciation of the acts which have made the expression disreputable, the electoral commission can be called little else than a national returning board. Wherein has it met the public expectations? Wherein has it sought to discover fraud or unearth villainy? Wherein has it answered the purposes of its creation? What act has it done which justice sanctions or truth approbates? Not one. With a blindness close akin to madness, with obdurate wickedness and intent to perpetrate wrong, step by step it has proceeded to the consummation of a fraud which had its conception in deliberate malice against the laws, the Constitution, and the verdict of the people.[2]

NOTES

1. The Avalon Project at Yale Law School, *Inaugural Addresses of the Presidents*, http://www.yale.edu/lawweb/avalon/presiden/inaug/hayes.htm (accessed on November 5, 2002).

2. *Congressional Record, Containing the Proceedings and Debates of the Forty-fourth*

Congress, First Session, Volume V, Part III (Washington, D.C.: Government Printing Office, 1876), Appendix to the Congressional Record, pp. 258–259.

THE ISSUE: THE NEW DEPARTURE

One of the policy platforms on which Hayes ran and to which he turned immediately upon his inauguration was that of the "New Departure." His New Departure program referred to the national government's relationship with the former Confederate states of the South. Since the end of the Civil War, the national government had remained a presence politically and militarily in the Southern states, imposing and maintaining order on the war-torn, economically crippled, and socially upended region. After over a decade of federal oversight in these states, Hayes believed it was time to end the Reconstruction-era occupation of the South—a plan intended from the very start to be temporary only— and allow the state and local governments to once again function on their own. Both his inaugural address and his personal diary reflected this position.

Two particular challenges existed as a result of the policies of Reconstruction. First, how could states that had been managed by national authority learn to manage themselves in the post–Civil War world? Second, how could the rights of former slaves, now free citizens, be protected from infringement if national power retreated? Hayes responded to each question separately in his New Departure plan.

First, Hayes believed that the atrophied muscles of Southern self-government would never grow strong enough to support the region unless the state and local governments were given a chance to exercise their powers and adapt to the new economic, social, and political realties of the post-Reconstruction United States. As it was, the South remained trapped in time with little opportunity to re-create itself and thereby grow its economy and society. Hayes appreciated that the transition would be difficult, but he also appreciated that the stopgap measure of federal supervision—and the presence of permanent U.S. troops, in particular—had to end in order for the South to progress. It had served its purpose years earlier: all of the formerly Confederate states had been administered as military districts and readmitted to the union by 1870.

Hayes knew not only that the practical goals of readmission and organization had been met, but also that the United States could not put the Civil War in the past either psychologically or financially (stationing U.S. troops in the South was, after all, an expensive proposition) until the artificial, imposed order of the Reconstruction administrations gave way to state and local self-government. He also knew that Southerners of both parties actively wanted the troops removed. Two months after his inauguration, Hayes thrilled Southerners by withdrawing U.S. troops from the South and effectively ending the Reconstruction era. Hayes followed this by appointing Southerners to federal positions and making financial appropriations for Southern improvements, thus further pulling the former Confederate states back into the national fold.

The second challenge was more complex and long lived. Although he believed the military occupation of the South should end, Hayes appreciated that the newly achieved rights of African Americans in the South required protection, especially during elections, when some citizens used violence and intimidation to discourage black men from exercising their right to vote. For this reason, Hayes's New Departure plan did not discourage all national involvement in the South, but rather allowed the federal supervision of elections in areas where local and state supervision failed to protect the rights of all. This satisfied Northerners but drew protests from Southerners like the Democratic Mississippi representative J. R. Chalmers, who felt the policy hypocritical, invasive, and unnecessary, and denounced it in the halls of Congress. In the end, Hayes's vocal concerns about enforcing the Fourteenth and Fifteenth Amendments held more bark than bite, and the South experienced very little in the way of involvement or oversight. The second challenge, then, met little resolution in Hayes's term. Although the removal of troops occurred swiftly, the question of African-American voting rights in the South plagued the nation for at least another century.

The President's Position: No Troops, But Some Federal Oversight

FROM HAYES'S INAUGURAL SPEECH
MARCH 5, 1877

The permanent pacification of the country upon such principles and by such measures as will secure the complete protection of all its citizens in the free enjoyment of all their constitutional rights is now the one subject in our public affairs which all thoughtful and patriotic citizens regard as of supreme importance.

Many of the calamitous efforts of the tremendous revolution which has passed over the Southern States still remain. The immeasurable benefits which will surely follow, sooner or later, the hearty and generous acceptance of the legitimate results of that revolution have not yet been realized. Difficult and embarrassing questions meet us at the threshold of this subject. The people of those States are still impoverished, and the inestimable blessing of wise, honest, and peaceful local self-government is not fully enjoyed. Whatever difference of opinion may exist as to the cause of this condition of things, the fact is clear that in the progress of events the time has come when such government is the imperative necessity required by all the varied interests, public and private, of those States. But it must not be forgotten that only a local government which recognizes and maintains inviolate the rights of all is a true self-government.

With respect to the two distinct races whose peculiar relations to each other have brought upon us the deplorable complications and perplexities which exist in those States, it must be a government which guards the interests of both races carefully and equally. It must be a government which submits loyally and heartily to the Constitution and the laws—the laws of the nation and the laws of the States themselves—accepting and obeying faithfully the whole Constitution as it is.

Resting upon this sure and substantial foundation, the superstructure of beneficent local governments can be built up, and not otherwise. In furtherance of such obedience to the letter and the spirit of the Constitution, and in behalf of all that its attainment implies, all so-called party interests lose their apparent importance, and party lines may well be permitted to fade into insignificance. The question we have to consider for the immediate welfare of those States of the Union is the question of government or no government; of social order and all the peaceful industries and the happiness that belongs to it, or a return to barbarism. It is a question in which every citizen of the nation is deeply interested, and with respect to which we ought not to be, in a partisan sense, either Republicans or Democrats, but fellow-citizens and fellowmen, to whom the interests of a common country and a common humanity are dear.

The sweeping revolution of the entire labor system of a large portion of our country and the advance of 4,000,000 people from a condition of servitude to that of citizenship, upon an equal footing with their former masters, could not occur without presenting problems of the gravest moment, to be dealt with by the emancipated race, by their former masters, and by the General Government, the author of the act of emancipation. That it was a wise, just, and providential act, fraught with good for all concerned, is not generally conceded throughout the country. That a moral obligation rests upon the National Government to employ its constitutional power and influence to establish the rights of the people it has emancipated, and to protect them in the enjoyment of those rights when they are infringed or assailed, is also generally admitted.

The evils which afflict the Southern States can only be removed or remedied by the united and harmonious efforts of both races, actuated by motives of mutual sympathy and regard; and while in duty bound and fully determined to protect the rights of all by every constitutional means at the disposal of my Administration, I am sincerely anxious to use every legitimate influence in favor of honest and efficient local self-government as the true resource of those States for the promotion of the contentment and prosperity of their citizens. In the effort I shall make to accomplish this purpose I ask the cordial cooperation of all who cherish an interest in the welfare of the country, trusting that party ties and the prejudice of race will be freely surrendered in behalf of the great purpose to be accomplished. In the important work of restoring the South it is not the political situation alone that merits attention. The material development of that section of the country has been arrested by the social and political revolution through which it has passed, and now needs and deserves the considerate care of the National Government within the just limits prescribed by the Constitution and wise public economy.

But at the basis of all prosperity, for that as well as for every other part of the country, lies the improvement of the intellectual and moral condition of the people. Universal suffrage should rest upon universal education. To this end, liberal and permanent provision should be made for the support of free schools by the State governments, and, if need be, supplemented by legitimate aid from national authority.

Let me assure my countrymen of the Southern States that it is my earnest desire to regard and promote their truest interest—the interests of the white and of the colored people both and equally—and to put forth my best efforts in behalf of a civil policy which will forever wipe out in our political affairs the color line and the distinction between North and South, to the end that we may have not merely a united North or a united South, but a united country.[3]

From his diary 22 April 1877   We got through with the South Carolina and Louisiana [problems]. At any rate, the troops are ordered away and I now hope for peace, and what is equally important, security and prosperity for the colored people. The result of my plans is to get from those

States by their governors, legislators, press, and people pledges that the Thirteenth, Fourteenth, and Fifteenth Amendments shall be faithfully observed; that the colored people shall have equal rights to labor, education, and the privileges of citizenship. I am confident this is a good work, Time will tell.[4]

Against the President's Position: No Federal Oversight

REPRESENTATIVE J. R. CHALMERS OF MISSISSIPPI
SPEECH IN HOUSE OF REPRESENTATIVES
JUNE 13, 1878

Mr. Chairman, I desire to say a few words in reply to the gentleman from New York, [Mr. Lapham,] who defends the use of the military of the United States in the election in South Carolina in 1876. I desire to answer him, first, because he has denounced the democratic campaign in South Carolina as one of violence and intimidation and has called it "the Mississippi plan;" second, because I have seen it stated in the newspapers that the sixth district of Mississippi, which I have the honor to represent, is one of the southern districts selected for northern interference in the coming election, and I have heard it said that the distinguished gentleman from New York [Mr. Lapham] has been selected as the missionary to teach the heathen of the sixth district their political duty. Sir, I hope this is true, and I extend to him a pressing invitation to come. I will promise to meet him on the northern border of "the shoestring district" and to escort him safely to its southern extremity, and he shall need no "boys in blue" to protect him. And if he will divide time fairly I will furnish him with foemen worthy of his steel in colored democratic orators who will teach him what their race has learned from northern interference in southern affairs.

This gentleman defends the use of the military of the United States in this election because the democrats of South Carolina wore red shirts; moved in organized bodies and carried pistols. The carrying of pistols is a custom practiced from time immemorial in the South—it is permitted by the constitutions of our States if not concealed—and every investigation into southern affairs shows that the wearing of pistols has no political significance. The organizations and the red shirts then formed the only distinguishing features of these political gatherings, and these it is said justified the use of United States troops in the elections. Let the gentleman recall the quasi-military organization of "the wide-awakes" in 1860, the Grand Army of the Republic to-day, and the thousand and one other politico-military organizations of his own party, and say whether the Army of the United States should be used to suppress them or to counteract the impression produced by them in their political demonstrations. The gentleman states the object and policy of the South Carolina campaign correctly when he says in the language of Mr. Moise it was "to make such exhibitions of power as they could but to avoid any actual violence." But the gentleman from New York denounces this purely defensive campaign and calls it one of intimidation and violence, and says "no one not moved by political prejudice or the love of clamor can find just cause of complaint at the use made of the military force." I answer that no one not blinded by the bitterest partisan prejudice or the love, not of clamor, but of bloodshed, could justify such use of the military force. But, rejoicing over this illegitimate use of the Army, he says, "the desperate men who had resolved to carry out the Mississippi plan in that State, to make as much exhibition of power as they could and awe the colored voters into submission to their will, quailed at the presence of 'the boys in blue.' "

In this statement the gentleman not only misrepresents the facts, but he shows that he has not the dignity of soul necessary to appreciate the motives of men who bow to the flag of their country though used for their oppression. In answer to his insinuation that southern men "quailed at the presence of the boys in blue," I answer in the language of John Wooley, a colored democrat of my district. A garrison of Federal soldiers was established in Port Gibson, and in their presence John Wooley, addressing his colored brethren, said, "If you expect these troops to intimidate me and to intimidate the democratic party, I tell you they wouldn't make a breakfast for the 'Brandywine Club.' "[5]

NOTES

3. The Avalon Project at Yale Law School, *Inaugural Addresses of the Presidents*, http://www.yale.edu/lawweb/avalon/presiden/inaug/hayes.htm   (accessed November 5, 2002).

4. J. F. Watts and Fred L. Israel, eds., *Presidential Documents: The Speeches, Proclamations, and Policies That Have Shaped the Nation from Washington to Clinton* (New York: Routledge, 2000), p. 158.

5. *Congressional Record, Containing the Proceedings and Debates of the Forty-fourth*

Congress, Second Session, Volume VII (Washington, D.C.: Government Printing Office, 1878), Appendix to the Congressional Record, p. 478.

THE ISSUE: RESUMPTION

Unlike the New Departure, which was a policy created and articulated by the president for his term, Hayes inherited the specific law regarding resumption from the previous administration. Like the New Departure's fundamental subject of Reconstruction, however, Hayes inherited the greater issue of resumption from the Civil War. When Congress passed the Resumption Act in 1875, it was another development in a long debate about the nature of money. So-called "soft money" advocates supported the use of Civil War–era paper money known as greenbacks, which were made legal tender by mandate of Congress, upheld by the Supreme Court, and still circulated widely more than a decade after their original introduction into the economy. "Hard money" advocates, however, wanted the U.S. government to redeem the paper money and resume a currency based on specie, or precious metals such as gold.

The Resumption Act of 1875 decided this debate in favor of hard money advocates, requiring the Secretary of the Treasury to do three things: (1) reduce the greenbacks in circulation to $300 million (from approximately $430 million) immediately; (2) replace the fractional paper currency known as "shinplasters" with silver coins immediately; and, most important for the Hayes administration, (3) redeem the legal-tender notes in specie beginning on January 1, 1879.

Soft money proponents fought against the act and succeeded in altering the Resumption Act's requirements in order to increase the number of paper bills allowed in circulation. These advocates, most of whom represented Midwestern and agricultural interests, formed the Greenback-Labor party, which elected 14 members to Congress in 1878 and gathered over 300,000 votes for its presidential candidate in 1880, the agrarian radical James B. Weaver. The party relied heavily on the rhetoric of region (Midwesterners vs. Easterners), class (labor vs. elite, agriculture vs. industry, debtors vs. creditors), and condition (poverty vs. wealth) to convey its message and draw support. The party could not get the Resumption Act repealed despite its best efforts, however, and eventually the leadership changed its focus to abandon the cause of greenbacks and instead support the unlimited coinage of silver. The Greenback-Labor party evolved into the People's party and Populist party, eventually merging with the Democratic party in the twentieth century.

Hayes favored hard money and supported the fact that the Resumption Act made greenbacks redeemable in gold in 1879. Hayes's support was passive rather than active, as excerpts from his inaugural and annual speeches show—it required him only to defend executing a law already on the books, and not to fight for new legislation or policy—but it was nevertheless controversial, especially since Congress was almost equally divided between those favoring soft money and those favoring hard money. Representatives such as Democratic congressman Thomas Ewing from Ohio vocally opposed the president's position in addresses to fellow legislators. Although Hayes succeeded with his execution of the Resumption Act, he would meet the issue of currency again in his administration through the Bland-Allison Act, and this time with less success.

The President's Position: For Resumption

FROM HAYES'S INAUGURAL SPEECH
MARCH 5, 1877

With respect to the financial condition of the country, I shall not attempt an extended history of the embarrassment and prostration which we have suffered during the past three years. The depression in all our varied commercial and manufacturing interests throughout the country, which began in September, 1873, still continues. It is very gratifying, however, to be able to say that there are indications all around us of a coming change to prosperous times.

Upon the currency question, intimately connected, as it is, with this topic, I may be permitted to repeat here the statement made in my letter of acceptance, that in my judgment the feeling of uncertainty inseparable from an irredeemable paper currency, with its fluctuation of values, is one of the greatest obstacles to a return to prosperous times. The only safe paper currency is one which rests upon a coin basis and is at all times and promptly convertible into coin.

I adhere to the views heretofore expressed by me in favor of Congressional legislation in behalf of an early resumption of specie payments, and I am satisfied not only that this is wise, but that the interests, as well as the public sentiment, of the country imperatively demand it.[6]

HAYES'S THIRD ANNUAL MESSAGE
DECEMBER 1, 1879

The most interesting events which have occurred in our public affairs since my last annual message to Congress are connected with the financial operations of the Government, directly affecting the business interests of the country. I congratulate Congress on the successful execution of the resumption act. At the time fixed, and in the manner contemplated by law, United States notes began to be redeemed in coin. Since the 1st of January last they have been promptly redeemed on presentation, and in all business transactions, public and private, in all parts of the country, they are received and paid out as the equivalent of coin. The demand upon the Treasury for gold and silver in exchange for United States notes has been comparatively small, and the voluntary deposit of coin and bullion in exchange for notes has been very large. The excess of the precious metals deposited or exchanged for United States notes over the amount of United States notes redeemed is about $40,000,000.

The resumption of specie payments has been followed by a very great revival of business. With a currency equivalent in value to the money of the commercial world, we are enabled to enter upon an equal competition with other nations in trade and production. The increasing foreign demand for our manufactures and agricultural products has caused a large balance of trade in our favor, which has been paid in gold, from the 1st of July last to November 15, to the amount of about $59,000,000. Since the resumption of specie payments there has also been a marked and gratifying improvement of the public credit. The bonds of the Government bearing only 4 per cent interest have been sold at or above par, sufficient in amount to pay off all of the national debt which was redeemable under present laws. The amount of interest saved annually by the process of refunding the debt since March 1, 1877, is $14,297,177. The bonds sold were largely in small sums, and the number of our citizens now holding the public securities is much greater than ever before. The amount of the national debt which matures within less than two years is $792,121,700, of which $500,000,000 bear interest at the rate of 5 per cent, and the balance is in bonds bearing 6 per cent interest. It is believed that this part of the public debt can be refunded by the issue of 4 per cent bonds, and, by the reduction of interest which will thus be effected, about $11,000,000 can be annually saved to the Treasury.[7]

Against the President's Position: Against Resumption

REPRESENTATIVE THOMAS EWING OF OHIO
HOUSE OF REPRESENTATIVES
JUNE 13, 1878

Mr. Speaker, on the 24th of November last the House passed the bill to repeal all that part of the act of January 14, 1875, which authorizes the Secretary of the Treasury to increase the bonded debt or use surplus revenues to provide for redemption in coin of United States notes on and after January 1, 1870. The Senate sends the bill back to us with all after the enacting clause stricken out and with two wholly different provisions inserted. They are, first, a provision to make greenbacks receivable in payments for 4 per cent, coin bonds; and, second, a provision to make greenbacks receivable for customs after October 1, 1878.

On Friday last, when the bill was received back from the Senate with these amendments, I moved to *non-concur*, and asked a committee of conference. The motion was defeated by nearly a tie vote. The gentleman from Illinois [Mr. Fort] now moves to concur in the amendments. I have a word or two to say why, in my opinion, that motion should not prevail.

We are told we can get no more than the Senate now offers, and if we fail to take this we shall get nothing. Sir, that is not the spirit with which we should maintain the rights of the people. If we are ready to accept a slight concession in lieu of a great right, we will henceforth be expected to sacrifice important measures by petty compromises. The Senate offers nothing desirable in these amendments except to make greenbacks receivable for customs. A separate bill for that single purpose, now in the hands of my colleague, [Mr. Southard,] will pass the House to-day or to-morrow. Let the Senate pass that bill by itself, and not offer us this "nubbin" as a condition of acquiescence in the gigantic wrong of forced resumption.

The only other proposition in the Senate amendments is a device of the Secretary of the Treasury to promote resumption. That is the provision giving him power to sell 4 per cent bonds for greenbacks *at his discretion*. There are two methods by which he hopes to maintain resumption. One is by hoarding coin to pay the greenbacks as they are presented for redemption; the other is to collect greenbacks from taxes or sales of bonds and withhold them from circulation, so as to make them scarce, and thus stop their flow to the Treasury for redemption. To the extent of *all the surplus moneys in the Treasury the greenbacks so received are appropriated by the resumption law to the uses of resumption.*

The Secretary does not construe the act passed this session stopping the further destruction of greenbacks and requiring their reissue as at all limiting the sweeping provision of the resumption law appropriating all surplus moneys to resumption purposes, as his telegram of to-day to my friend from Kansas [Mr. Phillips] very plainly shows. That appropriation applies to proceeds of sales of bonds as well as to surplus revenues. As the law now stands, he can only sell bonds for coin. Give him the power to sell them for greenbacks also, and you enable him to take legal-tenders out of circulation and hoard them in the Treasury without any limit except the limit of the popular demand for the bonds. The greenbacks now in private vaults throughout the country, awaiting a revival of business, would go largely into these bonds and be hoarded in the Treasury, to be paid out again only when, in the language of Mr. Sherman, "they can be maintained at par with coin." Hence, no matter how great the business demand for the reissue of greenbacks hoarded by the Secretary might become, the people could only get them in circulation again when their reissue, in his opinion, would not endanger resumption.

We have already increased our bonded debt $120,000,000 to aid resumption. This Senate amendment gives the Secretary new power and facilities to increase it indefinitely for that purpose. We have already contracted our currency seventy-five millions for resumption. This amendment gives him new power and facilities to contract it. It is therefore only a dangerous and pernicious enlargement of the powers of mischief conferred on the Secretary by the resumption law.

But there is a still further objection to this amendment. If resumption shall break down, as I am thoroughly convinced it will, gold will mount to a high premium. I would not be surprised to see it go to 50 per cent above par in greenbacks. Suppose it does; then we will be selling 4 per cent coin bonds for greenbacks worth but sixty-six and two-thirds cents on the dollar in coin, thus repeating in effect the 5.20 bond swindle.

If we concur in the amendment striking out all of our bill after the enacting clause we abandon our demand for the repeal of the resumption scheme. That demand was not made first by us, but by the people; and whatever changes may have recently come over this House, the people still demand it more unmistakably and vehemently than ever. The eight months during which this bill slept in the hostile hands of the Senate have been the most calamitous ever endured by the American people. Their business is being ruined, their fortunes swept away, their very means of subsistence stolen by the cunning devilry of this scheme of resumption—a scheme which not one in ten of its intelligent promoters believes can result in permanent specie payments, and the only certain effect of which is the robbery of the many and the enrichment of the few through an enormous decrease in the prices of commodities and increase in the purchasing power of money. Let us accept no substitute for the repeal of this most impractical and destructive law. Let us stand for repeal until the Senate and President yield to the voice of the people.[8]

NOTES

6. The Avalon Project at Yale Law School, *Inaugural Addresses of the Presidents*, http://www.yale.edu/lawweb/avalon/presiden/inaug/hayes.htm (accessed November 5, 2002).

7. Richardson, Volume X, pp. 4509–4510.

8. *Congressional Record, Containing the Proceedings and Debates of the Forty-fourth Congress, Second Session*, Volume VII (Washington, D.C.: Government Printing Office, 1878), Appendix to the Congressional Record, p. 466.

THE ISSUE: CIVIL SERVICE REFORM

Although it seemed fitting for a president who came to office amidst a controversial and nearly violent political conflict to embrace civil service reform, Rutherford B. Hayes was actually an advocate of civil service reform long before he became chief executive. As a Congressman from 1865 through 1867 and the Governor of Ohio from 1867 through 1876, Hayes fought to set a high moral tone in his behavior and held others, including his fellow officials, to a similar standard. His concern for leadership above reproach was heightened, however, by the two-term presidency of former general Ulysses S. Grant from 1869 to 1877, whose administration suffered from highly problematic and publicized accusations of corruption. When Hayes succeeded Grant, he placed civil service reform at the forefront of his policy initiatives.

Hayes's ideas about reforming the civil service included the notion of replacing the traditional system of political patronage—in which leaders rewarded the supporters who got them elected by gifting them with official positions in government—with examinations designed to determine merit in an objective and nonpartisan manner. Interestingly enough, Hayes's greatest obstacle to his plan came from the leadership of his own party in the form of Republican New York Senator Roscoe Conkling, who had supported Hayes's election to the presidency.

Conkling represented an old, entrenched, Jacksonian view of politics. First a lawyer and Whig party leader, Conkling became a Republican representative and then senator from New York. He believed in party loyalty and discipline; to achieve this, he held that senators needed control of all federal appointments within their state boundaries so that they could reward and punish party members and offer and withhold the positions at will. Hayes first crossed Conkling when he chose to extend an olive branch to the South in the form of federal appointments. The Republican senator not only distrusted the South, but saw those positions as lost political currency that could have been used for the good of the Republican party in the North.

The bitter struggle between Hayes and Conkling escalated when Hayes followed his reform agenda by demanding the resignation of two top officials, both of whom worked in the New York customhouse, which Conkling considered under his personal control. (Ironically, one of the officials was future president Chester Arthur.) Conkling, leading the conservative faction known as Stalwarts, in retaliation then supported a third term for former president Ulysses S. Grant at the 1880 Republican convention. Conkling's efforts at defeating Hayes did little good, however, as another civil service reformer, James A. Garfield, succeeded him in the White House.

The civil service reform issue would become increasingly volatile in the following administration, as would the significance of the Stalwart faction of the Republican party. During Hayes's time, the subject was significant because the president honestly sought specific, progressive answers and was actively blocked by members of his own party.

The President's Position: For Reform

FROM HAYES'S INAUGURAL SPEECH
MARCH 5, 1877

I ask the attention of the public to the paramount necessity of reform in our civil service—a reform not merely as to certain abuses and practices of so-called official patronage which have come to have the sanction of usage in the several Departments of our Government, but a change in the system of appointment itself; a reform that shall be thorough, radical, and complete; a return to the principles and practices of the founders of the Government. They neither expected nor desired from public officers any partisan service. They meant that public officers should owe their whole service to the Government and to the people. They meant that the officer should be secure in his tenure as long as his personal character remained untarnished and the performance of his duties satisfactory. They held that appointments to office were not to be made nor expected merely as rewards for partisan services, nor merely on the nomination of members of Congress, as being entitled in any respect to the control of such appointments.

The fact that both the great political parties of the country, in declaring their principles prior to the election, gave a prominent place to the subject of reform of our civil service, recognizing and strongly urging its necessity, in terms almost identical in their specific import with those I have here employed, must be accepted as a conclusive argument in behalf of these measures. It must be regarded as the expression of the united voice and will of the whole country upon this subject, and both political parties are virtually pledged to give it their unreserved support.

The President of the United States of necessity owes his election to office to the suffrage and zealous labors of a political party, the members of which cherish with ardor and regard as of essential importance the principles of their party organization; but he should strive to be always mindful of the fact that he serves his party best who serves the country best.

In furtherance of the reform we seek, and in other important respects a change of great importance, I recommend an amendment to the Constitution prescribing a term of six years for the Presidential office and forbidding a reelection.[9]

HAYES'S THIRD ANNUAL MESSAGE
DECEMBER 1, 1879

Very different considerations apply to the greater number of those who fill the subordinate places in the civil service. Their responsibility is to their superiors in official position. It is their duty to obey the legal instructions of those upon whom that authority is devolved, and their best public service consists in the discharge of their functions irrespective of partisan politics. Their duties are the same whatever party is in power and whatever policy prevails. As a consequence it follows that their tenure of office should not depend on the prevalence of any policy or the supremacy of any party, but should be determined by their capacity to serve the people most usefully quite irrespective of partisan interests. The same considerations that should govern the tenure should also prevail in the appointment, discipline, and removal of these subordinates. The authority of appointment and removal is not a perquisite, which may be used to aid a friend or reward a partisan, but is a trust, to be exercised in the public interest under all the sanctions which attend the obligation to apply the public funds only for public purposes.

Every citizen has an equal right to the honor and profit of entering the public service of his country. The only just ground of discrimination is the measure of character and capacity he has to make that service most useful to the people. Except in cases where, upon just and recognized principles—as upon the theory of pensions—offices and promotions are bestowed as rewards for past services, their bestowal upon any theory which disregards personal merit is an act of injustice to the citizen, as well as a breach of that trust subject to which the appointing power is held.

In the light of these principles it becomes of great importance to provide just and adequate means, especially for every Department and large administrative office, where personal discrimination on the part of its head is not practicable, for ascertaining those qualifications to which appointments and removals should have reference. To fail to provide such means is not only to deny the opportunity of ascertaining the facts upon which the most righteous claim to office depends, but of necessity to discourage all worthy aspirants by handing over appointments and removals to mere influence and favoritism. If it is the right of the worthiest claimant to gain the appointment and the interest of the people to bestow it upon him, it would seem clear that a wise and just method of ascertaining personal fitness for office must be an important and permanent function of every just and wise government. It has long since become impossible in the great offices for those having the duty of nomination and appointment to personally examine into the individual qualifications of more than a small proportion of those seeking office, and with the enlargement of the civil service that proportion must continue to become less.

In the earlier years of the Government the subordinate offices were so few in number that it was quite easy for those making appointments and promotions to personally ascertain the merits of candidates. Party managers and methods had not then become powerful agencies of coercion, hostile to the free and just exercise of the appointing power.

A large and responsible part of the duty of restoring the civil service to the desired purity and efficiency rests upon the President, and it is my purpose to do what is within my power to advance such prudent and gradual measures of reform as will most surely and rapidly bring about that radical change of system essential to make our administrative methods satisfactory to a free and intelligent people.[10]

Against the President's Position: Against Reform

SENATOR ROSCOE CONKLING'S ROCHESTER SPEECH NEW YORK, SEPTEMBER 1877

Exotic despotism revised and improved, will not grow in American soil. It will perish. It would be trodden out, if it did not die out. Who are these oracular censors so busy of late in brandishing the rod over me and every other Republican in this State? Some man has said, "I am of age in the Republican party." So am I. For the last twenty-two years I have labored for it and stood by its flag; and never in twenty-two years have I been false to its principles, its cause, or its candidates. Who are these men who, in newspapers and elsewhere, are cracking their whips over Republicans and playing school-master to the Republican party and its conscience and convictions? They are of various sorts and convictions. Some of them are . . . the dilettanti and carpet knights of politics, men whose efforts have been expended in denouncing and ridiculing and accusing honest men who, in storm and in sun, in war and peace, have clung to the Republican flag and defended it against those who have tried to trail and trample it in the dust. Some of them are men who, when they could work themselves into conventions, have attempted to belittle and befoul Republican administrations and to parade their own thin veneering of superior purity. Some of them are men who, by insisting it is corrupt and bad for men in office to take part in politics, are striving now to prove that the Republican party has been unclean and vicious all its life, and that the last campaign was venal and wrong and fraudulent, not in some of the States, but in all the States, North and South. For it is no secret that in all States office-holders, in committees, in organizations and everywhere, did all that men could fairly do to uphold the candidates of our party, and that they were encouraged and urged to do so. Some of these worthies masquerade as reformers. Their vocation and ministry is to lament the sins of other people. Their stock in trade is rancid, canting self-righteousness. They are wolves in sheep's clothing. Their real object is office and plunder. When Dr. Johnson defined patriotism as the last refuge of a scoundrel, he was unconscious of the then undeveloped capabilities and uses of the word "Reform." Yet long before Johnson lived something was known of a class of men who take the name of "reform" in vain.

A wise man wrote Christian precepts in China 500 years before Mary's son walked beneath the bending palms of Palestine. And this sage teacher warned his followers, with unerring point, against the very impostures and perversions which these days find employed to daze and bewilder the American people. . . . It seems to me public officers are entitled to presumptions in their favor, and ought never to be condemned until they and their acts have been fairly tried, and then only on clear evidence.[11]

NOTES

9. The Avalon Project at Yale Law School, *Inaugural Addresses of the Presidents*, http://www.yale.edu/lawweb/avalon/presiden/inaug/hayes.htm   (accessed November 5, 2002).

10. Richardson, Volume X, pp. 4514–4515.

11. Conkling, Alfred R., *The Life and Letters of Roscoe Conkling: Orator, Statesman, Advocate* (New York: Charles L. Webster and Company, 1889), pp. 540–542.

THE ISSUE: STRIKES

After avoiding what appeared to be a potential civil war caused by the uncertainty and protest surrounding the election of 1876, Hayes turned his attention to policy questions such as his position on the South and civil service reform. Neither he nor most other U.S. citizens at the time were prepared for the unprecedented violence and bloodshed that erupted in July of 1877, even though the problem in a sense dated back several years.

The panic of 1873 and its following depression created economic hardships on many in the United States, and the effects continued into the era of the Hayes administration. One sector of the economy that was hit hardest by this depression was the railroad industry. Seventy-six railroads failed in 1876 alone, while those surviving the 1873 to 1876 period cut operating expenses, including wages, by eighteen percent. In 1877, stock prices for the remaining major companies continued to fall. Industry leaders determined that individual companies had to cooperate and pool resources in order to spend less while charging more. Although this allowed some businesses to exist, they did so while employees worked twelve-hour days in dangerous conditions with decreased wages. Morale among workers plummeted as employees worked harder for less and yet observed company leaders colluding with each other and raising prices.

Strikes began in Baltimore on July 16, when the scheduled pay cuts for B&O Railroad workers took effect. Soon riots broke out in other surrounding areas, including West Virginia, while strikebreakers attempted to fill the positions left by those on strike and subsequently fired. Violence escalated until President Hayes sent federal troops to put down the rioters and restore order, which they did, but not until the strikes and associated violence had spread significantly.

Hayes himself was not sympathetic to the railroad industry's interests in particular, though he could hardly have been said to be a crusader on behalf of labor, either. Instead, Hayes championed the cause of public peace—in this case, the right of those in the community caught in the crossfire of violent strikes—and the cause of individuals to decide when and how they wished to work—in this instance, the nonstrikers or strikebreakers who wished to be employees of the railroad despite the planned pay cuts. Nonetheless, these causes and their practical outcome, the quick ending of the strikes, worked to the advantage of the railroad industry leaders.

Both sides had legitimate concerns. The railroad leaders genuinely wanted to stay in business, and felt justified in following the economic practices most likely to keep their companies afloat. On the other hand, railroad laborers had suffered the brunt of these policies time and again, and their perception of collusion at the highest levels of management between the railroad companies was based in fact. Perhaps most significantly, the decision to meet the laborers' force with national military force fed the paranoia and resolve of labor leaders, who utilized the image of a powerful nation taking deadly arms against its own honest and downtrodden workers in much of its subsequent rhetoric.

Although many supported Hayes's use of force to restore the peace, Hayes faced criticism not only from labor, but from other U.S. officials, as well. Leaders, such as Wisconsin representative C. G. Williams, urged the government to listen to the legitimate concerns of the strikers and go beyond merely discouraging violence to actively pursue policies that would decrease the financial and political pressure on the working people of the United States. In short, the president believed his role to be to end the disturbance and restore order, while his opposition believed this meant treating the symptom rather than curing the illness. Labor unrest would continue into the twentieth century.

The President's Position: End Strikes

BY THE PRESIDENT OF THE UNITED STATES OF AMERICA
A PROCLAMATION
JULY 21, 1877

Whereas it is provided in the Constitution of the United States that the United States shall protect every State in this Union, on application of the legislature, or of the executive (when the legislature can not be convened), against domestic violence; and

Whereas the governor of the State of Maryland has represented that domestic violence exists in said State at Cumberland, and along the line of the Baltimore and Ohio Railroad in said State, which the authorities of said State are unable to suppress; and

Whereas the laws of the United States require that in all cases of insurrection in any State or of obstruction to the laws thereof, whenever, in the judgment of the President, it becomes necessary to use the military forces to suppress such insurrection or obstruction to the laws, he shall forthwith, by proclamation, command such insurgents to disperse and retire peaceably to their respective abodes within a limited time:

Now, therefore, I, Rutherford B. Hayes, President of the United States, do hereby admonish all good citizens of the United States and all persons within the territory and jurisdiction of the United States against aiding, countenancing, abetting, or taking part in such unlawful proceedings; and I do hereby warn all persons engaged in or connected with said domestic violence and obstruction of the laws to disperse and retire peaceably to their respective abodes on or before noon of the 22nd day of July instant. . . .

PRESIDENT HAYES'S REFLECTIONS ON
THE GREAT RAILROAD STRIKES
AUGUST 5, 1877

The strikes have been put down by *force*, but now for the *real* remedy. Can't something [be] done by education of the strikers, by judicious control of the capitalists, by wise general policy to end or diminish the evil? The R.R. strikers, as a rule, are good men, sober, intelligent, and industrious.

The mischiefs are:

1. Strikers prevent men willing to work from doing so.
2. They seize and hold the property of their employees.
3. The consequent excitement furnishes an opportunity for the dangerous criminal classes to destroy life and property.

Now, "every man has a right, if he sees fit to, to quarrel with his own bread and butter, but he has no right to quarrel with the bread and butter of other people." Every man has a right to determine for himself the value of his own labor, but he has no right to determine for other men the value of their labor. (Not good.)

Every man has a right to refuse to work if the wages don't suit him, but he has no right to prevent others from working if they are suited with the wages.

Every man has a right to refuse to work, but no man has a right to refuse to work, but no man has a right to prevent others from working.

Every man has a right to decide for himself the question of wages, but no man has a right to decide that question for other men.[12]

HAYES'S FIRST ANNUAL MESSAGE
DECEMBER 3, 1877

The very serious riots which occurred in several of the States in July last rendered necessary the employment of a considerable portion of the Army to preserve peace and maintain order. In the States of West Virginia, Maryland, Pennsylvania, and Illinois these disturbances were so formidable as to defy the local and State authorities, and the National Executive was called upon, in the mode provided by the Constitution and laws, to furnish military aid. I am gratified to be able to state that the troops sent in response to these calls for aid in the suppression of domestic violence were able, by the influence of their presence in the disturbed regions, to preserve the peace and restore order without the use of force. In the discharge of this delicate and important duty both officers and men acted with great prudence and courage, and for their services deserve the thanks of the country.[13]

Against the President's Position: Listen to Strikers

REPRESENTATIVE C. G. WILLIAMS OF WISCONSIN IN THE HOUSE OF REPRESENTATIVES JUNE 13, 1878

Mr. Chairman, I think it was Macaulay who said in the great discussion upon the parliamentary reform bill of 1830–31 that the obstinacy of rulers was the opportunity of demagogues; that the people, when repulsed by those to whom they were accustomed to look for relief, naturally turned to unprincipled agitators and political charlatans, and that where a considerable number of the people had or fancied they had a real grievance, it was better to give them a respectful and considerate hearing, even though it might be impossible to afford them relief; and in enforcing this view upon Parliament he cited an instance in ancient English history where one hundred thousand armed insurgents assembled upon Black Heath demanding a leader; when the king himself appeared upon the scene, and, inquiring the cause of their grievances, responded: "I will be your leader!" and, yielding something to their demands, saved his realm from riot and pillage.

Now, sir, while Congress is neither king nor ruler, but the servant of the people, there is no disguising the fact that for a year and more the laboring masses of this country have been looking to Congress with a patience amounting almost to faith that it would do something to relieve their wants; and if this long session shall finally close, having done nothing in this direction, we may well remember the force of the old proverb: "Beware of the wrath of a patient man." It is just here, Mr. Chairman, that an American mob is more dangerous than any other on earth. Those who compose it are more accustomed to obey law, have greater reverence for established institutions, and an abiding faith in the ultimate justice of the Government. Let them lose confidence in these and become desperate enough to strike against recognized authority and law, and nothing restrains them. Many, therefore, maintain that we should be ready with ample military power to put down the mob at all hazards, as we undoubtedly should be, Mr. Chairman, because a mob is like a fire in a great city: it carries destruction everywhere, and should be put down by powder and ball if need be, without inquiry how it originated or who is to blame. A mob is as dangerous to itself as to society. It is the abnegation of all rightful authority. It is the dissolution and destruction of all forms of civil government. It is the restoration of the old and barbarous doctrine of might against reason, under which the weaker goes to the bottom and sinks deeper and deeper in distress. Re-establish and recrown it and the weak and the poor go back to serfdom and slavery. Hence the mob must be put down. But God grant that that other equally fatal and pernicious fallacy shall never gain foothold here, namely: that the American laborer can be pinned to his toil by the bayonet or the American artisan be made to walk to and from his labor between rows of bristling steel. Reason and the assent of the masses are the fount of power which sends the life-blood coursing through the veins of this nation. In dealing with our form of government or legislating for it let us not ignore the vital condition of its existence. Macaulay, again, said:

I understand how the peace is kept in New York; it is by the assent and support of the people. I understand also how the peace is kept at Milan; it is by the bayonets of the Austrian soldiers.

Sir, may we never accept the latter and reject the former. No, Mr. Chairman, these men must be heard and must be reasoned with and in return must be allowed to reason with us, for, while the triumphs of arms may be lost in a day, the convictions of reason last for eternity. Go out upon the eastern portico of this Capitol any of these evenings and you will see excited men addressing a more excited crowd, appealing to their prejudices and passions and telling them that this Congress does nothing but for money; that it legislates for the rich and cares nothing for the poor; that it is venal and corrupt; and that if things are to go on as they now are the laboring man can have no further interest in a Government which his labor supports and his valor defends. And have we nothing to say to these things uttered at the very doors of the Capitol? Have we nothing better to submit in reply than that these men be dispersed by the bayonet, and that we vote men and money enough to keep them dispersed?

Ah, Mr. Chairman, that will never do![14]

NOTES

12. Watts and Israel, p. 159.

13. Richardson, Volume IX, p. 4424.

14. *Congressional Record, Containing the Proceedings and Debates of the Forty-fourth Congress, Second Session,* Volume VII (Washington, D.C.: Government Printing Office, 1878), Appendix to the Congressional Record, pp. 486–487.

THE ISSUE: THE "INDIAN PROBLEM"

The oldest of the issues inherited by the Hayes administration pre-dated the creation of the United States itself. Ever since the country had come into being, presidents had wrestled with the question of how the United States should interact with the native nations of America. By the time Hayes came to the White House, much of forced Amerindian re-moval was completed and the so-called "Indian Wars" in the West were the last evidence of native resistance to U.S. expansion on the North American continent. Clearing the last lands for white settlers and ad-ministering the reservations were the primary goals for U.S. policy.

Hayes did not break the pattern of force used by the U.S. government against native nations. One example of this pattern was found in the case of the Nez Percé. The Nez Percé people formed the most powerful nation in the Pacific Northwest and retained friendly relations with the United States throughout the first half of the nineteenth century. Many con-verted to Christianity and were educated in English-speaking schools. Despite the fact that the Nez Percé had treaties with the United States, however, U.S. citizens in the Civil War era pressed westward, and the government attempted to pressure the nation into relocating to small and unattractive reservations in order to make way for more white settlers.

In 1877, the U.S. government backed this pressure with military force and attempted to remove the Nez Percé to a reservation in Idaho. Chief Joseph resisted and led his people toward Canada in an effort to escape the U.S. army and seek refuge with friendly groups. From June through September of 1877, Joseph and his followers traveled more than one thousand miles across Oregon, Washington, Idaho, and Montana, both eluding U.S. troops and at times defeating them in combat despite the fact that the Nez Percé were outnumbered at least ten to one. Contrary to popular notions of native savagery, Joseph's people treated prisoners humanely; cared for their own aged, sick, and weak; and purchased rather than stole supplies from white settlers. Though the behavior of the Nez Percé captured mainstream U.S. sympathy for their plight, the U.S. army continued to pursue them, captured them within forty miles of the Canadian border, and then exiled them on reservations far away from their ancestral homes. Despite Chief Joseph's traveling to Washington, D.C., to plead for his people's return to their land, Joseph and his nation remained held in reservations for the rest of their lives.

U.S. force against native Americans also extended beyond military removal campaigns to include so-called peacekeeping on reservations, though this often meant keeping starving men from hunting for food due to the inept administration of goods and services intended for the native populations. Though Hayes recognized the problem, and both native American leaders and U.S. officials protested the inefficiencies and inhumanities created by the system, the inherited pattern of force continued throughout the Hayes administration.

The President's Position: Force

HAYES'S FIRST ANNUAL MESSAGE
DECEMBER 3, 1877

The report of the Secretary of War shows that the Army has been actively employed during the year, and has rendered very important service in suppressing hostilities in the Indian country and in preserving peace and protecting life and property in the interior as well as along the Mexican border. A long and arduous campaign has been prosecuted, with final complete success, against the Nez Percé tribe of Indians. A full account of this campaign will be found in the report of the General of the Army. It will be seen that in its course several severe battles were fought, in which a number of gallant officers and men lost their lives. I join with the Secretary of War and the General of the Army in awarding to the officers and men employed in the long and toilsome pursuit and in the final capture of these Indians the honor and praise which are so justly their due.[15]

HAYES'S SECOND ANNUAL MESSAGE
DECEMBER 2, 1878

The annual reports of the Secretary of the Interior and of the Commissioner of Indian Affairs present an elaborate account of the present condition of the Indian tribes and of that branch of the public service which ministers to their interests. While the conduct of the Indians generally has been orderly and their relations with their neighbors friendly and peaceable, two local disturbances have occurred, which were deplorable in their character, but remained, happily, confined to a comparatively small number of Indians. The discontent among the Bannocks, which led first to some acts of violence on the part of some members of the tribe and finally to the outbreak, appears to have been caused by an insufficiency of food on the reservation, and this insufficiency to have been owing to the inadequacy of the appropriations made by Congress to the wants of the Indians at a time when the Indians were prevented from supplying the deficiency by hunting. After an arduous pursuit by the troops of the United States, and several engagements, the hostile Indians were reduced to subjection, and the larger part of them surrendered themselves as prisoners. In this connection I desire to call attention to the recommendation made by the Secretary of the Interior, that a sufficient fund be placed at the disposal of the Executive, to be used, with proper accountability, at discretion, in sudden emergencies of the Indian service.

The other case of disturbance was that of a band of Northern Cheyennes, who suddenly left their reservation in the Indian Territory and marched rapidly through the States of Kansas and Nebraska in the direction of their old hunting grounds, committing murders and other crimes on their way. From the documents accompanying the report of the Secretary of the Interior it appears that this disorderly band was as fully supplied with the necessaries of life as the 4,700 other Indians who remained quietly on the reservation, and that the disturbance was caused by men of a restless and mischievous disposition among the Indians themselves. Almost the whole of this band have surrendered to the military authorities; and it is a gratifying fact that when some of them had taken refuge in the camp of the Red Cloud Sioux, with whom they had been in friendly relations, the Sioux held them as prisoners and readily gave them up to the officers of the United States, thus giving new proof of the loyal spirit which, alarming rumors to the contrary notwithstanding, they have uniformly shown ever since the wishes they expressed at the council of September, 1877, had been complied with.

Both the Secretary of the Interior and the Secretary of War unite in the recommendation that provision be made by Congress for the organization of a corps of mounted "Indian auxiliaries," to be under the control of the Army and to be used for the purpose of keeping the Indians on their reservations and preventing or repressing disturbance on their part. I earnestly concur in this recommendation. It is believed that the organization of such a body of Indian cavalry, receiving a moderate pay from the Government, would considerably weaken the restless element among the Indians by withdrawing from it a number of young men and giving them congenial employment under the Government, it being a matter of experience that Indians in our service almost without exception are faithful in the performance of the duties assigned to them. Such an organization would materially aid the Army in the accomplishment of a task for which its numerical strength is sometimes found insufficient.

But while the employment of force for the prevention or repression of Indian troubles is of occasional necessity, and wise preparation should be made to that end, greater reliance must be placed on humane and civilizing agencies for the ultimate solution of what is called the Indian problem. It may be very difficult and require much patient effort to curb the unruly spirit of the savage Indian to the restraints of civilized life, but experience shows that it is not impossible. Many of the tribes which are now quiet and orderly and self-supporting were once as savage as any that at present roam over the plains or in the mountains of the far West, and were then considered inaccessible to civilizing influences. It may be impossible to raise them fully up to the level of the white population of the United States; but we should not forget that they are the aborigines of the country, and called the soil their own on which our people have grown rich, powerful, and happy.[16]

Against the President's Position: Peace

CHIEF JOSEPH
AT HIS SURRENDER IN THE BEAR PAW MOUNTAINS, 1877

The first white men of your people who came to our country were named Lewis and Clark. They brought many things which our people had never seen. They talked straight and our people gave them a great feast as proof that their hearts were friendly. They made presents to our chiefs and our people made presents to them. We had a great many horses of which we gave them what they needed, and they gave us guns and tobacco in return. All the Nez Percé made friends with Lewis and Clark and agreed to let them pass through their country and never to make war on white men. This promise the Nez Percé have never broken.

For a short time we lived quietly. But this could not last. White men had found gold in the mountains around the land of the Winding Water. They stole a great many horses from us and we could not get them back because we were Indians. The white men told lies for each other. They drove off a great many of our cattle. Some white men branded our young cattle so they could claim them. We had no friends who would plead our cause before the law councils. It seemed to me that some of the white men in Wallowa were doing these things on purpose to get up a war. They knew we were not strong enough to fight them. I labored hard to avoid trouble and bloodshed. We gave up some of our country to the white men, thinking that then we could have peace. We were mistaken. The white men would not let us alone. We could have avenged our wrongs many times, but we did not. Whenever the Government has asked for help against other Indians we have never refused. When the white men were few and we were strong we could have killed them off, but the Nez Percé wishes to live at peace. On account of the treaty made by the other bands of the Nez Percé the white man claimed my lands. We were troubled with white men crowding over the line. Some of them were good men, and we lived on peaceful terms with them, but they were not all good. Nearly every year the agent came over from Lapwai and ordered us to the reservation. We always replied that we were satisfied to live in Wallowa. We were careful to refuse the presents or annuities which he offered. Through all the years since the white man came to Wallowa we have been threatened and taunted by them and the treaty Nez Percé. They have given us no rest. We have had a few good friends among the white men, and they have always advised my people to bear these taunts without fighting. Our young men are quick tempered and I have had great trouble in keeping them from doing rash things. I have carried a heavy load on my back ever since I was a boy. I learned then that we were but few while the white men were many, and that we could not hold our own with them. We were like deer. They were like grizzly bears. We had a small country. Their country was large. We were contented to let things remain as the Great Spirit Chief made them. They were not; and would change the mountains and rivers if they did not suit them.

Perhaps you think the Creator sent you here to dispose of us as you see fit. If I thought you were sent by the Creator, I might be induced to think you had a right to dispose of me. Do not misunderstand me, but understand fully, with reference to my affection for the land. I never said the land was mine to do with as I choose. The one who has a right to dispose of it is the one who has created it. I claim a right to live on my land, and accord you the privilege to return to yours. Brother, we have listened to your talk coming from the father in Washington, and my people have called upon me to reply to you. And in the winds which pass through these aged pines we hear the moaning of their departed ghosts. And if the voices of our people could have been heard, that act would never have been done. But alas, though they stood around, they could neither be seen nor heard. Their tears fell like drops of rain. I hear my voice in the depths of the forest, but no answering voice comes back to me. All is silent around me. My words must therefore be few. I can say no more. He is silent, for he has nothing to answer when the sun goes down.

Tell General Howard that I know his heart. What he told me before I have in my heart. I am tired of fighting. Our chiefs are killed. Looking Glass is dead, Tu-hul-hil-sote is dead. The old men are all dead. It is the young men who now say yes or no. He who led the young men [Joseph's brother Alikut] is dead. It is cold and we have no blankets. The little children are freezing to death. My people—some of them have run away to the hills and have no blankets and no food. No one knows where they are—perhaps freezing to death. I want to have time to look for my children and see how many of them I can find. Maybe I shall find them among the dead. Hear me, my chiefs, my heart is sick and sad. From where the sun now stands I will fight no more forever.[17]

NOTES

15. Richardson, Volume IX, p. 4424.

16. Richardson, Volume IX, pp. 4454–4455.

17. Great Wisdom, http://dkoch332.tripod.com/QuotesHTML/wisdom.htm (accessed November 22, 2002).

THE ISSUE: THE BLAND-ALLISON ACT

The hard money and soft money forces met again during the Hayes administration on the issue of silver. Democratic Congressman Richard "Silver Dick" Bland restated the 1896 free-silver Democratic party platform by introducing a bill that called for the unlimited coinage of the old standard silver dollar. The bill passed the House of Representatives with enthusiastic support, including backing from such unusual sources as Republicans Charles Foster and Jacob Dolson Cox from President

Hayes's own state of Ohio, and William McKinley, future president and champion of the gold standard.

The bill lost some steam in the Senate Finance Committee, where Iowa Republican William B. Allison proposed an amendment. Instead of the bill calling for unlimited coinage of silver, Allison suggested that it require at least two million and up to four million silver dollars be coined monthly, at the discretion of the Secretary of the Treasury. Soft money advocates accepted this alteration—noting that although two to four million was not unlimited, it certainly was a lot—and the House of Representatives passed the Bland-Allison Act on February 21, 1878.

The policy on which Bland-Allison was based promoted inflation, which benefited debtors by decreasing the value of money; the deflation created by the gold standard preserved a high value for money, meaning that debtors gave a premium when they paid back their loans, in effect giving back more money than they had received since money was more valuable in a deflation economy. The opposite was equally true: inflation hurt creditors while deflation helped creditors. The "debtors vs. creditors" mentality created a false picture of the economy, however, since many individuals were in some way both debtors and creditors, and economic interests also diversified across a range of interests including manufacturing, agriculture, importing and exporting, and so on. More to the point, dramatic changes, such as sudden inflation, tended to throw the U.S. economy (and, through it, the Western economy and beyond) into short-term tumult as the market and the government strove for balance amid unstable economic currents, and such tumult ultimately benefited few people, if any.

The debtor/creditor mentality also oversimplified the complexity of issues such as the silver question. President Hayes, for example, came to the presidency deeply in debt since the panic of 1873 and remained a debtor through his term in the White House. Despite his own personal economic position, however, he remained an advocate of hard money. He came to his position through both his understanding of economics and his convictions about morality. Not only did he believe hard money was fiscally the most sound alternative, but he also believed that altering the value of money for public or personal economic advantage was dishonest and immoral, and he believed such behavior would reduce international faith and respect in the United States and its citizens. Not only did he worry about the disorder sudden inflation would bring, but he also feared the dishonor he felt would come with the artificial manipulation of currency value for the benefit of some over others.

Hayes's protests fell on deaf ears. Although he vetoed the Bland-Allison Act, Congressmen such as Democratic representative Richard P. Bland of Missouri, known as "Silver Dick" because of his support for inflated silver currency, argued against and immediately overturned the veto and made the act law.

The President's Position: Against the Act

VETO MESSAGE
EXECUTIVE MANSION

February 28, 1878
To the House of Representatives:

After a very careful consideration of the House bill No. 1093, entitled "An act to authorize the coinage of the standard silver dollar and to restore its legal-tender character," I feel compelled to return it to the House of Representatives, in which it originated, with my objections to its passage.

Holding the opinion, which I expressed in my annual message, that "neither the interests of the Government nor of the people of the United States would be promoted by disparaging silver as one of the two precious metals which furnish the coinage of the world, and that legislation which looks to maintaining the volume of intrinsic money to as full a measure of both metals as their relative commercial values will permit would be neither unjust nor inexpedient," it has been my earnest desire to concur with Congress in the adoption of such measures to increase the silver coinage of the country as would not impair the obligation of contracts, either public or private, nor injuriously affect the public credit. It is only upon the conviction that this bill does not meet these essential requirements that I feel it my duty to withhold from it my approval. . . .

The bill provides for the coinage of silver dollars of the weight of 412 grains each, of standard silver, to be a legal tender at their nominal value for all debts and dues, public and private, except where otherwise expressly stipulated in the contract. It is well known that the market value of that number of grains of standard silver during the past year has been from 90 to 92 cents as compared with the standard gold dollar. Thus the silver dollar authorized by this bill is worth 8 to 10 per cent less than it purports to be worth, and is made a legal tender for debts contracted when the law did not recognize such coins as lawful money.

The right to pay duties in silver or in certificates for silver deposits will, when they are issued in sufficient amount to circulate, put an end to the receipt of revenue in gold, and thus compel the payment of silver for both the principal and interest of the public debt. One billion one hundred and forty-three million four hundred and ninety-three thousand four hundred dollars of the bonded debt now outstanding was issued prior to February, 1873, when the silver dollar was unknown in circulation in this country, and was only a convenient form of silver bullion for exportation; $583,440,350 of the funded debt has been issued since February, 1873, when gold alone was the coin for which the bonds were sold, and gold alone was the coin in which both parties to the contract understood that the bonds would be paid. These bonds entered into the markets of the world. They were paid for in gold when silver had greatly depreciated, and when no one would have bought them if it had been understood that they would be paid in silver. The sum of $225,000,000 of these bonds has been sold during my Administration for gold coin, and the United States received the benefit of these sales by a reduction of the rate of interest to 4 per cent. During the progress of these sales a doubt was suggested as to the coin in which payment of these bonds would be made. The public announcement was thereupon authorized that it was "not to be anticipated that any future legislation of Congress or any action of any department of the Government would sanction or tolerate the redemption of the principal of these bonds or the payment of the interest thereon in coin of less value than the coin authorized by law at the time of the issue of the bonds, being the coin exacted by the Government in exchange for the same." . . .

It is said that the silver dollar made a legal tender by this bill will under its operation be equivalent in value to the gold dollar. Many supporters of the bill believe this, and would not justify an attempt to pay debts, either public or private, in coin of inferior value to the money of the world. The capital defect of the bill is that it contains no provision protecting from its operation preexisting debts in case the coinage which it creates shall continue to be of less value than that which was the sole legal tender when they were contracted. If it is now proposed, for the purpose of taking advantage of the depreciation of silver in the payment of debts, to coin and make a legal tender a silver dollar of less commercial value than any dollar, whether of gold or paper, which is now lawful money in this country, such measure, it will hardly be questioned, will, in the judgment of mankind, be an act of bad faith. As to all debts heretofore contracted, the silver dollar should be made a legal tender only at its market value. The standard of value should not be changed without the consent of both parties to contract. National promises should be kept with unflinching fidelity. There is no power to compel a nation to pay its just debts. Its credit depends on its honor. The nation owes what it has led or allowed its creditors to expect. I can not approve a bill which in my judgment authorizes the violation of sacred obligations. The obligation of the public faith transcends all questions of profit or public advantage. Its unquestionable maintenance is the dictate as well of the highest expediency as of the most necessary duty, and should ever be carefully guarded by the Executive, by Congress, and by the people.

It is my firm conviction that if the country is to be benefited by a silver coinage it can be done only by the issue of silver dollars of full value, which will defraud no man. A currency worth less than it purports to be worth will in the end defraud not only creditors, but all who are engaged in legitimate business, and none more surely than those who are dependent on their daily labor for their daily bread.[18]

Against the President's Position: For the Act

REPRESENTATIVE RICHARD P. BLAND OF MISSOURI
HOUSE OF REPRESENTATIVES
DECEMBER 13, 1876

Mr. Speaker, it has been urged by the opponents of this bill that this measure has been forced upon the House and the country without due consideration. Sir, this bill was pending at the last session of this Congress six weeks; it has been discussed throughout the country in the public press and in nearly every congressional district in the country, and when the gentleman from Ohio claims that here, without consideration, we are endeavoring to pass a measure of this importance, and compares it to the explosion of Hell Gate, I apprehend that he has probably forgotten that when silver was demonetized in this country it was a Hell Gate explosion, and that he helped to apply the torch. The country was not informed of the fact that such a measure was pending in the House at that time.

Mr. Speaker, the gentleman from Iowa [Mr. Kasson] and the gentleman from New York [Mr. Hewitt] pleaded for time, for consideration, but I apprehend the fact that the pleading is for an extension of time wherein to oppress the debtor class of this country. It is simply a question, as was remarked by the gentleman from Pennsylvania [Mr. Kelley,] that instead of one day's work paying a certain amount of debt we shall require two days' work; that is the effect of establishing a single standard of values. It is not a matter of history that a famine occurred in Ireland which nearly swept the people of that green isle from the face of the earth because its people depended upon one standard of food!

If it were possible by legislation to decree that nothing but wheat should be used for bread, would it not be a consequence that the price of wheat would be double? But when there are two or three articles that may be used, the actual effect is that the price of the one governs the other and there is a medium standard established between the two. . . .

Pleading for time is pleading for the creditor class against the debtor. . . . The gentlemen who oppose this bill pretend to be especial advocates on this floor—and especially the gentleman from Iowa [Mr. Kasson]— of the workingmen, the widows, and orphans. He is not representing that class upon this floor, and I venture to assert that if you ask the workingmen, the widows, and orphans what they demand in this country there would be a unanimous voice in favor of this bill. But if he asks the creditor class, the men who hold the obligations of the country in behalf of public and private debts, they would demand payment in gold coin. He refers to the report of the Director of the Mint on this question of the variation of the prices of gold and silver, and the whole argument is an assumption when they undertake to say that gold is the only standard. It is merely an assumption, because gold has appreciated and was occasioned by the demonetizing of silver in Germany and the United States. Mr. Groschen, on behalf of the British Parliament, expressed himself with reference to these commodities having appreciated. I hope that this Government will in restoring to us a double standard, compel Germany to retrace her steps in that regard. . . .[19]

NOTES

18. James D. Richardson, ed., *A Compilation of the Messages and Papers of the Presidents*, Volume IX (New York: Bureau of National Literature, Inc., 1897), pp. 4438–4440.

19. *Congressional Record, Containing the Proceedings and Debates of the Forty-fourth Congress, First Session*, Volume V, Part I (Washington, D.C.: Government Printing Office, 1876), pp. 171–172.

RECOMMENDED READINGS

Barnard, Harry. *Rutherford B. Hayes, and His America*. Indianapolis: Bobbs-Merrill, 1954.

Barney, William L. *The Civil War and Reconstruction: A Student Companion*. New York: Oxford University Press, 2001.

Davison, Kenneth E. *The Presidency of Rutherford B. Hayes*. Westport, CT: Greenwood Press, 1972.

Geer, Emily Apt. *First Lady: The Life of Lucy Webb Hayes*. Kent: Kent State University Press: Rutherford B. Hayes Presidential Center, 1984.

Hoogenbloom, Ari. *The Presidency of Rutherford B. Hayes*. Lawrence: University Press of Kansas, 1988.

———. *Rutherford B. Hayes: One of the Good Colonels*. Abilene, TX: McWhiney Foundation Press, 1999.

Simpson, Brooks D. *The Reconstruction Presidents*. Lawrence: University Press of Kansas, 1998.

Williams, T. Harry. *Hayes of the Twenty-third: The Civil War Volunteer Officer*. New York: Knopf, 1965.

2

JAMES A. GARFIELD

(1881)

Public mourning and expressions of grief following the September 19, 1881 death of President James A. Garfield outshone even U.S. reaction to Abraham Lincoln's death less than two decades earlier, though Lincoln had led the nation through war, preserved the union, and met a tragic end. Garfield in effect ushered in a new aspect of the presidency—the chief executive as a celebrity—due to his long, courageous, and ultimately unsuccessful battle against an assassin's bullet, and due to the enduring question of what might have been had the leader had more time in the White House.

Like Hayes before him, Garfield was the son of an Ohio farmer. He was the last president to be born in a log cabin. When Garfield's father died two years after he was born, his mother assumed the task of running the family farm. The family lived in poverty, and Garfield soon went to work on a boat on the Ohio Canal. Garfield's ambitions, however, eventually took him in a number of different professional directions. After graduating from Williams College, he became first a professor of ancient languages and then the president of Western Reserve Eclectic Institute, which later became Hiram College. Garfield also studied law and was ordained a minister in the Disciples of Christ church. His interests led him to the infant Republican party, as a member of which he served in the Ohio state legislature. Distinguished military service during the Civil War in campaigns such as the Battle of Shiloh and the Battle of Chickamauga won him the rank of major general in the Union army. Elected to the U.S. House of Representatives, Garfield served the state of Ohio for nine terms until he was elected Senator in 1880.

When he attended the Republican presidential convention later that same year, Garfield had no intention of running for office. Instead, he sought to thwart the aspirations of the conservative Stalwart faction, led by New York Senator Roscoe Conkling, who supported former president Ulysses S. Grant, and the moderate Half-Breed faction that supported Maine Senator James G. Blaine, by backing the Secretary of the Treasury John Sherman as the best candidate for the White House. With Hayes's refusal to be renominated, the field of candidates was wide open. Garfield's impressive presence at the convention, and his eloquent nomination speech for Sherman, stole the spotlight from Sherman and the other candidates, however. When none of the three major contenders could win a majority of votes from the delegates, Garfield's name appeared. Even as Garfield was trying to remove himself from consideration by the electors, he won the party's nomination on the 36th ballot. In effect, the Republican party drafted the newly elected Senator Garfield to run for the presidency.

Though at first unwilling to accept the nomination, Garfield at last enthusiastically threw himself into the campaign. He capitalized on his "rags to riches" story of success and highlighted his role as a military hero. With the support of his adviser and wife, Lucretia Randolph Garfield, he conducted the first modern bid for the presidency, wooing the press, penning slogans, and orchestrating a "front porch" campaign headquartered in his Ohio home, where members of the media and voting public came to hear his platform and speeches. He defeated his opponents from the Democratic and Greenback parties by a clear, if not sizeable, margin.

Rather than following the traditional spoils system approach of rewarding personal supporters with official positions, Garfield tried to assemble a cabinet that represented all the divisions of the Republican party. Perhaps the most influential of his cabinet officials was former Republican presidential candidate Blaine, who served as Secretary of State. Despite his attempt to unify his party, Garfield, like Hayes, soon ran into conflict with Conkling over appointments in New York that challenged Conkling's patronage machine. Conkling resigned in the end. The civil service reform issue was one of several issues Garfield inherited from Hayes; the problems of monetary policy and race relations in the South both survived into Garfield's administration. Garfield echoed Hayes's position on each issue, though perhaps at times with more force.

Garfield had no opportunity to enact his policies, however. After only four months in office, he was shot in the back on July 2, 1881, by a rejected and irate civil service applicant as the president was planning to take a train from the capital to visit his wife, who lay ill in New Jersey. The shooter, Charles J. Guiteau, surrendered to the police, admitting, "I am a Stalwart. Arthur is now president of the United States." There could have been no better illustration of the need for civil service reform than Guiteau's partisan rationale for assassinating the chief executive.

But Arthur was not president. Garfield quietly and painfully fought for life for eighty days, enduring excruciating medical procedures (some of which were responsible for the wound proving fatal, as the assembled doctors bickered and competed and in some cases reinvented the term malpractice even according to the standards of the day) with remarkable composure and dignity. His survival, though heroic, left the executive branch in an uncertain position. The U.S. Constitution was vague as to whether the vice president should assume the power of the wounded president or displace Garfield altogether as leader of the nation. Garfield's vice president, Conkling Stalwart Chester Arthur, was horrified by Garfield's plight and unwilling to promote himself, so, since Congress was not in session at the time, the matter drifted, unresolved. At last a cabinet meeting agreed that no action would be taken without consulting Garfield; Garfield's doctors, however, refused any access to the dying man, and so the situation continued to flounder. Each department head took responsibility for that section's management, but the nation as a whole remained effectively leaderless. In the meantime, the U.S. public was riveted by the daily news about Garfield's battle for survival.

Finally, Garfield succumbed to slow blood poisoning on September 19, 1881, leaving his vice president to respond to the news with "childlike sobs."[1] Arthur, who at some level had been a tool of his party's faction throughout much of his political life, appeared transformed by the tragedy of Garfield's death and the overwhelming challenge left him in the presidency, becoming more of a leader than even his supporters believed he would be. The outpouring of national grief was tremendous, and was later made worse by the fact that Garfield's death was not the last in this new era of assassinations.

THE ISSUE: CIVIL SERVICE REFORM

The civil service reform issue, raised by Hayes and blocked in particular by Senator Roscoe Conkling, bled into the Garfield administration.

Garfield strongly supported Hayes's position that the spoils system of rewarding political supporters with government jobs led to corruption. His public speeches and private diary reflected this. He also saw the bureaucratic system that political patronage created, one that made the constant doling out of political appointments one of the major time-consuming duties of the chief executive, as a crippling inefficiency at the government's highest level. Garfield called for regulations and limitations on civil service to solve the problems. Like Hayes, Garfield met significant resistance to his reform goals in his own party. Unlike Hayes, however, Garfield eventually outlasted Conkling and his followers. Although he had made sure that Hayes's efforts at reform were mostly blocked, Conkling spent his political capital against his fellow party members; in 1881, he resigned from office in protest of Hayes, Garfield, and their position on patronage.

The aggressive office-seeking mentality that Garfield believed was produced by the uncontrolled and unaccountable spoils system soon was highlighted for the entire nation to see. On July 2, 1881, a frustrated office seeker approached Garfield in the Washington, D.C., railroad station and shot him in the back. The president lingered for over two months before he died. The assassin, Charles J. Guiteau, explained his actions in terms of party faction loyalty, noting that his action moved fellow Stalwart Chester A. Arthur to the White House.

Garfield's death at the hands of a frustrated player in the spoils system game meant that Chester A. Arthur, a conservative Republican of the same Stalwart faction that produced Roscoe Conkling (indeed, Arthur was one of the civil servants whose resignation Hayes had demanded during his own attempt to reform the civil service), became chief executive. Interestingly enough, however, this did not mean the end of Garfield's plan for reform. In fact, popular outrage about the assassination and its cause forced the issue into the spotlight. Mourners of the late president demanded that action be taken. Arthur then was able to harness the favorable public sentiment about the fallen Garfield to support and sign into law the Pendleton Civil Service Act in 1883.

The Pendleton act created the precedent and mechanism for permanent federal employment of individuals based not on political activity or even party membership itself, but rather on individual merit and suitability for a given job. The act established the Civil Service Commission as the independent body responsible for the open selection of employees who competed fairly without regard to politics, religion, race, or national origin. Although the law applied only to approximately ten percent of federal positions at the time it was passed, it was a first step in the direction both Hayes and Garfield had desired, and it left the door open for almost every succeeding president to expand the scope and applicability of the law. What Hayes had begun and Garfield had hoped to do, Arthur was able to accomplish; but not without a national tragedy to underscore the problem, end the debate, and create consensus about the issue.

The President's Position: Civil Service Reform

FROM GARFIELD'S INAUGURAL SPEECH
MARCH 4, 1881

The civil service can never be placed on a satisfactory basis until it is regulated by law. For the good of the service itself, for the protection of those who are intrusted with the appointing power against the waste of time and obstruction to the public business caused by the inordinate pressure for place, and for the protection of incumbents against intrigue and wrong, I shall at the proper time ask Congress to fix the tenure of the minor offices of the several Executive Departments and prescribe the grounds upon which removals shall be made during the terms for which incumbents have been appointed.[2]

PRESIDENT GARFIELD'S REFLECTIONS ON POLITICAL
PATRONAGE
FROM HIS DIARY
MARCH–MAY 1881

Wednesday, 16. [March 1881]   Got on fairly well through the day, with the usual rush; the numbers are smaller, but the appetite for office apparently keener. It will cost me some struggle to keep from despising the office seeker. Worked off many minor appointments, and some of importance.

Wednesday, 6. [April 1881]   The rush of visitors was greater today than usual. I sent in some nominations of marshals and postmasters. In the evening Gen. and Mrs. Logan dined with us, and after dinner, I had a long conversation with the General *de rebus certaminis inter Senatores meque* [about certain matters between the Senators and me]. Conkling alleges that Robertson is his bitter personal enemy.

I summed up the case in reply to allegation. 1. The Robertson appointment is mine not another's. 2. The office is national, not local. 3. Having given all the other places to Conkling's friends, he is neither magnanimous nor just, in opposing this one friend of mine. 4. He has raised a question of veracity with me and it shall be tried—by the Senate. Senator Ferry and Representative Pound called. The only exercise I had today was billiards and casino. Retired at 11pm.

Monday, 16. [May 1881]   . . . At 12 Senators Conkling and Platt tendered their resignations as senators, a very weak attemp[t] at the heroic. If I do not mistake, it will be received with guffaws of laughter. They appeal to a legislature which they think is already secured. Even in this they may fail. The[y] have wounded the self love of their brother Senators, and will lose by it. Late at night the Associated Press sent me their letter to Gov. Cornell, giving their reasons for resigning. It is a weak attempt at masquerading as injured innocents and Civil Service reformers. They are neither. I go on without disturbance. Having done all I fairly could to avoid a fight, I now fight to the end. Retired at midnight.[3]

6–13 June 1881 [On 6 June after three days absence from Washington] The stream of callers which was damned up by absence became a torrent and swept away my day.

[8 June]   My day in the office was very like its predecessors. Once or twice I felt like crying out in the agony of my soul against the greed for office and its consumption of my time. My services ought to be worth more to the government than to be spent thus.

[13 June]   I am feeling greatly dissatisfied for my lack of opportunity for study. My day is frittered away by the personal seeking of people, when it ought to be given to the great problem[s] which concern the whole country. Four years of this kind of intellectual dissipation may cripple me for the remainder of my life. What might not a vigorous thinker do, if he could be allowed to use the opportunities of a Presidential term in vital, useful activity! Some Civil Service Reform will come by necessity after the weariness of some years of wasted Presidents have paved the way for it.[4]

Against the President's Position: Against Civil Service Reform

SENATOR ROSCOE CONKLING'S LETTER OF RESIGNATION

Washington, D.C., May 14, 1881
Sir:

Transmitting, as we do, our resignations, respectively, of the great trusts with which New York has honoured us, it is fit that we acquaint you, and through you the Legislature and people of the State, with the reasons which, in our judgment, make such a step respectful and necessary.

Some weeks ago the President sent to the Senate in a group the nominations of several persons for public offices already filled. One of these offices is the Collectorship of the port of New York, now held by General Merritt; another is the Consul-Generalship at London, now held by General Badeau; another is Chargé d'Affaires to Denmark, held by Mr. Cramer; another is the mission to Switzerland, held by Mr. Fish, a son of the former distinguished Secretary of State. Mr. Fish had, in deference to an ancient practice, placed his position at the disposal of the new Administration, but, like the other persons named, he was ready to remain at his post if permitted to do so. All of these officers, save only Mr. Cramer, are citizens of New York. It was proposed to displace them all, not for any alleged fault of theirs, or for any alleged need or advantage of the public service, but in order to give the great office of Collector of the port of New York to Mr. William H. Robertson as a "reward" for certain acts of his, said to have "aided in making the nomination of General Garfield possible." The chain of removals thus proposed was broken by General Badeau's promptly declining to accept the new place to which he was to be sent.

These nominations summoned every member of the Senate to say on his oath whether he "advised" such a transaction. The movement was more than a surprise. . . . After earnest reflection and consultation we believed the proceeding unwise and wrong, whether considered wholly in relation to the preservation and integrity of the public service and the public example to be set, or in relation also to the integrity of the Republican party. No public utterance of comment or censure was made by either of us in the Senate or elsewhere; on the contrary, we thought that the President would reconsider an action so sudden and hasty, and would at least adopt a less hurtful and objectionable mode of requiting personal or individual service.

In this hope the following paper was prepared and signed, and presented by Mr. James to the President, who was subsequently informed that you had authorized your named to be added also:
To The President.

We beg leave to remonstrate against the change in the Collectorship at New York by the removal of Mr. Merritt and the appointment of Mr. Robertson. The proposal was wholly a surprise. We heard of it only when the several nominations involved in the plan were announced in the Senate. We had only two days before this had been informed from you that a change in the Customs office at New York was not contemplated; and, quite ignorant of a purpose to take any action now, we had no opportunity, until after the nominations, to make the suggestions we now present. We do not believe that the interests of the public service will be promoted by removing the present Collector and putting Mr. Robertson in his stead. Our opinion is quite the reverse, and we believe no political advantage can be gained for either the Republican party or its principles. Believing that no individual has claims or obligations which should be liquidation in such a mode, we earnestly and respectfully ask that the nomination of Mr. Robertson be withdrawn.

Chester A. Arthur
T. C. Platt
Thomas L. James
Roscoe Conkling

. . . Immediately after the nominations were published, letters and telegrams in great numbers came from every part of the State, from its leading citizens, protesting against the proposed changes and condemning them on many grounds. Several thousand of the leading mercantile firms of New York—constituting, we are informed, a majority of every branch of trade—sent us remonstrances. Sixty of the eighty-one Republican members of the Assembly, by letter or memorial, made objection. Representatives in Congress, State officials, business men, professional men, commercial, industrial and political organizations, are among the remonstrants, and they speak from every section of the State. Besides the nominations already referred to, there were awaiting the action of the Senate several citizens of New York named for offices connected with the courts, district-attorneys and marshals. These were all reappointments. Most of them had been originally commissioned by Mr. Hayes. They were certified by the judges of the courts and many other eminent persons, who attested the faithfulness and merit of their service, and recommended their continuance. They were not presented by us.

We have not attempted to "dictate," nor have we asked the nomination of one person to any office in the State. Indeed, with the sole exception of the written request set forth above, we have never even expressed an opinion to the President in any case unless questioned in regard to it. . . .

With a profound sense of the obligation we owe, with devotion to the Republican party and its creed of liberty and right, with reverent attachment to the great State whose interests and honor are dear to us, we hold it respectful and becoming to make room for those who may correct all the errors we have made, and interpret aright all the duties we have misconceived.

We, therefore, inclose [sic] our resignations, but hold fast the privilege, as citizens and Republicans, to stand for the constitutional rights of all men, and of all representatives, whether of the States, the nation, or the people.

> We have the honor to be,
> Very respectfully, your obedient servants,
> Roscoe Conkling
> Thomas C. Platt
> To His Excellency Governor Cornell, Albany, N.Y.

NOTES

1. Justus D. Doenecke, *The Presidencies of James A. Garfield and Chester A. Arthur* (Lawrence: University Press of Kansas, 1981), p. 54.

2. The Avalon Project at Yale Law School, *Inaugural Addresses of the Presidents*, http://www.yale.edu/lawweb/avalon/presiden/inaug/garfield.htm (accessed November 5, 2002).

3. James A. Garfield, *The Diary of James A. Garfield*, Volume IV: 1878–1881, Harry James Brown and Frederick D. Williams, eds. (Detroit: Michigan State University Press, 1981), pp. 559, 570, 593.

4. Watts and Israel, p. 160.

THE ISSUE: RESUMPTION

As with the political issue of civil service reform, the economic issue of resumption survived from the Hayes administration into Garfield's term. Like Hayes, Garfield was a hard money advocate. Not only did he support resumption from his inaugural address onward, but he questioned whether the government even had (or had ever had) the authority to issue greenbacks in the first place. He was a bimetallist; in other words, he believed the government should use both gold and silver to make legal tender coins. His position did not endear many, though. Many bimetallists, like the greenbackers to whom they were politically related, sought inflation as a means of alleviating the economic problems of agriculture and debtor interests as well as other sectors that had been hurt by depression. In order to create inflation, they called for unlimited coinage of and artificially adjusted value for silver coins. Garfield, however, found this morally dishonest and fiscally irresponsible, and instead called for bimetallism at an absolutely free exchange rate, which meant that gold, the more scarce and precious metal, would always be worth more and therefore be more in demand.

In short, Garfield's position, like Hayes's, supported a stable, market-driven economy of competing specie currencies based on a confidence in the gold standard. His policy played into the existing rhetoric and platform of the Greenback-Labor party and similar groups that framed the monetary issue as one of creditors vs. debtors, agriculture vs. industry, labor vs. elite, the Midwest vs. the East, and poverty vs. wealth. Not only did they think the current system failed to benefit them, but the Greenback-Labor party and associated groups also believed it was the product of an active conspiracy by those in power in Washington and New York—and even overseas interests in scheming foreign nations— to oppress the common people, eradicate their values and ways of life, and maintain the elite in its position of privilege.

Not all of the president's opposition came from those who advocated greenbacks and/or free silver. That side of the political spectrum, grass-roots populism, arose essentially as a reaction against change: an agrarian backlash against industrialism, a political backlash against the elite, a distrust of innovators and outsiders, such as foreigners and economic competitors who threatened a traditional way of life. This populism often called for increased governmental involvement in all aspects of everyday activity. On the other end of the spectrum was anarchism, based on the ideal of noncoercion, which spawned much social, political, and economic experimentation. This anarchism often called for limited or no government involvement in individual affairs. If the greenback and free silver advocates opposed Garfield's economic plan because they wished the government to do more for the "common people," anarchists opposed Garfield's economic plan because they believed the government was already doing too much.

The political activist and theorist Lysander Spooner was one such anarchist. In his many works of political thought, he wrote about government monopolies that concentrated power in the hands of the few. In the case of bimetallism, he argued that the government's decision to sanction only gold and silver as legal tender gave those coins unnatural value, in effect robbing honest citizens and arbitrarily rewarding those who hoarded the government-sponsored money. Like populists, anarchists like Spooner perceived collusion among those in power; unlike populists, anarchists like Spooner did not believe those leaders sought to destroy any individual way of life in favor of another newer one. Instead, Spooner argued that government leaders' ultimate goal was simply to obtain and wield power.

Garfield did not live long enough to make any substantial contribution to economic policy. The question of resumption, the issues of greenbacks and bimetallism, would continue to play a key role in economic debates into the twentieth century.

The President's Position: For Resumption

GARFIELD'S INAUGURAL ADDRESS
MARCH 4, 1881

Enterprises of the highest importance to our moral and material well-being unite us and offer ample employment of our best powers. Let all our people, leaving behind them the battlefields of dead issues, move forward and in their strength of liberty and the restored Union win the grander victories of peace.

The prosperity which now prevails is without parallel in our history. Fruitful seasons have done much to secure it, but they have not done all. The preservation of the public credit and the resumption of specie payments, so successfully attained by the Administration of my predecessors, have enabled our people to secure the blessings which the seasons brought.

By the experience of commercial nations in all ages it has been found that gold and silver afford the only safe foundation for a monetary system. Confusion has recently been created by variations in the relative value of the two metals, but I confidently believe that arrangements can be made between the leading commercial nations which will secure the general use of both metals. Congress should provide that the compulsory coinage of silver now required by law may not disturb our monetary system by driving either metal out of circulation. If possible, such an adjustment should be made that the purchasing power of every coined dollar will be exactly equal to its debt-paying power in all the markets of the world.

The chief duty of the National Government in connection with the currency of the country is to coin money and declare its value. Grave doubts have been entertained whether Congress is authorized by the Constitution to make any form of paper money legal tender. The present issue of United States notes has been sustained by the necessities of war; but such paper should depend for its value and currency upon its convenience in use and its prompt redemption in coin at the will of the holder, and not upon its compulsory circulation. These notes are not money, but promises to pay money. If the holders demand it, the promise should be kept.

The refunding of the national debt at a lower rate of interest should be accomplished without compelling the withdrawal of the national-bank notes, and thus disturbing the business of the country.

I venture to refer to the position I have occupied on financial questions during a long service in Congress, and to say that time and experience have strengthened the opinions I have so often expressed on these subjects.

The finances of the Government shall suffer no detriment which it may be possible for my Administration to prevent.

The interests of agriculture deserve more attention from the Government than they have yet received. The farms of the United States afford homes and employment for more than one-half our people, and furnish much the largest part of all our exports. As the Government lights our coasts for the protection of mariners and the benefit of commerce, so it should give to the tillers of the soil the best lights of practical science and experience.

Our manufacturers are rapidly making us industrially independent, and are opening to capital and labor new and profitable fields of employment. Their steady and healthy growth should still be matured.[5]

Against the President's Position: Against Resumption/ Against Government Monopoly on Money

1880 GREENBACK-LABOR PARTY PLATFORM

Civil government should guarantee the divine right of every laborer to the results of his toil, thus enabling the producers of wealth to provide themselves with the means for physical comfort, and the facilities for mental, social and moral culture; and we condemn as unworthy of our civilization the barbarism which imposes upon the wealth-producers a state of perpetual drudgery as the price of bare animal existence. Notwithstanding the enormous increase of productive power, and the universal introduction of laborsaving machinery, and the discovery of new agents for the increase of wealth, the task of the laborer is scarcely lightened, the hours of toil are but little shortened; and few producers are lifted from poverty into comfort and pecuniary independence. The associated monopolies, the international syndicate and other income classes demand dear money and cheap labor: a "strong government," and hence a weak people.

Corporate control of the volume of money has been the means of dividing society into hostile classes, of the unjust distribution of the products of labor, and of building up monopolies of associated capital endowed with power to confiscate private property. It has kept money scarce, and scarcity of money enforces debt, trade and public and corporate loans. Debt engenders usury, and usury ends in the bankruptcy of the borrower. Other results are deranged markets, uncertainty in manufacturing enterprise and agriculture, precarious and intermittent employment for the laborers, industrial war, increasing pauperism and crime, and the consequent intimidation and disfranchisement of the producer and a rapid declension into corporate feudalism; therefore, we declare:

First—That the right to make and issue money is a sovereign power to be maintained by the people for the common benefit. The delegation of this right to corporations is a surrender of the central attribute of sovereignty, [void] of constitutional sanction, conferring upon a subordinate and irresponsible power absolute dominion over industry and commerce. All money, whether metallic or paper, should be issued and its volume controlled by the Government, and not by or through banking corporations, and when so issued should be a full legal-tender for all debts, public and private.

Second—That the bonds of the United States should not be refunded, but paid as rapidly as practicable, according to contract. To enable the Government to meet these obligations, legal tender currency should be substituted for the notes of the National banks, the National banking system abolished, and the unlimited coinage of silver, as well as gold, established by law.

. . . Thirteenth—We demand a government of the people, by the people, and for the people, instead of a government of the bondholder, by the bondholder, and for the bondholder; and we denounce every attempt to stir up sectional strife as an effort to conceal monstrous crimes against the people.

Fourteenth—In the furtherance of these ends we ask the co-operation of all fair-minded people. We have no quarrel with individuals, wage no war upon classes, but only against vicious institutions. We are not content to endure further discipline from our present actual rulers, who, having dominion over money, over transportation, over land and labor, and largely over the press and machinery of Government, wield unwarrantable power over our institutions, and over our life and property.[6]

"GOLD AND SILVER AS STANDARDS OF VALUE: THE FLAGRANT CHEAT IN REGARD TO THEM" LYSANDER SPOONER 1878

All the usurpation, and tyranny, and extortion, and robbery, and fraud, that are involved in the monopoly of money are practised, and attempted to be justified, under the pretence of maintaining the standard of value. This pretence is intrinsically a false one throughout. And the whole motive for it is to afford some color of justification for such a monopoly of money as will enable the few holders of gold and silver coins (or of such other money as may be specially licensed and substituted for them) to extort, in exchange for them, more of other men's property than the coins (or their substitutes) arc naturally and truly worth. . . .

If it should be said—as it constantly is said—that the fact of the coins being made money, and the further fact of prohibitions or limitations being imposed upon all other money, have given the coins "a purchasing power" far above their true and natural value as metals, the answer is that such a "purchasing power" is an unjust and extortionate power—a mere power of robbery—arbitrarily granted to the holders of the coins, from no motive whatever but to enable them to get more for their coins than they are really worth; or, what is the same thing, to enable them to coerce all other persons into selling their property to the holders of the coins for less than it is worth. And this is really the only motive that was ever urged against the free purchase and sale of all other money in competition with the coins. . . .

This supposed case . . . gives a fair illustration of the sense, motives, and honesty of all that class of men who are continually crying out for prohibitions or limitations upon all money except gold and silver coins, or some other privileged money, under pretence of maintaining the standard of value. They all have but one and the same motive,—namely, the monopoly of money, and the power which that monopoly gives them to rob everybody else.[7]

NOTES

5. The Avalon Project at Yale Law School, *Inaugural Addresses of the Presidents*, www.yale.edu/lawweb/avalon/presiden/inaug/garfield.htm (accessed November 5, 2002).

6. Greenback-Labor Party Platform 1880, www.geocities.com/CollegePark/Quad/6460/doct/880glp.html (accessed November 22, 2002).

7. Lysander Spooner, www.lysanderspooner.org/goldandsilver.htm (accessed November 22, 2002).

THE ISSUE: RACE IN THE SOUTH

The Hayes administration had changed the face of the U.S. South by withdrawing federal troops from the former Confederate states and returning local and state rule to the area. Although Hayes reminded the states that they had to uphold the Fourteenth and Fifteenth Amendments and cultivate good relationships between the races, he backed this with little federal supervision to make certain that it happened. The South that Garfield inherited was still experiencing the social, economic, and political upheaval of both the Civil War experience and the Reconstruction military occupation. Those who suffered most from the upheaval were often those with the least power: African Americans.

In his inaugural address, Garfield outlined his concern for the active citizenship and participation of Southern blacks. He knew that the right to vote—carefully protected and responsibly exercised—would be an important power for progress in the South in general and in the lives of African-American Southerners in particular. At the heart of the issue, in Garfield's opinion, was education. An educated black electorate, he believed, had to be one of the most important goals for the South and the country.

Looking back on this time, African-American educator and activist W. E. B. DuBois, an influential writer and co-founder of the National Association for the Advancement of Colored People (NAACP), criticized Garfield's vision as "incomplete and over-simple." He argued that it was impossible to expect blacks to emerge from generations of slavery without psychological, social, and economic scars. Simply learning to read would not put them on the same level political playing field as their white neighbors, he believed, not when the African-American community and even the family unit were the casualties of a long campaign against them. DuBois argued that as long as racism remained—as evidenced in lynching, segregation, race riots, discriminatory Jim Crow laws, and other phenomena in the South and nationwide—only agitation and protest could adequately secure rights and opportunity.

Other black leaders such as Booker T. Washington disagreed with Garfield's vision in a different way. Rather than rejecting his view of the vote as not enough, these leaders encouraged the African-American community to move slowly and steadily, to give up political power in the short term and focus instead on practical, industrial education. By accepting the system of segregation and discrimination, and through patience and hard work achieving stability and self-sufficiency, Washington believed, blacks would win the respect of the white majority, and thus social acceptance and political power.

In short, both sides of the African-American community found Garfield's prescription for a solution to the Southern race problem ineffective: some believed his "educated vote" goal too simplistic and unambitious to secure political equality, and some believed it entailed too much too soon to be practical. Garfield's untimely death denied him the opportunity to pursue his policy further. His desire for equal opportunity did appear somewhat before its time, however; over a decade later in the 1896 *Plessy v. Ferguson* case, the Supreme Court upheld racial segregation in schools, begging the question of how "equal" such separate facilities could be.

The President's Position: For Education

GARFIELD'S INAUGURAL ADDRESS
MARCH 4, 1881

The elevation of the negro race from slavery to the full rights of citizenship is the most important political change we have known since the adoption of the Constitution of 1787. NO thoughtful man can fail to appreciate its beneficent effect upon our institutions and people. It has freed us from the perpetual danger of war and dissolution. It has added immensely to the moral and industrial forces of our people. It has liberated the master as well as the slave from a relation which wronged and enfeebled both. It has surrendered to their own guardianship the manhood of more than 5,000,000 people, and has opened to each one of them a career of freedom and usefulness. It has given new inspiration to the power of self-help in both races by making labor more honorable to the one and more necessary to the other. The influence of this force will grow greater and bear richer fruit with the coming years.

No doubt this great change has caused serious disturbance to our Southern communities. This is to be deplored, though it was perhaps unavoidable. But those who resisted the change should remember that under our institutions there was no middle ground for the negro race between slavery and equal citizenship. There can be no permanent disfranchised peasantry in the United States. Freedom can never yield its fullness of blessings so long as the law or its administration places the smallest obstacle in the pathway of any virtuous citizen.

The emancipated race has already made remarkable progress. With unquestioning devotion to the Union, with a patience and gentleness not born of fear, they have "followed the light as God gave them to see the light." They are rapidly laying the material foundations of self-support, widening their circle of intelligence, and beginning to enjoy the blessings that gather around the homes of the industrious poor. They deserve the generous encouragement of all good men. So far as my authority can lawfully extend they shall enjoy the full and equal protection of the Constitution and the laws.

The free enjoyment of equal suffrage is still in question, and a frank statement of the issue may aid its solution. It is alleged that in many communities negro citizens are practically denied the freedom of the ballot. In so far as the truth of this allegation is admitted, it is answered that in many places honest local government is impossible if the mass of uneducated negroes are allowed to vote. These are grave allegations. So far as the latter is true, it is the only palliation that can be offered for opposing the freedom of the ballot. Bad local government is certainly a great evil, which ought to be prevented; but to violate the freedom and sanctities of the suffrage is more than an evil. It is a crime which, if persisted in, will destroy the Government itself. Suicide is not a remedy. If in other lands it be high treason to compass the death of the king, it shall be counted no less a crime here to strangle our sovereign power and stifle its voice.

It has been said that unsettled questions have no pity for the repose of nations. It should be said with the utmost emphasis that this question of the suffrage will never give repose or safety to the States or to the nation until each, within its own jurisdiction, makes and keeps the ballot free and pure by the strong sanctions of the law.

But the danger which arises from ignorance in the voter can not be denied. It covers a field far wider than that of negro suffrage and the present condition of the race. It is a danger that lurks and hides in the sources and fountains of power in every state. We have no standard by which to measure the disaster that may be brought upon us by ignorance and vice in the citizens when joined to corruption and fraud in the suffrage.

The voters of the Union, who make and unmake constitutions, and upon whose will hang the destinies of our governments, can transmit their supreme authority to no successors save the coming generation of voters, who are the sole heirs of sovereign power. If that generation comes to its inheritance blinded by ignorance and corrupted by vice, the fall of the Republic will be certain and remediless.

The census has already sounded the alarm in the appalling figures which mark how dangerously high the tide of illiteracy has risen among our voters and their children.

To the South this question is of supreme importance. But the responsibility for the existence of slavery did not rest upon the South alone. The nation itself is responsible for the extension of the suffrage, and is under special obligations to aid in removing the illiteracy which it has added to the voting population. For the North and South alike there is but one remedy. All the constitutional power of the nation and of the

States and all the volunteer forces of the people should be surrendered to meet this danger by the savory influence of universal education.

It is the high privilege and sacred duty of those now living to educate their successors and fit them, by intelligence and virtue, for the inheritance which awaits them.

In this beneficent work sections and races should be forgotten and partisanship should be unknown. Let our people find a new meaning in the divine oracle which declares that "a little child shall lead them," for our own little children will soon control the destinies of the Republic.

My countrymen, we do not now differ in our judgment concerning the controversies of past generations, and fifty years hence our children will not be divided in their opinions concerning our controversies. They will surely bless their fathers and their fathers' God that the Union was preserved, that slavery was overthrown, and that both races were made equal before the law. We may hasten or we may retard, but we can not prevent, the final reconciliation. Is it not possible for us now to make a truce with time by anticipating and accepting its inevitable verdict?[8]

Against the President's Position: Against Oversimplification of the Problem

STRIVINGS OF THE NEGRO PEOPLE
BY W. E. BURGHARDT DU BOIS
ATLANTIC MONTHLY, 1897

... Years have passed away, ten, twenty, thirty. Thirty years of national life, thirty years of renewal and development, and yet the swarthy ghost of Banquo sits in its old place at the national feast. ... The freedman has not yet found in freedom his promised land. Whatever of lesser good may have come in these years of change, the shadow of a deep disappointment rests upon the Negro people,—a disappointment all the more bitter because the unattained ideal was unbounded save by the simple ignorance of a lowly folk.

The first decade was merely a prolongation of the vain search for freedom, the boom that seemed ever barely to elude their grasp,—like a tantalizing will-o'-the-wisp, maddening and misleading the headless host. The holocaust of war, the terrors of the Kuklux Klan, the lies of carpet-baggers, the disorganization of industry, and the contradictory advice of friends and foes left the bewildered serf with no new watchword beyond the old cry for freedom. As the decade closed, however, he began to grasp a new idea. The ideal of liberty demanded for its attainment powerful means, and these the Fifteenth Amendment gave him. The ballot, which before he had looked upon as a visible sign of freedom, he now regarded as the chief means of gaining and perfecting the liberty with which war had partially endowed him. And why not?

Had not votes made war and emancipated millions? Had not votes enfranchised the freedmen? Was anything impossible to a power that had done all this? A million black men started with renewed zeal to vote themselves into the kingdom. The decade fled away,—a decade containing, to the freedman's mind, nothing but suppressed votes, stuffed ballot-boxes, and election outrages that nullified his vaunted right of suffrage. And yet that decade from 1875 to 1885 held another powerful movement, the rise of another ideal to guide the unguided, another pillar of fire by night after a clouded day. It was the ideal of "book-learning;" the curiosity, born of compulsory ignorance, to know and test the power of the cabalistic letters of the white man, the longing to know. Mission and night schools began in the smoke of battle, ran the gauntlet of reconstruction, and at last developed into permanent foundations. Here at last seemed to have been discovered the mountain path to Canaan; longer than the highway of emancipation and law, steep and rugged, but straight, leading to heights high enough to overlook life.

Up the new path the advance guard toiled, slowly, heavily, doggedly; only those who have watched and guided the faltering feet, the misty minds, the dull understandings of the dark pupils of these schools know how faithfully, how piteously, this people strove to learn. It was weary work. The cold statistician wrote down the inches of progress here and there, noted also where here and there a foot had slipped or some one had fallen. To the tired climbers, the horizon was ever dark, the mists were often cold, the Canaan was always dim and far away. If, however, the vistas disclosed as yet no goal, no resting-place, little but flattery and criticism, the journey at least gave leisure for reflection and self-examination; it changed the child of emancipation to the youth with dawning self-consciousness, self-realization, self-respect. In those sombre forests of his striving his own soul rose before him, and he saw himself,—darkly as through a veil; and yet he saw in himself some faint revelation of his power, of his mission. He began to have a dim feeling that, to attain his place in the world, he must be himself, and not another. For the first time he sought to analyze the burden he bore upon his back, that dead-weight of social degradation partially masked behind a half-named Negro problem. He felt his poverty; without a cent, without a home, without land, tools, or savings, he had entered into competition with rich, landed, skilled neighbors. To be a poor man is hard, but to be a poor race in a land of dollars is the very bottom of hardships. He felt the weight of his ignorance,—not simply of letters, but of life, of business, of the humanities; the accumulated sloth and shirking and awkwardness of decades and centuries shackled his hands and feet. Nor was his burden all poverty and ignorance. The red stain of bastardy, which two centuries of systematic legal defilement of Negro women had stamped upon his race, meant not only the loss of ancient African chastity, but also the hereditary weight of a mass of filth from white whore-mongers and adulterers, threatening almost the obliteration of the Negro home.

A people thus handicapped ought not to be asked to race with the world, but rather allowed to give all its time and thought to its own social problems. But alas! while sociologists gleefully count his bastards and his prostitutes, the very soul of the toiling, sweating black man is darkened by the shadow of a vast despair. . . .

Thus the second decade of the American Negro's freedom was a period of conflict, of inspiration and doubt, of faith and vain questionings, of Sturm and Drang. The ideals of physical freedom, of political power, of school training, as separate all-sufficient panaceas for social ills, became in the third decade dim and overcast. They were the vain dreams of credulous race childhood; not wrong, but incomplete and over-simple. The training of the schools we need to-day more than ever,—the training of deft hands, quick eyes and ears, and the broader, deeper, higher culture of gifted minds. The power of the ballot we need in sheer self-defense, and as a guarantee of good faith. We may misuse it, but we can scarce do worse in this respect than our whilom masters. Freedom, too, the long-sought, we still seek,—the freedom of life and limb, the freedom to work and think. Work, culture, and liberty,—all these we need, not singly, but together; for to-day these ideals among the Negro people are gradually coalescing, and finding a higher meaning in the unifying ideal of race,—the ideal of fostering the traits and talents of the Negro, not in opposition to, but in conformity with, the greater ideals of the American republic, in order that some day, on American soil, two world races may give each to each those characteristics which both so sadly lack. Already we come not altogether empty-handed: there is to-day no true American music but the sweet wild melodies of the Negro slave; the American fairy tales are Indian and African; we are the sole oasis of simple faith and reverence in a dusty desert of dollars and smartness. . . .

Merely a stern concrete test of the underlying principles of the great republic is the Negro problem, and the spiritual striving of the freedmen's sons is the travail of souls whose burden is almost beyond the measure of their strength, but who bear it in the name of an historic race, in the name of this land of their fathers' fathers, and in the name of human opportunity.[9]

NOTES

8. The Avalon Project at Yale Law School, *Inaugural Addresses of the Presidents*, www.yale.edu/lawweb/avalon/presiden/inaug/garfield.htm (accessed November 5, 2002).

9. W. E. B. Du Bois, "Strivings of the Negro People," http://eserver.org/race/strivings.txt (accessed November 22, 2002).

RECOMMENDED READINGS

Booraem, Hendrik, V. *The Road to Respectability: James A. Garfield and His World, 1844–1852.* Lewisburg, PA: Bucknell University Press; Cleveland, OH: Western Reserve Historical Society Press, 1987.

Brooks, Stewart M. *Our Murdered Presidents: The Medical Story.* New York: F. Fell, 1966.

Doenecke, Justus D. *The Presidencies of James A. Garfield and Chester A. Arthur.* Lawrence: University Press of Kansas, 1981.

Feis, Ruth Stanley-Brown. *Mollie Garfield in the White House.* Chicago: Rand McNally, 1963.

Peskin, Allan. *Garfield: A Biography.* Kent: Kent State University Press, 1999.

Rupp, Robert O. *James A. Garfield: A Bibliography.* Westport, CT: Greenwood Press, 1997.

Shaw, John, ed. *Crete and James: Personal Letters of Lucretia and James Garfield.* East Lansing: Michigan State University Press, 1994.

Taylor, John M. *Garfield of Ohio: The Available Man.* New York: Norton, 1970.

3

CHESTER A. ARTHUR

(1881–1885)

Brought to and taken from the White House by circumstances beyond his control and against his desire, Chester A. Arthur's presidential story is one of dramatic transformation and tremendous tragedy. Born the son of a Baptist minister on October 5, 1829, Arthur graduated from Union College in Schenectady, New York. He worked as a schoolteacher as he studied for the bar, and after passing in 1854, he joined a New York City law firm. His strong abolitionist beliefs led him to take a number of important race-related cases, the most notable of which was the suit of an African-American woman against a Brooklyn streetcar company that reserved vehicles for whites only and denied her a seat. Arthur's courtroom victory in this case led to a state law against discrimination in public transportation. He continued his active role in the state by serving as New York's quartermaster general during the Civil War.

Arthur's political beginnings were somewhat less savory than his legal work, however. As a New York Republican, Arthur quickly fell under the sway of party machine leader Roscoe Conkling, who rewarded Arthur's faithful support by persuading then-president Ulysses S. Grant to give him the important position of customs collector for the lucrative port of New York City. During Hayes's term in the White House, Arthur was one of the officials singled out by the president as an example of civil service gone wrong, since he held his job as a result of the spoils system and used political patronage as the criteria for hiring—or, more correctly, overhiring—to fill his staff positions. Hayes demanded Arthur's resignation and eventually suspended him. In turn, Arthur backed the reelection bid of his scandal-ridden mentor Ulysses S. Grant in the following presidential campaign of 1880, a move that no doubt would have provided him with another presidential appointment had Grant won his party's nomination.

The Republican party nominated dark horse candidate James A. Garfield instead of Grant, however. To placate Conkling and his Stalwart faction, who were unhappy with the defeat of Grant, leaders chose Arthur as Garfield's running mate. Arthur's lack of leadership experience and close connection to Conkling and scandal brought him little public enthusiasm, but despite his lukewarm reception, the Garfield-Arthur duo won national election and found themselves in Washington.

Political victory marked the beginning of public and personal pain for Arthur. Shortly after the election, his wife, the former Ellen Lewis Herndon, died of pneumonia. Only a few months later, Garfield was downed by an attacker's bullet. As the president lay dying, Arthur, in shock and ill-prepared, refused to accept executive authority and instead allowed a kind of leadership limbo to carry the nation as the citizenry waited for the inevitable. When Garfield at last succumbed, a mournful Arthur accepted the presidency with reluctance.

Arthur, who had never held any kind of national position before, was well aware not only of his inexperience but also of how the public perceived his past ties to the Stalwarts in general and Conkling in particular. Rather than prove the public's fears of his corruption and return to the status quo as justified, Arthur reinvented himself, using Garfield's political goals and untimely end as his reference points. Arthur became convinced, as many U.S. citizens were, that Garfield's assassination by a frustrated office seeker was the product of an uncontrollable civil service organization whose patronage system encouraged the worst kinds of collusion, dishonesty, inefficiency, and motivations. Rather than reverting back to the spoils system himself, Arthur broke free of Conkling's sway and championed the civil service reform position Garfield had held. This move led to the passage of the landmark Pendleton Civil Service Act of 1883, which created the Civil Service Commission to oversee the open hiring of employees based on merit instead of political affiliation, race, creed, or national origin. Conkling saw Arthur's move as a betrayal, but the majority of the U.S. public saw Arthur's transformation as political maturation and integrity, a trial by fire endured and passed.

Arthur inherited issues other than civil service reform from his predecessors. He followed public sentiment in his condemnation of the ongoing existence of Mormon polygamy, a stand that led to the Edmunds

Act for the suppression of polygamy, the forced abandonment of the practice by Mormons, and eventual statehood for Utah. When Congress passed the Chinese Exclusion Act with its twenty-year ban on immigration, Arthur held legislators accountable to a good faith reading of U.S. treaty agreements with China despite the widespread growth of the public's anti-immigrant and anti-Asian sentiment. Arthur then persuaded Congress to lower the ban to a less severe ten years before agreeing to sign the act. He became the next president, and one of the last, to apply a strict constructionist reading of the U.S. Constitution, along with a sense of fair play and fiscal conservatism, to the issue of internal improvements and to decide that national funds should not be used to back expensive regional projects. He also wrestled with the so-called "Indian Problem" and articulated a policy known as allotment. Although no action followed during his administration, Arthur's idea was the basis for the ground breaking but ultimately unsuccessful Dawes Severalty Act of 1887. Although much of his policy followed with public sentiment, he never failed to win heartfelt backing of another Republican faction's leadership after the Stalwarts abandoned him for his crusade for civil service reform.

The death of the woman he loved and the president he respected opened Arthur's administration with tragedy. His own health ended his days in office with further sorrow. Afflicted with a painful, incurable kidney illness known as Bright's disease, Arthur carefully hid his condition from the U.S. public even as his health declined. When party leaders asked him to run for reelection, he refused, admitting that he would not survive the entirety of a second term; at their persistence, he finally decided not to fight the nomination. His illness, coupled with the divisions in his party created in part by his snubbing of the Stalwart faction, made the 1885 campaign half-hearted at best. When he failed to defeat Democratic opposition Grover Cleveland, he retired to New York in relief and died the following year.

THE ISSUE: MORMON POLYGAMY

The question of the Utah territory predated Arthur's arrival to the White House. From 1845 to 1847, Mormons searched for a homeland in the West away from religious and political persecution. They found it in the valley of the Great Salt Lake, where leader Brigham Young and his followers decided to settle and transform the desert into a habitable and hospitable land. In a territory that stretched from the Rocky Mountains to the Sierra Nevada and from the Columbia River to the Gila River, the Mormons dispatched organized groups of colonists based on skills, experience, and leadership abilities. By 1860, they had established over 150 self-sustaining societies. The unique political and social system of the Mormons, which in some places included the practice of polygamy, soon clashed with the U.S. government. As early as 1857, President James Buchanan sent troops to the territory to establish U.S. sovereignty in the area and end what he considered a state of rebellion in Utah. A miners' rush to the territory during the Civil War era led many non-Mormons to the area, and tensions flared between the two groups and their ways of life. Six separate bids for the creation of a Mormon state to join the union failed.

By the time Arthur became president, it was clear that the U.S. government would not allow Utah to gain statehood as long as it was in effect a Mormon theocracy. Arthur, in his speeches, was the mouthpiece for a nearly nationwide consensus that several things had to change before the territory could progress further politically: (1) the Mormon Church, through its vehicle the People's party, had to discontinue its active role in Utah politics; (2) Mormon leaders had to disavow the economic practice of conducting business only with fellow Mormons; and, most importantly, (3) the practice of polygamy had to end. Popular anti-Mormon rhetoric, including Arthur's, focused especially on the practice of polygamy, which struck the mainstream U.S. public as immoral and uncivilized, and helped paint the Mormons as foreign, exotic, and frightening. Arthur's vigorous support of anti-Mormonism led to legislation such as the 1882 Edmunds Act for the suppression of polygamy. With the entire weight of the U.S. government marshaled against the Utah territory, Mormons soon realized that they had to choose between the opportunity to exercise their rights as citizens (such as voting, for example) and the chance to practice their religion as they saw fit.

By withholding individual civil liberties, such as voting and the corporate opportunity for statehood, the U.S. government eventually forced the Mormons to submit to its demands. Utah finally gained statehood in 1896. In the process that led to statehood, however, many Mormon leaders and laypersons faced jail, economic hardships, and other forms of suffering. Their pleas and petitions to the national government fell on deaf ears. The Mormon faith changed as, by necessity, its followers relinquished some of their religious practices due to pressure from the U.S. government. The nation's legal ban on polygamy survives to this day.

The President's Position: Outlaw Polygamy

ARTHUR'S FIRST ANNUAL MESSAGE
DECEMBER 6, 1881

For many years the Executive, in his annual message to Congress, has urged the necessity of stringent legislation for the suppression of polygamy in the Territories, and especially in the Territory of Utah. The existing statute for the punishment of this odious crime, so revolting to the moral and religious sense of Christendom, has been persistently and contemptuously violated ever since its enactment. Indeed, in spite of commendable efforts on the part of the authorities who represent the United States in that Territory, the law has in very rare instances been enforced, and, for a cause to which reference will presently be made, is practically a dead letter.

The fact that adherents of the Mormon Church, which rests upon polygamy as its corner stone, have recently been peopling in large numbers Idaho, Arizona, and other of our Western Territories is well calculated to excite the liveliest interest and apprehension. It imposes upon Congress and the Executive the duty of arraying against this barbarous system all the power which under the Constitution and the law they can wield for its destruction.

Reference has been already made to the obstacles which the United States officers have encountered in their efforts to punish violations of law. Prominent among these obstacles is the difficulty of procuring legal evidence sufficient to warrant a conviction even in the case of the most notorious offenders.

Your attention is called to a recent opinion of the Supreme Court of the United States, explaining its judgment of reversal in the case of Miles, who had been convicted of bigamy in Utah. The court refers to the fact that the secrecy attending the celebration of marriages in that Territory makes the proof of polygamy very difficult, and the propriety is suggested of modifying the law of evidence which now makes a wife incompetent to testify against her husband.

This suggestion is approved. I recommend also the passage of an act providing that in the Territories of the United States the fact that a woman has been married to a person charged with bigamy shall not disqualify her as a witness upon his trial for that offense. I further recommend legislation by which any person solemnizing a marriage in any of the Territories shall be required, under stringent penalties for neglect or refusal, to file a certificate of such marriage in the supreme court of the Territory.

Doubtless Congress may devise other practicable measures for obviating the difficulties which have hitherto attended the efforts to suppress this iniquity. I assure you of my determined purpose to cooperate with you in any lawful and discreet measures which may be proposed to that end.[1]

ARTHUR'S THIRD ANNUAL MESSAGE
DECEMBER 4, 1883

The Utah Commission has submitted to the Secretary of the Interior its second annual report. As a result of its labors in supervising the recent election in that Territory, pursuant to the act of March 22, 1882, it appears that persons by that act disqualified to the number of about 18,000, were excluded from the polls. This fact, however, affords little cause for congratulation, and I fear that it is far from indicating any real and substantial progress toward the extirpation of polygamy. All the members elect of the legislature are Mormons. There is grave reason to believe that they are in sympathy with the practices that this Government is seeking to suppress, and that its efforts in that regard will be more likely to encounter their opposition than to receive their encouragement and support. Even if this view should happily be erroneous, the law under which the commissioners have been acting should be made more effective by the incorporation of some such stringent amendments as they recommend, and as were included in bill No. 2238 on the calendar of the Senate at its last session.

I am convinced, however, that polygamy has become so strongly intrenched in the Territory of Utah that it is profitless to attack it with any but the stoutest weapons which constitutional legislation can fashion. I favor, therefore, the repeal of the act upon which the existing government depends, the assumption by the National Legislature of the entire political control of the Territory, and the establishment of a commission with such powers and duties as shall be delegated by law.[2]

Against the President's Position: Amnesty

PETITION FOR AMNESTY
DECEMBER 19, 1891

"We, the First Presidency and Apostles of the Church of Jesus Christ of Latter-day Saints, beg respectfully to represent to your Excellency the following facts:

"We formerly taught to our people that polygamy, or celestial marriage as commanded by God through Joseph Smith, was right; that it was a necessity to man's highest exaltation in the life to come. That doctrine was publicly promulgated by our President, the late Brigham Young, forty years ago, and was steadily taught and impressed upon the Latter-day Saints up to a short time before September, 1890. Our people are devout and sincere, and they accepted the doctrine, and many personally embraced and practiced polygamy.

"When the Government sought to stamp the practice out, our people, almost without exception, remained firm, for they, while having no desire to oppose the Government in anything, still felt that their lives and their honor as men were pledged to a vindication of their faith; and that their duty towards those whose lives were a part of their own was a paramount one, to fulfill which they had no right to count anything, not even their [64] own lives, as standing in the way. Following this conviction hundreds endured arrest, trial, fine and imprisonment, and the immeasurable suffering borne by the faithful people, no language can describe. That suffering, in abated form, still continues.

"More, the Government added disfranchisement to its other punishments for those who clung to their faith and fulfilled its covenants.

"According to our faith the head of our Church receives, from time to time, revelations for the religious guidance of his people.

"In September, 1890, the present head of the Church, in anguish and prayer, cried to God for help for his flock, and received permission to advise the members of the Church of Jesus Christ of Latter-day Saints, that the law commanding polygamy was henceforth suspended.

"At the great semi-annual conference which was held a few days later, this was submitted to the people, numbering many thousands and representing every community of the people of Utah, and was by them in the most solemn manner accepted as the future rule of their lives.

"They have since been faithful to the covenant made that day. At the last October conference, after a year had passed by, the matter was once more submitted to the thousands of people gathered together, and they again in the most potential manner, ratified the solemn covenant.

"This being the true situation and believing that the object of the government was simply the vindication of its own authority and to compel obedience to its laws, and that it takes no pleasure in persecution, we respectfully pray that full amnesty may be extended to all who are under disabilities because of the operation of the so-called Edmunds and Edmunds-Tucker laws. Our people are scattered; homes are made desolate; many are still imprisoned; others are banished or in hiding. Our hearts bleed for those. In the past they followed our counsels, and while they are thus afflicted our souls are in sack cloth and ashes.

"We believe there are nowhere in the Union a more loyal people than the Latter-day Saints. They know no other country except this. They expect to live and die on this soil.

"When the men of the South, who were in rebellion against the government in 1865, threw down their arms and asked for recognition along the old lines of citizenship, the Government [65] hastened to grant their prayer.

"To be at peace with the Government and in harmony with their fellow citizens who are not of their faith, and to share in the confidence of the government and people, our people have voluntarily put aside something which all their lives they have believed to be a sacred principle. Have they not the right to ask for such clemency as comes when the claims of both law and justice have been fully liquidated? As shepherds of a patient and suffering people, we ask amnesty for them, and pledge our faith and honor for their future.

"And your petitioners will ever pray."

Wilford Woodruff	George Q. Cannon	Joseph F. Smith
Lorenzo Snow	Franklin D. Richards	Moses Thatcher
Francis M. Lyman	H. J. Grant	John Henry Smith[3]
John W. Taylor	M. W. Merrill	
Anthon H. Lund	Abraham H. Cannon	

NOTES

1. Richardson, Volume X, pp. 4644–4645.

2. Richardson, Volume X, p. 4771.

3. Petition for Amnesty, www.polygamyinfo.com/Petition%20For%20Amnesty.htm (accessed November 22, 2002).

THE ISSUE: THE CHINESE EXCLUSION ACT

The question of Mormon polygamy was a particularly complex issue; although a legitimate question was raised—Should a state politically controlled by one church be allowed to achieve statehood?—it was couched in and clouded by extreme, sometimes even hysterical prejudice against Mormons and their lifestyle. The same was true of the Chinese Exclusion Act. At its heart was an understandable anxiety about what a large influx of one kind of immigrant would do to the society and economy of a given U.S. region. This concern, however, was often lost behind outright racism and anti-Asian bigotry.

The United States faced unparalleled immigration after the Civil War. Over 9,000,000 immigrants entered the country in the last two decades of the twentieth century alone. This sudden flood of individuals, many of whom did not speak English, caused some U.S. leaders to question the nation's traditional policy of welcoming virtually all who came, regardless of background, race, nationality, or creed. The 1870s, in particular, saw a rise of agitation from citizens of California who feared and resented the large number of Chinese immigrants who made their home on the Pacific coast.

A number of factors fed this concern. First, the volume of immigrants meant that entire communities of Chinese quickly emerged, and these communities challenged the expected model of immigration that guaranteed that any immigrant would have to assimilate into the larger culture quickly in order to be successful. If these immigrants did not have to learn English or interact with mainstream U.S. citizens on a daily basis, some wondered how they would become "Americanized." Others worried that the immigrants' ability to live frugally and their willingness to work for modest wages would render U.S. citizens unable to compete in. the labor market. Furthermore, others feared the sheer exoticness of the Chinese and what it would mean for the European heritage and culture shared by many U.S. citizens (after all, though the Italians, Germans, and Irish had very different cultural backgrounds, they were all European).

In response to the concerns, primarily of Californians, Congress passed a Chinese Exclusion Act in 1879, but Hayes vetoed it on the grounds that it contradicted rights guaranteed to the Chinese by the United States in the Burlingame Treaty of 1868. In 1880, the treaty provisions were revised to permit the United States to suspend Chinese immigration for a limited time. In 1882, Congress once again passed a Chinese Exclusion Act thanks to the support of congressmen such as Democratic representative George D. Wise of Virginia. Arthur vetoed it, arguing that a twenty-year suspension of immigration exceeded the good faith limits of the revised Burlingame Treaty. Finally a revised act, suspending immigration for only ten years, became law. The act was renewed in 1892 for another decade-long period. In 1902, the suspension of Chinese immigration became indefinite. The act remained a symbol of U.S. uncertainty about its role as a cultural "melting pot," a reflection of nativist xenophobia and protectionism, and a symbol of the growing pains the nation endured as it tried to find a new image and a role for itself as it entered the world stage.

The President's Position: Veto

Washington, April 4, 1882
To the Senate of the United States:

After careful consideration of Senate bill No. 71, entitled "An act to execute certain treaty stipulations relating to Chinese," I herewith return it to the Senate, in which it originated, with my objections to its passage.

A nation is justified in repudiating its treaty obligations only when they are in conflict with great paramount interests. Even then all possible reasonable means for modifying or changing those obligations by mutual agreement should be exhausted before resorting to the supreme right of refusal to comply with them.

These rules have governed the United States in their past intercourse with other powers as one of the family of nations. I am persuaded that if Congress can feel that this act violates the faith of the nation as pledged to China it will concur with me in rejecting this particular mode of regulating Chinese immigration, and will endeavor to find another which shall meet the expectations of the people of the United States without coming in conflict with the rights of China.

The present treaty relations between that power and the United States spring from an antagonism which arose between our paramount domestic interests and our previous relations.

The treaty commonly known as the Burlingame treaty conferred upon Chinese subjects the right of voluntary emigration to the United States for the purposes of curiosity or trade or as permanent residents, and was in all respects reciprocal as to citizens of the United States in China. It gave to the voluntary emigrant coming to the United States the right to travel there or to reside there, with all the privileges, immunities, or exemptions enjoyed by the citizens or subjects of the most favored nation.

Under the operation of this treaty it was found that the institutions of the United States and the character of its people and their means of obtaining a livelihood might be seriously affected by the unrestricted introduction of Chinese labor. Congress attempted to alleviate this condition by legislation, but the act which it passed proved to be in violation of our treaty obligations, and, being returned by the President with his objections, failed to become law.

Diplomatic relief was then sought. A new treaty was concluded with China. Without abrogating the Burlingame treaty, it was agreed to modify it so far that the Government of the United States might regulate, limit, or suspend the coming of Chinese laborers to the United States or their residence therein, but that it should not absolutely prohibit them, and that the limitation or suspension should be reasonable and should apply only to Chinese who might go to the United States as laborers, other classes not being included in the limitations. This treaty is unilateral, not reciprocal. It is a concession from China to the United States in limitation of the rights which she was enjoying under the Burlingame treaty. It leaves us by our own act to determine when and how we will enforce those limitations. China may therefore fairly have a right to expect that in enforcing them we will take good care not to overstep the grant and take more than has been conceded to us.

It is but a year since this new treaty, under the operation of the Constitution, became part of the supreme law of the land, and the present act is the first attempt to exercise the more enlarged powers which it relinquishes to the United States. . . .

Our intercourse with China is of recent date. Our first treaty with that power is not yet forty years old. It is only since we acquired California and established a great deal of commerce on the Pacific that we may be said to have broken down the barriers which fenced in that ancient Monarchy. The Burlingame treaty naturally followed. Under the spirit which inspired it many thousand Chinese laborers came to the United States. No one can say that the country has not profited by their work. They were largely instrumental in constructing the railways which connect the Atlantic with the Pacific. The States of the Pacific Slope are full of evidences of their industry. Enterprises profitable alike to the capitalist and to the laborer of Caucasian origin would have lain dormant but for them. A time has now come when it is supposed that they are not needed, and when it is thought by Congress and by those most acquainted with the

subject that it is best to try to get along without them. There may, however, be other sections of the country where this species of labor may be
advantageously employed without interfering with the laborers of our
own race. In making the proposed experiment it may be the part of
wisdom as well as of good faith to fix the length of the experimental
period with reference to this fact.

Experience has shown that the trade of the East is the key to national
wealth and influence. The opening of China to the commerce of the
whole world has benefited no section of it more than the States of our
own Pacific Slope. The State of California, and its great maritime port
especially, have reaped enormous advantages from this source. Blessed
with an exceptional climate, enjoying an unrivaled harbor, with the
riches of a great agricultural and mining State in its rear and the wealth
of the whole Union pouring into it over its lines of railway, San Francisco
has before it an incalculable future if our friendly and amicable relations
with Asia remain undisturbed. It needs no argument to show that the
policy which we now propose to adopt must have a direct tendency to
repel Oriental nations from us and to drive their trade and commerce
into more friendly lands. It may be that the great and paramount interest
of protecting our labor from Asiatic competition may justify us in a permanent adoption of this policy; but it is wiser in the first place to make
a shorter experiment, with a view hereafter of maintaining permanently
only such features as time and experience may commend.[4]

Against the President's Position: For the Act

REPRESENTATIVE GEORGE D. WISE OF VIRGINIA
U.S. HOUSE OF REPRESENTATIVES
MARCH 22, 1882

Mr. Speaker: The question under consideration has been so fully and
exhaustively discussed in this and in the other ed of the Capitol that I
hesitate to trespass even for a brief space of time upon the patience and
indulgence of this House. I do not hope to be able to make any new or
striking presentation of it, my purpose in rising to speak simply being
to place myself more emphatically upon the record as in sympathy with
the object proposed to be accomplished by this bill than I could by a
simple vote. This question is of a gravity to demand our most serious
consideration, and the problem too important to be treated with levity

or indifference. Immigration exerts a wonderful influence upon our civilization and upon our growth and development as a nation, and the subject is worthy of the study and reflection of our wisest statesmen.

The people on the Pacific slope have spoken with no uncertain sound, and with a unanimity almost unexampled. I am unwilling to believe that in their loud and earnest demands for relief they have been controlled by blind passion and unreasoning prejudices. These appeals to Congress for the application of a remedy for what is considered as a great and growing evil come to us from men in every walk and grade of life, and I am convinced that a real and not an imaginary cause exists to produce them. These bitter complaints come to us not alone from the laboring classes, who in their various callings are confronted with an unequal and degrading competition, but from others also whose conclusions are the result of intelligent observation and reflection.

The object sought to be accomplished by this bill is the suspension of the immigration of Chinese laborers for the period of twenty years. There are some who hold to the opinion that a suspension for so many years is unreasonable and amounts to prohibition, and therefore is violative of the stipulation of our treaty with the Government of China. . . . By the terms of thus treaty the United States may limit or suspend, but may not prohibit. "Such suspension shall be reasonable," and that is the only limitation upon our right to stop for a time at least the immigration of Chinese laborers. In the treaty it is recognized and conceded that the necessity for a "suspension" may arise, and when it shall the Government of the United States is authorized to act as may be deemed best for the interests of the country, its welfare and prosperity.

The remedy must be commensurate with the disease, and its application must be for such time as will produce the desired results. I am at a loss to discover by what process of reasoning, by what rule of interpretation gentlemen have arrived at the conclusion that a suspension for ten years would be reasonable but for twenty years would not be. . . .

I shall always steadily and firmly resist those whose utterances are in the interest of capital against labor, of monopolies against the rights of man. In the competition between the Caucasian and Asiatic races the conditions are all opposed to the former and advantages in favor of the latter.

The Chinese are not encumbered with families, and they lived huddled together, in large numbers, in the same room, so that they require no more for their subsistence than has been found sufficient for the maintenance of convicts in our prisons. I cannot entertain the opinion that blessings will flow from degradation of our working people to such a condition, and I can tell gentlemen that the intelligent representatives of the Negro race are as much opposed to it as are the whites. While I would not fan the fires of passion and prejudice, I tell gentlemen plainly that the laboring classes will not tamely submit to what they feel to be a wrong and injustice, and that discords and sanguinary results are inevitable.

The honorable gentleman from Ohio, Mr. Taylor, whose presentation of his side of the case is not exceeded, in my humble judgment, in ability and eloquence by that of any other opponent of this measure, was careful to express in this connection his convictions in language too plain to be mistaken. He is reported in the RECORD as having said:

> The reason I object to the bill chiefly and finally is because it changes our condition before the world. It is taking upon us an exclusiveness that has not belonged to us in the past, and for one I am not willing to do that. But, Mr. Speaker, permit me to say in justice to myself I hope my remarks have not been understood as favoring a further immigration of the Chinese. I deplore their presence here as much as any man. I have not been addressing myself to that branch of the subject. I want no more of them.

If it is not desirable to have more of them, if "unrestricted immigration is an evil of great magnitude," and their presence here is something to be deplored, I cannot see why we should hesitate to change our condition before the world and to take upon ourselves an exclusiveness in regard to them that has not belonged to us in the past. Their presence here is to be deplored, says the honorable gentleman. We have the statement of the joint special committee, appointed by the two Houses of Congress to investigate this subject, "that the influx of Chinese us a standing menace to republican institutions on the Pacific and the existence there of Christian civilization." We have the concurrent testimony of hundreds of intelligent witnesses, unbiased by prejudice, that it is a great and growing evil, demanding the application of a speedy remedy, and yet we are gravely told that we must continue in a ruinous policy because a departure from it "changes our condition before the world." . . . I hold it to be a duty to provide against that which is dangerous to the existence of our free institutions, to Christian civilization, and to social order.[5]

NOTES

4. Richardson, Volume X, pp. 4699–4700, 4704–4705.

5. *Congressional Record, Containing the Proceedings and Debates of the Forty-seventh Congress, First Session*, Volume XIII (Washington, D.C.: Government Printing Office, 1882), Appendix to the Congressional Record, pp. 63–64.

THE ISSUE: INTERNAL IMPROVEMENTS

The question of internal improvements and the proper role for the national government to play in them was an issue that dated as far back as the presidency of James Madison (1809–1817). In 1817, the U.S. Congress passed the Bonus Bill, which earmarked federal funds for regional projects. Madison, who favored a strict construction, or narrow reading, of the U.S. Constitution, vetoed the bill. He argued that the Constitution made no provision for using national money for improvements that failed to benefit the entire country. In order for Congress to allot federal funds for regional projects, he believed, a constitutional amendment would be necessary to grant that power to the legislature. He did not interpret the "general welfare" clause of the Constitution to be a catchall phrase covering every power not enumerated as belonging to Congress. Not only did Madison's action offer a clear illustration of strict constructionism in action, but it also opened the door for future presidents to use the veto power of executive office more often and more aggressively.

In 1882, Arthur was put in a similar situation to that faced by Madison in 1817. Congress passed a bill providing national funds for public works with a regional flavor, namely improvements on certain rivers and harbors. Proponents of the bill, such as Republican representative Robert T. Van Horn of Missouri, argued for it on two fronts: first, swift improvements were very necessary; and second, the positive effects of inexpensive travel and trade routes benefited not only the region in which they were located but, indirectly, the nation as a whole.

Arthur found these arguments unpersuasive for two reasons. First, he argued, it was unfair to use national money on projects that benefited a region or locality—solely or predominantly—instead of the entire country. Not only did this reward those who did not care for their own areas with their own state or locally gathered funds, but it punished those states or localities that practiced frugal, forward-thinking administration of their funds. Moreover, he believed, agreeing to such internal improvements would start an endless cycle in which other areas with legitimate needs would see one get national funds and then demand equal national funds for themselves. Where would the spending end? If fairness was a guiding principle, he argued, every regional need would have to be met if the nation favored one region with federal funds.

Second, Arthur viewed the amount of funds requested, and the idea of significant national government spending in general, to be troublesome. Each dollar used by the government, he said, was a dollar taken from the hands of the citizens, all of whom could find other uses for it. He did not want Congress to get into the habit of spending money with ease or without serious reflection.

That said, Arthur offered a compromise to Congress. If the expenditures listed in the bill were reduced significantly, and if the projects funded were only those with direct national benefits (in this case, as stipulated by the Secretary of War), he would support the bill. This position marked Arthur as the direct descendent of presidents such as Madison, but one of a dying breed. By the early twentieth century, strict constructionism and federal thrift were replaced by a broad reading of the U.S. Constitution and the rise of a national government eager to appropriate funds for both national and regional purposes, a practice that made state and local governments increasingly dependent on Washington.

The President's Position: Veto

August 1, 1882
To the House of Representatives:

Having watched with much interest the progress of House bill No. 6242, entitled "An act making appropriations for the construction, repair, and preservation of certain works on rivers and harbors, and for other purposes," and having since it was received carefully examined it, after mature consideration I am constrained to return it herewith to the House of Representatives, in which it originated, without my signature and with my objections to its passage.

Many of the appropriations in the bill are clearly for the general welfare and most beneficent in their character. Two of the objects for which provision is made were by me considered so important that I felt it in my duty to direct to them the attention of Congress. In my annual message in December last I urged the vital importance of legislation for the reclamation of the marshes and for the establishment of the harbor lines along the Potomac front. In April last, by special message, I recommended an appropriation for the improvement of the Mississippi River. It is not necessary that I say that when my signature would make the bill appropriating for these and other valuable national objects a law it is with great reluctance and only under a sense of duty that I withhold it.

My principal objection to the bill is that it contains appropriations for purposes not for the common defense or general welfare, and which do not promote commerce among the States. These provisions, on the contrary, are entirely for the benefit of the particular localities in which it is proposed to make the improvements. I regard such appropriation of the public money as beyond the powers given by the Constitution to Congress and the President.

I feel the more bound to withhold my signature from the bill because of the peculiar evils which manifestly result from this infraction of the Constitution. Appropriations of this nature, to be devoted purely to local objects, tend to an increase in number and amount. As the citizens of one State find that money, to raise which they in common with the whole country are taxed, is to be expended for local improvements in another State, they demand similar benefits for themselves, and it is not unnatural that they should seek to indemnify themselves for such use of the public funds by securing appropriations for similar improvements in their own neighborhood. Thus as the bill becomes more objectionable it secures more support. This result is invariable and necessarily follows a neglect to observe the constitutional limitations imposed upon the lawmaking power.

The appropriations for river and harbor improvements have, under the influences to which I have alluded, increased year by year out of proportion to the progress of the country, great as that has been. In 1870 the aggregate appropriation was $3,975,900; in 1875, $6,648,517.50; in 1880, $8,976,500; and in 1881, $11,451,000; while by the present act there is appropriated $18,743,875.

While feeling every disposition to leave to the Legislature the responsibility of determining what amount should be appropriated for the purposes of the bill, so long as the appropriations are confined to objects indicated by the grant of power, I can not escape the conclusion that, as a part of the lawmaking power of the Government, the duty devolves upon me to withhold my signature from a bill containing appropriations which in my opinion greatly exceed in amount the needs of the country for the present fiscal year. It being the usage to provide money for these purposes by annual appropriation bills, the President is in effect directed to expend so large an amount of money within so brief a period that the expenditure can not be made economically and advantageously.

The extravagant expenditure of public money is an evil not to be measured by the value of that money to the people who are taxed for it. They sustain a greater injury in the demoralizing effect produced upon those who are intrusted with official duty through all the ramifications of government.

These objections could be removed and every constitutional purpose readily attained should Congress enact that one-half only of the aggregate amount provided for in the bill be appropriated for expenditure during the fiscal year, and that the sum so appropriated be expended only for such objects named in the bill as the Secretary of War, under the direction of the President, shall determine; provided that in no case shall the expenditure for any one purpose exceed the sum now designated by the bill for that purpose.

I feel authorized to make this suggestion because of the duty imposed upon the President by the Constitution "to recommend to the consideration of Congress such measures as he shall judge necessary and expedient," and because it is my earnest desire that the public works which are in progress shall suffer no injury. Congress will also convene again in four months, when this whole subject will be open for their consideration.[6]

Against the President's Position: For Improvements

REPRESENTATIVE ROBERT T. VAN HORN OF MISSOURI
U.S. HOUSE OF REPRESENTATIVES
JUNE 15, 1882

Mr Chairman: The question of the improvement of the internal navigable waters of the United States has assumed an importance in the extent and cost of the work required as to mark a new era in our policy in that direction. Once they were regarded as local, and only the tidal waters were treated as national. While the situation is not reversed, the former have assumed the leading place in magnitude and cost. The food supply as to surplus is now where, when Henry Clay inaugurated the American system, the wilderness was unbroken. He heart of the nation is now in the valley of the Mississippi, and the policy once adapted to the coast-line is no longer applicable.

Other changes have tended to transform our policy in regard to the sea-ports of the country. Steam has increased the size and draught of vessels until the deepening of our harbor entrances has become for them a vital question. We cannot longer legitimate for sections in this respect. If we must have deep harbor approaches, we must have deeper rivers upon which to float to the great vessels cheap and abundant cargoes. Commerce always cheapens by abundance, and competition to be successful and desirable must be based upon cheap bread—not upon cheap labor. The economy which renders it impossible for labor to acquire independence at forty-five years is a false one, and in the end brings social disaster.

There is another view of this question, as affecting the right of the people of the West, the agricultural people, to demand legislation in this direction. We are met with the policy of protection to the industrial interests of the country engaged in manufactures, and skilled labor employed in the useful arts. Many of us in the West recognize the justice and policy of this demand, and for the last twenty years our tariff laws have given the home markets to this class of industry. The most efficient protection that can be given to the great agricultural interests of the West—the labor and capital employed in the development of the soil—is by cheap transportation. There is nothing offered for sale that represents more labor value in proportion to price than a bushel of wheat. It is nearly all labor. Cheap transportation, then, is one form of protection, because it enables us to secure the highest possible price for the labor bestowed upon the product. As now, it often costs two bushels of corn to get one to market. If by the improvement of our natural water-ways we can send two bushels at the cost of one, the situation is reversed; we get double the money for our corn. If this is not protection direct, it is the same in effect, and by means entirely in harmony with the fundamental methods of civilization—the development of natural facilities by the application of intelligent labor. And it is in harmony with the elementary duties of government—the improvement of natural resources for the uses of man.

Again, we have the right to demand it, because out of the common fund of all the people—the lands of the nation and taxes—vast sums have been expended in aid of capital in the construction of our interstate and transcontinental system of railways. In this way the agricultural interest has furnished the basis of credit for the immense loans that capital secured, and the fruits of which it now enjoys, to build these lines. I am not referring to these expenditures in any fault-finding sense. For many of these grants I have voted as a member of this House, and as a citizen I have given the full measure of effort and support wherever I could toward the construction of these lines of traffic, and am ready to do so again when necessary. Their influence has been for progress, and the results from their construction and operation are among the greatest of the great wonders of the last twenty years.

But I do not think we ought to stop here. Nor, strongly as I would deprecate hostile legislation, and little sympathy as I have with crusades preached against these greatest of all modern agents of material progress, yet they are not all that we require or all that we should foster in the way of transportation. Artificial as they are, they must be owned by corporate and private interests, controlled primarily for individual profit, and at times are felt as oppressive upon the interests of the people—as to the masses and very largely so against localities. The law of competition in their case acts unequally—where it is against rival lines to the benefit of competing points, but where free from this against the people having no other channel of transport. And always the rail is owned by a close corporation—its use paid for by the people.

But the river is free. Any man who chooses can launch his craft upon its waters and float to the sea or to the interior markets. Its dangers are removable, its obstacles avoidable, and its benefits accessible to all. It is a gift of nature, free of tolls, unvexed by management, and supplies transport at the lowest cost. If industry is protected by customs duties, if railroads have been built by grants of land and national, State, and municipal taxation for the benefit of mechanical and manufacturing industry and corporate capital, surely the improvement of natural waterways of the nation for the benefit of agricultural industry, general commerce, and the cheapening of food for all is not only a proper subject for legislation but a duty involving the most enlightened statesmanship. It is but meting out to the great agricultural interests of the nation the equal measure of favor it has in common with all others bestowed upon its sister interests. We ask nothing but what we concede; we require but a hundredth part of what has been given.[7]

NOTES

6. Richardson, Volume X, pp. 4708–4709.

7. *Congressional Record, Containing the Proceedings and Debates of the Forty-seventh Congress, Second Session*, Volume XIII (Washington, D.C.: Government Printing Office, 1882), Appendix to the Congressional Record, p. 420.

THE ISSUE: ALLOTMENT

Arthur, like all U.S. presidents before him, faced the so-called "Indian Problem," the challenge of defining the relationship between the federal government and the native nations of America. The problem was exacerbated in Arthur's time not only due to the final throes of the "Indian wars" and the discontent on reservations, but also by the fact that U.S. citizens were continuing to push West and look for new territories to settle, including areas previously set aside by the government for Amerindians who had been removed from their original homelands. Arthur believed two things: the natives had to be "civilized," and they had to be protected.

The policy he created to match both goals was known as allotment. Rather than requiring native Americans to remain within general boundaries of areas held in common for one or more native nations as a group, Arthur believed that these individuals should each be given a specific plot of land to own and improve. This policy hearkened back to Thomas Jefferson's idea of the yeoman farmer and the conviction that land ownership and cultivation created self-supporting, independent individuals capable of being good citizens and fulfilled human beings. Allotment would allow Amerindians to experience this "American" (or rather "U.S.") dream, Arthur believed. Individual titles to land would also make it simpler to protect the property rights of native Americans from infringement by greedy settlers.

Arthur's ideas were not realized during his administration, but they set in motion policy that culminated in the Dawes Severalty Act of 1887, which made allotment a reality. Senator Henry L. Dawes, the act's author, revisited Arthur when he stated that allotment would be a key step in changing Amerindian lifestyles, saying that post-allotment, civilized native Americans would "wear civilized clothes . . . cultivate the ground, live in houses, ride in Studebaker wagons, send children to school, drink whiskey [and] own property."[8]

The Dawes Act failed to meet either of its goals, however. The property rights of native Americans were not protected. In fact, Amerindians actually lost land in the allotment process; as reservation land was divided into individual plots, millions of "surplus" acres ended up in white rather than native American hands. This combination of dishonesty and mismanagement led Senator Henry M. Teller to ascribe less than noble motivations to the act, saying "The real aim of [the Dawes Act] is to get at the Indians' land and open it up for resettlement."[9] Many failed to receive any land at all, due to either government incompetence or native American unwillingness to go on the required rolls, which some feared might lead authorities to those who had escaped forced relocation in the past, and often required individuals to Anglicize their names legally, forever losing a link to their home culture. Even worse, the opportunity for land ownership that some enjoyed was short lived, as the Indian Reorganization Act overturned completely the policy of allotment.

For vocal Amerindian leaders such as Chief Joseph, the assumption about civilization and the anxiety over property rights protection that undergirded the Dawes Act was sadly ironic, since it overlooked the fact that native nations had owned land either individually or corporately and lost it when the United States itself violated their property rights. These leaders opposed allotment because it put them one step further from their goal, which was a peaceable return to and respect for their homelands.

The President's Position: For Allotment

ARTHUR'S THIRD ANNUAL MESSAGE
DECEMBER 4, 1883

This question [of managing "Indian affairs"] has been a cause of trouble and embarrassment from the infancy of the Government. . . .

It has been easier to resort to convenient makeshifts for tiding over temporary difficulties than to grapple with the great permanent problem. . . . It was natural, at a time when the national territory seemed almost illimitable and contained many millions of acres far outside the bounds of civilized settlements, that a policy should have been initiated . . . of relegating them by treaty stipulations to the occupancy of immense reservations in the West, and of encouraging them to live the savage life, undisturbed by any earnest and well-directed efforts to bring them under the influences of civilization.

The unsatisfactory results which have sprung from this policy are becoming apparent to all.

As the white settlements have crowded the borders of the reservations, the Indians, sometimes contentedly and sometimes against their will, have been transferred to other hunting grounds, from which they have again been dislodged whenever their newfound homes have been desired by the adventurous settlers.

These removals and the frontier collisions by which they have often been preceded have led to frequent and disastrous conflicts between the races. It is profitless to discuss here which of them has been chiefly responsible for the disturbances. . . .

We have to deal with the appalling fact that though thousands of lives have been sacrificed and hundreds of millions of dollars expended in the attempt to solve the Indian problem, it has until within the past few years seemed scarcely nearer a solution that it was half a century ago. . . .

[To alleviate the "Indian problem," I propose] . . . to introduce among the Indians the customs and pursuits of civilized life and gradually to absorb them into the mass of our citizens, sharing their rights and holden to their responsibilities. . . .

First. I recommend the passage of an act making the laws of the various states and Territories applicable to Indian reservations within their borders. . . . The Indian should receive the protection of the law. He should be allowed to maintain in court the rights of person and property. He has repeatedly begged for this privilege. Its exercise would be very valuable to him in his progress towards civilization.

Second. . . . Permitting the allotment in severalty to . . . [Indians] of a reasonable quantity of land secured to them by patent, and for their own protection made inalienable for twenty or twenty five years, is demanded for their present welfare and their permanent advancement.

In return for such considerate action on the part of Government, there is reason to believe that the Indians in large numbers would be persuaded to sever their tribal relations and to engage at once in agricultural pursuits. Many of them realize that their hunting days are over and that it is now for their best interests to conform their manner of life to the new order of things. . . .

[Allotting Indians personal title to land] would have a direct and powerful influence in dissolving the tribal bond, which is so prominent a feature of savage life, and which tends so strongly to perpetuate it.

Third. I advise a liberal appropriation for the support of Indian schools, because of my confident belief that such a course is consistent with the wisest economy. . . .[10]

THE DAWES SEVERALTY ACT (1887)

Be it enacted by the Senate and House of Representatives of the United States of America in Congress assembled, That in all cases where any tribe or band of Indians has been, or shall hereafter be, located upon any reservation created for their use, either by treaty stipulation or by virtue of an act of Congress or executive order setting apart the same for their use, the President of the United States be, and he hereby is, authorized, whenever in his opinion any reservation or any part thereof of such Indians is advantageous for agricultural and grazing purposes, to cause said reservation, or any part thereof, to be surveyed, or resurveyed if necessary, and to allot the lands in said reservation in severalty to any Indian located thereon in quantities as follows:

To each head of a family, one-quarter of a section;
To each single person over eighteen years of age, one-eighth of a section;
To each orphan child under eighteen years of age, one-eighth of a section; and
To each other single person under eighteen years now living, or who may be born prior to the date of the order of the President directing an allotment of the lands embraced in any reservation, one-sixteenth of a section. . . .

The United States does and will hold the land thus allotted, for the period of twenty-five years, in trust for the sole use and benefit of the Indian to whom such allotment shall have been made . . . and that at the expiration of said period the United States will convey the same by patent to said Indian. . . .

That upon the completion of said allotments and the patenting of the lands to said allottees, each and every member of the respective bands or tribes of Indians to whom allotments have been made shall have the benefit of and be subject to the laws, both civil and criminal, of the State or Territory in which they may reside; and no Territory shall pass or enforce any law denying any such Indian within its jurisdiction the equal protection of the law. And every Indian born within the territorial limits of the United States to whom allotments shall have been made under the provisions of this act, or under any law or treaty, and every Indian born within the territorial limits of the United States who has voluntarily taken up, within said limits, his residence separate and apart from any tribe of Indians therein, and has adopted the habits of civilized life, is hereby declared to be a citizen of the United States, and is entitled to all the rights, privileges, and immunities of such citizens, whether said Indian has been or not, by birth or otherwise, a member of any tribe of

Indians within the territorial limits of the United States without in any manner affecting the right of any such Indian to tribal or other property.[11]

Against the President's Position: Equal Rights

CHIEF JOSEPH, ON A VISIT TO WASHINGTON, D.C., 1879

At last I was granted permission to come to Washington and bring my friend Yellow Bull and our interpreter with me. I am glad I came. I have shaken hands with a good many friends, but there are some things I want to know which no one seems able to explain. I cannot understand how the Government sends a man out to fight us, as it did General Miles, and then breaks his word. Such a government has something wrong about it. I cannot understand why so many chiefs are allowed to talk so many different ways, and promise so many different things. I have seen the Great Father Chief [President Hayes]; the Next Great Chief [Secretary of the Interior]; the Commissioner Chief; the Law Chief; and many other law chiefs [Congressmen] and they all say they are my friends, and that I shall have justice, but while all their mouths talk right I do not understand why nothing is done for my people. I have heard talk and talk but nothing is done. Good words do not last long unless they amount to something. Words do not pay for my dead people. They do not pay for my country now overrun by white men. They do not protect my father's grave. They do not pay for my horses and cattle. Good words do not give me back my children. Good words will not make good the promise of your war chief, General Miles. Good words will not give my people a home where they can live in peace and take care of themselves. I am tired of talk that comes to nothing. It makes my heart sick when I remember all the good words and all the broken promises. There has been too much talking by men who had no right to talk. Too many misinterpretations have been made; too many misunderstandings have come up between the white men and the Indians. If the white man wants to live in peace with the Indian he can live in peace. There need be no trouble. Treat all men alike. Give them the same laws. Give them all an even chance to live and grow. All men were made by the same Great Spirit Chief. They are all brothers. The earth is the mother of all people, and all people should have equal rights upon it. You might as well expect all rivers to run backward as that any man who was born a free man should be contented penned up and denied liberty to go where he pleases. If you tie a horse to a stake, do you expect he will grow fat? If you pen an Indian up on a small spot of earth and compel him to stay there, he will not be contented nor will he grow and prosper. I have asked some of the Great White Chiefs where they get their authority to say to the Indian that he shall stay in one place, while he sees white men going where they please. They cannot tell me. I only ask of the Government to be treated as all other men are treated. If I cannot go to my own home, let me have a home in a country where my people will not die so fast. I would like to go to Bitter Root Valley. There my people would be happy; where they are now they are dying. Three have died since I left my camp to come to Washington. When I think of our condition, my heart is heavy. I see men of my own race treated as outlaws and driven from country to country, or shot down like animals. I know that my race must change. We cannot hold our own with the white men as we are. We only ask an even chance to live as other men live. We ask to be recognized as men. We ask that the same law shall work alike on all men. If an Indian breaks the law, punish him by the law. If a white man breaks the law, punish him also. Let me be a free man, free to travel, free to stop, free to work, free to trade where I choose, free to choose my own teachers, free to follow the religion of my fathers, free to talk, think and act for myself—and I will obey every law or submit to the penalty. Whenever the white man treats the Indian as they treat each other then we shall have no more wars. We shall be all alike—brothers of one father and mother, with one sky above us and one country around us and one government for all. Then the Great Spirit Chief who rules above will smile upon this land and send rain to wash out the bloody spots made by brothers' hands upon the face of the earth. For this time the Indian race is waiting and praying. I hope no more groans of wounded men and women will ever go to the ear of the Great Spirit Chief above, and that all people may be one people. Hin-mah-too-yah-lat-kekht has spoken for his people.[12]

NOTES

8. The Dawes Act, www-personal.umich.edu/jamarcus/dawes.html (accessed November 11, 2002).

9. The Dawes Act, www-personal.umich.edu/jamarcus/dawes.html (accessed November 11, 2002).

10. The Fieldston School United States History Survey, www.pinzler.com/ushistory/dawesactsupp.html (accessed November 11, 2002).

11. The Avalon Project at Yale Law School, *Statutes of the United States Concerning Native Americans*, www.yale.edu/lawweb/avalon/statutes/native/dawes.htm (accessed November 11, 2002).

12. Great Wisdom, http://dkoch332.tripod.com/QuotesHTML/wisdom.htm (accessed November 22, 2002).

RECOMMENDED READINGS

Doenecke, Justus D. *The Presidencies of James A. Garfield and Chester A. Arthur*. Lawrence: University Press of Kansas, 1981.

Jordan, David M. *Roscoe Conkling of New York: Voice in the Senate*. Ithaca, NY: Cornell University Press, 1971.

Prucha, Francis Paul. *The Great Father: The United States Government and the American Indians*. Lincoln: University of Nebraska Press, 1984.

Reeves, Thomas C. *Gentleman Boss: The Life of Chester Alan Arthur*. New York: Knopf, 1975.

Wiebe, Robert H. *The Search for Order, 1877–1920*. New York: Hill and Wang, 1967.

4

GROVER CLEVELAND

(1885–1889)

In polls conducted of presidential historians and books compiled by the same, Grover Cleveland is consistently ranked the highest of all U.S. presidents of the Reconstruction Era and Gilded Age (roughly 1866–1900), regardless of whether he is ranked "near great" or simply "above average" in relation to all chief executives across the entire history of the nation.[1] Some of his policies did resonate in the U.S. consciousness—his idea that the unfair practice of levying protectionist tariffs had to be abandoned, his conviction that the gold standard had to be maintained or the nation would suffer economic disaster—but overall his accomplishments seem somewhat thin compared to the acclaim he has gathered. What, then, causes Cleveland to stand out among his peers?

Scholars tend to agree that the answer lies not as much with Cleveland's achievements as in his personality and character. A plain-spoken, independent man, Cleveland restored an impartiality to a White House that had been tainted by scandal, corruption, and patronage. He actively fought political machines and refused patronage. Cleveland did not court the press; on the contrary, he took strong stands even when the timing spelled political suicide, and remained honest even about his own personal foibles. His rhetoric carried little affectation: if he viewed a certain faction as robbers, he called its members robbers, plainly and clearly. In a sense, what the public saw with Cleveland was what the public got, and that immovability and solidity was both reassuring and refreshing.

Cleveland's rise to executive office was unusual. He was born the son of an itinerant Presbyterian minister in 1837. Upon his father's death in

1853, Cleveland dropped out of school to support his mother and sisters. Despite this setback, he eventually studied law, passed the bar, and became an active member of the Democratic party. When the Civil War began, he followed the legal procedure to hire a substitute to serve in his place so he could remain at home and care for his mother. After the war he served first as his county's assistant district attorney and then as its sheriff, but he stepped down from his position in 1873 to practice law quietly. Much of what he accomplished was thrust upon him. His early years fail to reflect the single-minded ambition and drive characteristic of so many other young chief executives in the making.

Eight years later, Democrats who remembered Cleveland from his tenure as sheriff nominated him as their mayoral candidate for the city of Buffalo, New York. As mayor, Cleveland began his trademark practice of vetoing spending measures he found inefficient and unnecessary. A year later, state Democrats nominated him for governor. He won the position, notably without seeking or gaining the support of the infamous Tammany Hall Democratic machine that ran New York City. It was Cleveland's defiance of Tammany Hall and other patronage machines that caught national attention; he remained in the spotlight by using his veto often and adhering consistently to his political positions.

In 1884, the Democratic party leadership believed Cleveland presented a clear contrast to Washington insider and Republican presidential nominee James G. Blaine. After Cleveland's nomination as the Democratic presidential candidate, however, the press uncovered a ten-year-old child Cleveland had allegedly fathered out of wedlock. Cleveland's response to the Republican taunt "Ma, Ma, where's my pa?" was to be honest; he admitted his past affair and explained how he had taken financial responsibility for the child. The novel approach of disclosing rather than hiding or denying past fault took the sting from the story. Soon the Democrats had a taunt of their own that capitalized on Cleveland's forthrightness: "Blaine, Blaine, James G. Blaine, the continental liar from the state of Maine!" Though the vote was uncomfortably close, the election hinged on the electoral votes of Cleveland's home state of New York, and he took the White House. He arrived in Washington very much as he later left it: with no "brain trust" or inner-circle panel of advisers, and little love for relations with the press; in short, quite alone, a condition that Cleveland often found to be a strength rather than a liability.

During Cleveland's first term, challenges to the government came from the theoretical as well as the practical realm. Anarchists questioned the legitimacy not only of lawmakers who claimed to create law rather than discover it, but also of the contract of the U.S. Constitution when no living citizen had signed his name or consented to it. Cleveland however believed that the U.S. system, when limited in power and applied to all equally, was legitimate; he cited the peaceful transfer of power from one faction to another as proof of the government's viability and virtue.

As he did in his capacity as mayor and governor, Cleveland used his veto power vigorously to oppose measures he found wasteful or unfair, such as the Civil War Pensions Bill. As president, Cleveland vetoed more legislation than all other previous presidents combined. He likewise was consistent in his support of the gold standard against advocates of soft money who sought the inflation caused by unlimited silver coinage.

During Cleveland's first term, the federal government enacted two important measures that came to be linked to his name. The first was the Interstate Commerce Act of 1887, which established the nation's first regulatory agency, the Interstate Commerce Commission. The second was the Dawes Severalty Act, also of 1887, which carried out former president Arthur's call for the redistribution of reservation land into allotments for native American individuals.

The most important issue of Cleveland's first term was the protectionist tariff. Cleveland believed that the fundamental premise behind protectionism—using the public power to tax for the benefit of private interests such as key industries who wished to stack the tables against overseas competitors—was unfair as well as economically unsound. He defied conventional political wisdom and maintained a strong position on the controversial issue though his bid for reelection drew near. In the end, his Republican challenger Benjamin Harrison won the financial backing of pro-tariff industries and managed to capture the electoral college vote despite Cleveland winning the popular election. The tariff issue cost Cleveland reelection, but he left office a well-liked leader who could afford to wait until Harrison's administration self-destructed. Cleveland then returned to the White House, the first and only U.S. president to be elected to two non-consecutive terms in office.

NOTES

1. Morton Borden, ed., *America's Ten Greatest Presidents* (Chicago: Rand McNally, 1961); Richard E. Welch, Jr., *The Presidencies of Grover Cleveland* (Lawrence: University Press of Kansas, 1988).

THE ISSUE: LEGITIMACY OF U.S. GOVERNMENT

Not all of the challenges faced by Cleveland came from the realm of policy; others came from the realm of political theory. Some proponents of one of these theories, anarchism, not only questioned Garfield as a leader but also questioned the very foundations of U.S. government.

Composed of many differing strains of thought (such as mutualism, anarcho-individualism, anarcho-socialism, and anarcho-communism), anarchism revolves around the concept of noncoercion and the belief that force is illegitimate and unethical. Anarchism traveled from Europe to the United States in the mid-nineteenth century in the persons of political philosophers Josiah Warren, Robert Owen, and Lysander Spooner. Spooner, in particular, was both an activist and a theorist. His brand of anarchism was anarcho-individualism. This theory holds that the individual is the building block of the world, and that each person possesses rights that no other person or group of persons can violate. These rights, sometimes called natural rights, include rights such as the right to live, to control one's own body, and to speak one's own mind. From these rights, Spooner and others believed, other rights follow, such as the right to be creative and to own what one has produced. If people are independent thinkers and producers, then, the main way individuals interact socially is through exchange (buying, selling, and trading) and contract.

It was with contracts that Spooner, who was a trained and practiced attorney, was particularly interested. He argued that the U.S. system was illegitimate in part because it coerced individuals to follow laws that they themselves did not make or agree to obey; in that sense, the Constitution was a contract between the U.S. founders, but later generations never had the opportunity to choose or reject it. He attacked the idea of "lawmakers," arguing that natural laws—from gravity to the right to live— were not made by any government, but were either respected and protected or ignored and infringed upon. Most U.S. lawmakers, Spooner continued, actively found ways to violate natural law rather than preserve it. Perhaps most scathingly, Spooner, who had been an avid abolitionist, noted that many would challenge Cleveland's description of the U.S. governmental system as one providing "equal and exact justice to all men."

Cleveland, however, did view the government as legitimate, and called the U.S. Constitution and the system it created "the manifestation of the will of a great and free people." In particular, he viewed the peaceful transfer of power from one chief executive to another—especially in that trying time when one president had left office through assassination, and then in the following election when the White House transferred from Republican to Democratic control—as evidence of the justice and efficacy of the federal government. Cleveland did not persuade the anarchists of his position. In fact, the pull of the different strains of anarchism continued, especially thanks to economic uncertainty and the rise of organized labor, and would play a crucial role in the tragic end of another presidential administration. Anarchist, particularly anarcho-individualist, critiques of the legitimacy of the U.S. government continue to this day.

The President's Position: Legitimate

First Inaugural Address, March 4, 1885
Fellow-Citizens:

In the presence of this vast assemblage of my countrymen I am about to supplement and seal by the oath which I shall take the manifestation of the will of a great and free people. In the exercise of their power and right of self-government they have committed to one of their fellow-citizens a supreme and sacred trust, and he here consecrates himself to their service.

This impressive ceremony adds little to the solemn sense of responsibility with which I contemplate the duty I owe to all the people of the land. Nothing can relieve me from anxiety lest by any act of mine their interests may suffer, and nothing is needed to strengthen my resolution to engage every faculty and effort in the promotion of their welfare.

Amid the din of party strife the people's choice was made, but its attendant circumstances have demonstrated anew the strength and safety of a government by the people. In each succeeding year it more clearly appears that our democratic principle needs no apology, and that in its fearless and faithful application is to be found the surest guaranty of good government.

But the best results in the operation of a government wherein every citizen has a share largely depend upon a proper limitation of purely partisan zeal and effort and a correct appreciation of the time when the heat of the partisan should be merged in the patriotism of the citizen.

To-day the executive branch of the Government is transferred to new keeping. But this is still the Government of all the people, and it should be none the less an object of their affectionate solicitude. At this hour the animosities of political strife, the bitterness of partisan defeat, and the exultation of partisan triumph should be supplanted by an ungrudging acquiescence in the popular will and a sober, conscientious concern for the general weal. Moreover, if from this hour we cheerfully and honestly abandon all sectional prejudice and distrust, and determine, with manly confidence in one another, to work out harmoniously the achievements of our national destiny, we shall deserve to realize all the benefits which our happy form of government can bestow.

On this auspicious occasion we may well renew the pledge of our devotion to the Constitution, which, launched by the founders of the Republic and consecrated by their prayers and patriotic devotion, has for almost a century borne the hopes and the aspirations of a great people through prosperity and peace and through the shock of foreign conflicts and the perils of domestic strife and vicissitudes.

By the Father of his Country our Constitution was commended for adoption as "the result of a spirit of amity and mutual concession." In that same spirit it should be administered, in order to promote the lasting welfare of the country and to secure the full measure of its priceless benefits to us and to those who will succeed to the blessings of our national life. The large variety of diverse and competing interests subject to Federal control, persistently seeking the recognition of their claims, need give us no fear that "the greatest good to the greatest number" will fail to be accomplished if in the halls of national legislation that spirit of amity and mutual concession shall prevail in which the Constitution had its birth. If this involves the surrender or postponement of private interests and the abandonment of local advantages, compensation will be found in the assurance that the common interest is subserved and the general welfare advanced.

In the discharge of my official duty I shall endeavor to be guided by a just and unstrained construction of the Constitution, a careful observance of the distinction between the powers granted to the Federal Government and those reserved to the States or to the people, and by a cautious appreciation of those functions which by the Constitution and laws have been especially assigned to the executive branch of the Government.

But he who takes the oath today to preserve, protect, and defend the Constitution of the United States only assumes the solemn obligation which every patriotic citizen—on the farm, in the workshop, in the busy marts of trade, and everywhere—should share with him. The Constitution which prescribes his oath, my countrymen, is yours; the Government you have chosen him to administer for a time is yours; the suffrage which executes the will of freemen is yours; the laws and the entire scheme of our civil rule, from the town meeting to the State capitals and the national capital, is yours. Your every voter, as surely as your Chief Magistrate, under the same high sanction, though in a different sphere, exercises a public trust. Nor is this all. Every citizen owes to the country a vigilant watch and close scrutiny of its public servants and a fair and reasonable estimate of their fidelity and usefulness. Thus is the people's will impressed upon the whole framework of our civil polity—municipal, State, and Federal; and this is the price of our liberty and the inspiration of our faith in the Republic.

. . . In the administration of a government pledged to do equal and exact justice to all men there should be no pretext for anxiety touching the protection of the freedmen in their rights or their security in the enjoyment of their privileges under the Constitution and its amendments. . . .

These topics and the constant and ever-varying wants of an active and enterprising population may well receive the attention and the patriotic endeavor of all who make and execute the Federal law. Our duties are practical and call for industrious application, an intelligent perception of the claims of public office, and, above all, a firm determination, by united action, to secure to all the people of the land the full benefits of the best form of government ever vouchsafed to man. And let us not trust to human effort alone, but humbly acknowledging the power and goodness of Almighty God, who presides over the destiny of nations, and who has at all times been revealed in our country's history, let us invoke His aid and His blessings upon our labors.[2]

Against the President's Position: Illegitimate

A LETTER TO GROVER CLEVELAND ON HIS FALSE INAUGURAL ADDRESS, THE USURPATIONS AND CRIMES OF LAWMAKERS AND JUDGES, AND THE CONSEQUENT POVERTY, IGNORANCE, AND SERVITUDE OF THE PEOPLE BY LYSANDER SPOONER

1886

To Grover Cleveland:

SIR,—Your inaugural address is probably as honest, sensible, and consistent a one as that of any president within the last fifty years, or, perhaps, as any since the foundation of the government. If, therefore, it is false, absurd, self-contradictory, and ridiculous, it is not (as I think) because you are personally less honest, sensible, or consistent than your predecessors, but because the government itself—according to your own description of it, and according to the practical administration of it for nearly a hundred years—is an utterly and palpably false, absurd, and criminal one. Such praises as you bestow upon it are, therefore, necessarily false, absurd, and ridiculous.

Thus you describe it as "a government pledged to do equal and exact justice to all men."

Did you stop to think what that means? Evidently you did not; for nearly, or quite, all the rest of your address is in direct contradiction to it.

Let me then remind you that justice is an immutable, natural principle; and not anything that can be made, unmade, or altered by any human power.

It is also a subject of science, and is to be learned, like mathematics, or any other science. It does not derive its authority from the commands, will, pleasure, or discretion of any possible combination of men, whether calling themselves a government, or by any other name.

It is also, at all times, and in all places, the supreme law. And being everywhere and always the supreme law, it is necessarily everywhere and always the only law.

Lawmakers, as they call themselves, can add nothing to it, nor take anything from it. Therefore all their laws, as they call them,—that is, all the laws of their own making,—have no color of authority or obligation. It is a falsehood to call them laws; for there is nothing in them that either creates men's duties or rights, or enlightens them as to their duties or rights. There is consequently nothing binding or obligatory about them. And nobody is bound to take the least notice of them, unless it be to trample them under foot, as usurpations. If they command men to do justice, they add nothing to men's obligation to do it, or to any man's right to enforce it. They are therefore mere idle wind, such as would be commands to consider the day as day, and the night as night. If they command or license any man to do injustice, they are criminal on their face. If they command any man to do anything which justice does not require him to do, they are simple, naked usurpations and tyrannies. If they forbid any man to do anything, which justice could permit him to do, they are criminal invasions of his natural and rightful liberty. In whatever light, therefore, they are viewed, they are utterly destitute of everything like authority or obligation. They are all necessarily either the impudent, fraudulent, and criminal usurpations of tyrants, robbers, and murderers, or the senseless work of ignorant or thoughtless men, who do not know, or certainly do not realize, what they are doing.

This science of justice, or natural law, is the only science that tells us what are, and what are not, each man's natural, inherent, inalienable, individual rights, as against any and all other men. And to say that any, or all, other men may rightfully compel him to obey any or all such other laws as they may see fit to make, is to say that he has no rights of his own, but is their subject, their property, and their slave.

For the reasons now given, the simple maintenance of justice, or natural law, is plainly the one only purpose for which any coercive power— or anything bearing the name of government—has a right to exist.

It is intrinsically just as false, absurd, ludicrous, and ridiculous to say that lawmakers, so-called, can invent and make any laws, of their own, authoritatively fixing, or declaring, the rights of individuals, or that shall be in any manner authoritative or obligatory upon individuals, or that individuals may rightfully be compelled to obey, as it would be to say that they can invent and make such mathematics, chemistry, physiology, or other sciences, as they see fit, and rightfully compel individuals to conform all their actions to them, instead of conforming them to the mathematics, chemistry, physiology, or other sciences of nature.

Lawmakers, as they call themselves, might just as well claim the right to abolish, by statute, the natural law of gravitation, the natural laws of light, heat, and electricity, and all the other natural laws of matter and mind, and institute laws of their own in the place of them, and compel conformity to them, as to claim the right to set aside the natural law of justice, and compel obedience to such other laws as they may see fit to manufacture, and set up in its stead.

Let me now ask you how you imagine that your so-called lawmakers can "do equal and exact justice to all men," by any so-called laws of their own making. If their laws command anything but justice, or forbid anything but injustice, they are themselves unjust and criminal. If they simply command justice, and forbid injustice, they add nothing to the natural authority of justice, or to men's obligation to obey it. It is, therefore, a simple impertinence, and sheer impudence, on their part, to assume that their commands, as such, are of any authority whatever. It is also sheer impudence, on their part, to assume that their commands are at all necessary to teach other men what is, and what is not, justice. The science of justice is as open to be learned by all other men, as by themselves; and it is, in general, so simple and easy to be learned, that there is no need of, and no place for, any man, or body of men, to teach it, declare it, or command it, on their own authority.

For one, or another, of these reasons, therefore, each and every law, so-called, that forty-eight different congresses have presumed to make, within the last ninety-six years, have been utterly destitute of all legitimate authority. That is to say, they have either been criminal, as commanding or licensing men to do what justice forbade them to do, or as forbidding them to do what justice would have permitted them to do; or else they have been superfluous, as adding nothing to men's knowledge of justice, or to their obligation to do justice, or abstain from injustice.

What excuse, then, have you for attempting to enforce upon the people that great mass of superfluous or criminal laws (so-called) which ignorant and foolish, or impudent and criminal, men have, for so many years, been manufacturing, and promulgating, and enforcing, in violation of justice, and of all men's natural, inherent, and inalienable rights?[3]

NOTES

2. The Avalon Project at Yale Law School, *Inaugural Addresses of the Presidents*, www.yale.edu/lawweb/avalon/presiden/inaug/cleve1.htm (accessed November 5, 2002).

3. LysanderSpooner.org, www.lysanderspooner.org/bib_new.htm (accessed November 4, 2002).

THE ISSUE: THE GOLD STANDARD

The financial concerns that began with the Panic of 1873 continued to plague the United States into Cleveland's administration, when the central economic debate continued to be that between hard money, or gold, advocates and the interests of soft money, or silver and bimetallism. Despite the fact he was a Democrat, Cleveland, like Arthur and other Republicans before him, was a staunch defender of hard money. He worried that the law required the national government to coin silver and pay out gold, noting that the government would soon fail to have adequate gold in its stores and would be dependent on the private individuals who had hoarded gold and who would return it at a premium. This accumulation of silver and loss of gold by the U.S. government, in Cleveland's opinion, was particularly dangerous in terms of international relations. He warned that the time could come when the country would not be able to pay its foreign debts in the gold that other nations expected, meaning that the nation would either have to pay in inflated silver money, a bad faith act costing the United States much in terms of international confidence and goodwill, or not pay at all, thus adding to the interest already owed. Neither outcome was positive or desirable.

Reminding the laboring class that no one, not even the debtors and poor, benefited from an unstable currency, Cleveland unsuccessfully called for the repeal of the Bland-Allison Act of 1878, which expanded the U.S. Treasury's purchase of silver bullion and restored silver coins as legal tender. The issue remained unresolved during Cleveland's term, but he would revisit it again when he returned to the White House after a four-year absence.

As Cleveland argued for the demonitization of silver, soft money proponents such as Sarah E. V. Emery argued that it was the 1873 demonetization of silver that caused the original economic crisis. Just as Cleveland feared the hoarding of gold by speculators under Bland-Allison, silver advocates believed the rich and powerful had engineered the demonetization in order to increase the value of the gold they had hoarded. Cleveland worried about how the currency question would affect the United States' economic standing abroad with its trading partners, soft money supporters believed such concerns reflected undue foreign, especially British, influence and control of U.S. policy. Because they tended to frame all questions in terms of black-and-white opposites such as creditors vs. debtors, Midwesterners vs. Easterners, farmers vs. bankers, and the poor vs. the wealthy, almost any challenge or contradiction to their theories could fit into their conspiracy mentality. By turning those who disagreed with them into robbers, liars, and sneaking schemers intent on oppressing part of the popular for their own self-aggrandizement, those who favored free silver ensured that no real compromise or persuasion could take place. The class hostility and, at times, paranoia grew and informed the agrarian and labor movements at the turn of the century and beyond.

The President's Position: For the Gold Standard

CLEVELAND'S FIRST ANNUAL MESSAGE
DECEMBER 8, 1885

Nothing more important than the present condition of our currency and coinage can claim your attention.

Since February, 1878, the Government has, under the compulsory provisions of law, purchased silver bullion and coined the same at the rate of more than $2,000,000 every month. By this process up to the present date 215,759,431 silver dollars have been coined. . . .

Every month two millions of gold in the public Treasury are paid out for two millions or more of silver dollars, to be added to the idle mass already accumulated.

If continued long enough, this operation will result in the substitution of silver for all the gold the Government owns applicable to its general purposes. It will not do to rely upon the customs receipts of the Government to make good this drain of gold, because the silver thus coined having been made legal tender for all debts and dues, public and private, at times during the last six months 58 per cent of the receipts for duties has been in silver or silver certificates, while the average within that period has been 20 per cent. The proportion of silver and its certificates received by the Government will probably increase as time goes on, for the reason that the nearer the period approaches when it will be obliged to offer silver in payment of its obligations the greater inducement there will be to hoard gold against depreciation in the value of silver or for the purpose of speculating.

This hoarding of gold has already begun.

When the time comes that gold has been withdrawn from circulation, then will be apparent the difference between the real value of the silver dollar and a dollar in gold, and the two coins will part company. Gold, still the standard of value and necessary in our dealings with other countries, will be at a premium over silver; banks which have substituted gold for the deposits of their customers may pay them with silver bought with such gold, thus making a handsome profit; rich speculators will sell their hoarded gold to their neighbors who need it to liquidate their foreign debts, at a ruinous premium over silver, and the laboring men and women of the land, most defenseless of all, will find that the dollar received for the wage of their toil has sadly shrunk in its purchasing power. It may be said that the latter result will be but temporary, and that ultimately the price of labor will be adjusted to the change; but even if this takes place the wage-worker can not possibly gain, but must inevitably lose, since the price he is compelled to pay for his living will not only be measured in a coin heavily depreciated and fluctuating and uncertain in its value, but this uncertainty in the value of the purchasing medium will be made the pretext for an advance in prices beyond that justified by actual depreciation. . . .

The condition in which our Treasury may be placed by a persistence in our present course is a matter of concern to every patriotic citizen who does not desire his Government to pay in silver such of its obligations as should be paid in gold. Nor should our condition be such as to oblige us, in a prudent management of our affairs, to discontinue the calling and payment of interest-bearing obligations which we have the right now to discharge, and thus avoid the payment of further interest thereon.

The so-called debtor class, for whose benefit the continued compulsory coinage of silver is insisted upon, are not dishonest because they are in debt, and they should not be suspected of a desire to jeopardize the financial safety of the country in order that they may cancel their present debts by paying the same in depreciated dollars. Nor should it be forgotten that it is not the rich nor the money lender alone that must submit to such a readjustment, enforced by the Government and their debtors. The pittance of the widow and the orphan and the incomes of helpless beneficiaries of all kinds would be disastrously reduced. The depositors in savings banks and in other institutions which hold in trust the savings of the poor, when their little accumulations are scaled down to meet the new order of things, would in their distress painfully realize the delusion of the promise made to them that plentiful money would improve their condition.

We now have on hand all the silver dollars necessary to supply the present needs of the people and to satisfy those who from sentiment wish to see them in circulation, and if their coinage is suspended they can be readily obtained by all who desire them. If the need of more is at any time apparent, their coinage may be renewed.

That disaster has not already overtaken us furnishes no proof that danger does not wait upon a continuation of the present silver coinage. We have been saved by the most careful management and unusual expedients, by a combination of fortunate conditions, and by a confident expectation that the course of the Government in regard to silver coinage would be speedily changed by the action of Congress.

Prosperity hesitates upon our threshold because of the dangers and uncertainties surrounding this question. Capital timidly shrinks from trade, and investors are unwilling to take the chance of the questionable shape in which their money will be returned to them, while enterprise halts at a risk against which care and sagacious management do not protect.

As a necessary consequence, labor lacks employment and suffering and distress are visited upon a portion of our fellow-citizens especially entitled to the careful consideration of those charged with the duties of legislation. No interest appeals to us as strongly for a safe and stable currency as the vast army of the unemployed.

I recommend the suspension of the compulsory coinage of silver dollars, directed by the law passed in February, 1878.[4]

Against the President's Position: Against the Gold Standard

"DEMONETIZATION OF SILVER"
BY SARAH E. V. EMERY (2ND ED., 1888)

Having refunded and made payable in gold the bonds which had not cost their holders more than sixty cents on the dollar, the casual observer is satisfied that the last robbery has been perpetrated. But the busy brain of avarice is ever reaching out—not after new truths—but for gain, *gain*, GAIN; and we next find these civilized brigands have consummated a scheme for the *demonetization of silver*. This act, passed in 1873, destroyed the money quality of silver, and thus produced a farther contraction of the currency. The object of this act was first to prevent the payment of the bond, and second, to increase their value.

Never in this country had there been an investment so safe and yet so reliable. Shylock, with his hoarded millions, could rest on beds of down. Neither fire, flood, mildew nor blight brought anxiety to him. He seemed to rest in assurance of the Divine favor, having obeyed the injunction to "lay up his treasure where moth and rust could not corrupt, nor thieves break through and steal." Indeed, the entire country had become sponsor for his wealth, for under the law every producer and millions of wage-workers had been instituted a vigilance committee to look after his welfare. Why should he not be opposed to having his bond investment disturbed? The government held that property in safe keeping, and did not charge a cent for the favor; it collected his interest and paid it over to him free of charge; it paid his gold interest in advance and exempted him from taxation; the insurance agent and tax gatherer were strangers to him, they did not molest or make him afraid, and being thus fortified, he was content to let the producers of wealth eke out a miserable existence while he fared sumptuously every day. But it was not the American capitalist alone who entered into this murderous scheme for demonetizing silver. In the *Banker's Magazine* of August, 1873, we find the following on this subject:

> In 1872, silver being demonetized in France, England and Holland, a capital of $500,000 was raised, and Ernest Seyd of London was sent to this country with this fund, as agent of the foreign bond holders and capitalists, to effect the same object (demonetization of silver), which was accomplished.

There you have it, a paid agent of English capitalists sent to this country with $500,000 to buy the American Congress and rob the American people. . . .

God of our fathers! A British capitalist sent here to make laws for the American people. England failed to subjugate us by the bullet, but she stole into our Congressional halls and by the crafty use of gold, obtained possession of the ballot, and to-day American industry pays tribute to England, despite our blood-bought seal of independence.

Not only did the demonetization of silver prevent, or at least retard the payment of the bonds, but it added to the value of the gold in which these bonds were to be paid. Every dollar taken from circulation adds to the value of that which is left, hence the demonetization of silver increased the value of gold. After England had demonetized silver, our silver dollar, containing 412 grains, was not worth as much in that country by at least ten cents on the dollar, as our gold dollar containing 25.8 grains of gold. By destroying the money quality of silver, bonds became payable in gold only, thus adding immensely to their value. A British capitalist, holding $100,000,000 of our four per cent bonds, received an annual interest of $4,000,000, which paid in standard silver would be worth ten per cent, or $400,000 less than it would be if paid in gold. This would make a difference in his daily interest of $1,096. Is it not clear why English capitalists were anxious for the United States to demonetize silver? and why they could afford to send Ernest Seyd to this country with a capital of $500,000 to accomplish this object? . . .

The injury to the people of this country through the demonetization of silver can never, perhaps, be justly estimated. The panic of 1873, which ensued was one of the most disastrous that ever befell any people. Language fails in a description of the blighting misery that desolated the country, the ravages of war are scarcely comparable with it. From the demonetization of silver, in 1873, to its remonetization in 1878, may well be called the dark days of our Republic. Bankruptcies and financial disaster brought in train their legitimate offspring, and the statistics of those and the ensuing years are voluminous with the most startling and loathsome crimes, murder, insanity, suicide, divorce, drunkenness, and all forms of immorality and crime have increased from that day to this in the most appalling ratio. Will any man say that legislation has had nothing to do with the startling increase of crime in our country? Every result is produced from certain causes, and it is no more certain that like begets like than that the increase of misery and crime in our country are the direct result of evil legislation. And it is impossible for a nation long to remain free whose laws are made granting special privileges to the few and ignoring the rights of the many. The contraction of the currency, commencing with the destruction of the greenbacks in 1866, and the stringency increased by the demonetization of silver in 1873, has been productive of more misery and crime to the people of this country than all the wars, pestilence, and famine with which they have ever been afflicted. . . .

To whom, then, shall we charge these calamities that have come upon us like a flood? Is it the extravagance of the people? Is it because too many of the necessaries of life have been produced? Because the farmer has been too industrious and prudent, or the manufacturers employed too many laborers in the production of his commodities? . . . No, it is none of these circumstances that have brought such disaster upon our country, but it is a selfish and criminal legislation that has overwhelmed us with these alarming conditions.[5]

NOTES

4. Richardson, Volume X, pp. 4927–4928, 4930–4931.
5. Sarah E. V. Emery, "Demonetization of Silver," in George Brown Tindall, ed., *A Populist Reader: Selections from the Works of American Populist Leaders* (New York: Harper & Row, 1966), pp. 52–57.

THE ISSUE: CIVIL WAR PENSIONS

Cleveland's economic conservatism revealed itself again in the issue of the Civil War Pensions Bill. In 1887, congressmen such as Republican Byron M. Cutcheon of Michigan argued for and passed a bill providing pensions for the relief of disabled and dependent veterans of the Union army during the Civil War. The argument for the bill was simple: the nation owed U.S. veterans a debt of gratitude for preserving the union, and in a time of particular economic difficulty it was especially important to be certain that veterans who could not provide for themselves were cared for appropriately. The bill's supporters relied on sentiment—gratitude, sympathy, and patriotism—to rally others behind the cause. Despite the emotional rhetoric and obvious good intentions of the bill's proponents, however, Cleveland vetoed the measure.

Cleveland's argument against the bill was threefold. First, the bill referred to veterans who were disabled for any reason whatsoever as recipients of the pension. Cleveland pointed out that veterans who were dependent due to their service in the military and the related disabilities they sustained had been provided for in past legislation; in other words, anyone from the Union forces who was unable to support himself because of war-related injuries already had government resources to help him. Those left, then, were veterans who just happened to be dependent for separate reasons, not veterans who were dependent as a result of their service to the country. Cleveland felt it important to link military service and disabilities as a criteria for the receipt of such a government pension.

Second, Cleveland pointed to the precedent of past veteran pension bills that did not link disabilities with military service. Though they existed, such legislation was inevitably passed at such a late date after the conflict in question that the only surviving veterans were elderly and in need of care because of their very advanced age. This was not the case with the Civil War Pensions Bill, which was passed only a little over twenty years after the war. Many veterans were not elderly; in fact, many were barely middle-aged. Cleveland could see no reason why veterans who were not disabled in the conflict and were of a reasonable age to be self-sufficient needed additional funds from the national government.

Third, and perhaps most importantly, Cleveland saw this bill as an opening of the floodgates, a measure that would cost the country a great deal in a time when the economy was anything but balanced and the currency was in a state of flux. Not only was the proposition expensive, but it also was expensive at the worst time imaginable for the nation to incur more debt and spend more precious funds. The president sympathized with the charitable and public-spirited sentiment behind the bill, but for practical, ultimately economic questions, he opposed the measure. His practicality and willingness to say no—Cleveland vetoed more legislation than all other preceding presidents combined—became a trademark of his administration in both of his terms, and helped to make the presidency a more powerful institution. Congress did not override the veto, and the bill ultimately died.

The President's Position: Against the Civil War Pensions Bill

February 11, 1887
To the House of Representatives:

I herewith return without my approval House bill No. 10457, entitled "An act for the relief of dependent parents and honorably discharged soldiers and sailors who are now disabled and dependent upon their own labor for support."

This is the first general bill that has been sanctioned by the Congress since the close of the late civil war permitting a pension to the soldiers and sailors who served in that war upon the ground of service and present disability alone, and in the entire absence of any injuries received by the casualties or incidents of such service.

While by almost constant legislation since the close of this war there has been compensation awarded for every possible injury received as a result of military service in the Union Army, and while a great number of laws passed for that purpose have been administered with great liberality and have been supplemented by numerous private acts to reach special cases, there has not until now been an avowed departure from the principle thus far adhered to respecting Union soldiers, that the bounty of the Government in the way of pensions is generously bestowed when granted to those who, in this military service and in the line of military duty, have to a greater or less extent been disabled.

But it is a mistake to suppose that service pensions, such as are permitted by the second section of the bill under consideration, are new to our legislation. In 1818, thirty-five years after the close of the Revolutionary War, they were granted to the soldiers engaged in that struggle, conditional upon service until the end of the war or for a term not less than nine months, and requiring every beneficiary under the act to be one "who is, or hereafter by reason of his reduced circumstances in life shall be, in need of assistance from his country for support." Another law of a like character was passed in 1828, requiring service until the close of the Revolutionary War; and still another, passed in 1832, provided for those persons not included in the previous statute, but who served two years at some time during the war, and giving a proportionate sum to those who had served not less than six months.

A service-pension law was passed for the benefit of the soldiers of 1812 in the year 1871, fifty-six years after the close of that war, which required only sixty days' service; and another was passed in 1878, sixty-three years after the war, requiring only fourteen days' service.

The service-pension bill passed at this session of Congress, thirty-nine years after the close of the Mexican War, for the benefit of the soldiers of that war, requires either some degree of disability or dependency or that the claimant under its provisions should be 62 years of age, and in either case that he should have served sixty days or been actually engaged in a battle.

It will be seen that the bill of 1818 and the Mexican pension bill, thus passed nearer the close of the wars in which its beneficiaries were engaged than the others—one thirty-five years and the other thirty-nine years after the termination of such wars—embraced persons who were quite advanced in age, assumed to be comparatively few in number, and whose circumstances, dependence, and disabilities were clearly defined and could be quite easily fixed.

The other laws referred to appear to have been passed at a time so remote from the military service of the persons which they embraced that their extreme age alone was deemed to supply a presumption of dependency and need . . .

If this bill should become a law, with its tremendous addition to our pension obligation, I am thoroughly convinced that further efforts to reduce the Federal revenue and restore some part of it to our people will, and perhaps should, be seriously questioned.

It has constantly been a cause of pride and congratulation to the American citizen that his country is not put to the charge of maintaining a large standing army in times of peace. Yet we are now living under a war tax which has been tolerated in peaceful times to meet the obligations incurred in war. But for years past, in all parts of the country, the demand for the reduction of the burdens of taxation upon our labor and production has increased in volume and urgency.

I am not willing to approve a measure presenting the objections to which this bill is subject, and which, moreover, will have the effect of disappointing the expectation of the people and their desire and hope for relief from war taxation in time of peace.

In my last annual message the following language was used:

Every patriotic heart responds to a tender consideration for those who, having served their country long and well, are reduced to destitution and dependence, not as an incident of their service, but with advancing age or through sickness or misfortune. We are all tempted by the contemplation of such a condition to supply relief and are often impatient of the limitations of public duty. Yielding to no one in the desire to indulge this feeling of consideration, I can not rid myself of the conviction that if these ex-soldiers are to be relieved they and their cause are entitled to an enactment under which relief may be claimed as a right, and that such relief should be granted under the sanction of law, not in evasion of it; nor should such worthy objects of care, all equally entitled, be remitted to the unequal operation of sympathy or the tender mercies of social and political influence, with their unjust discrimination.

I do not think that the objects, the conditions, and the limitations thus suggested are contained in the bill under consideration.[6]

Grover Cleveland

Against the President's Position: For the Civil War Pensions Bill

REPRESENTATIVE BYRON M. CUTCHEON OF MICHIGAN
HOUSE OF REPRESENTATIVES
JULY 12, 1888

. . . And now, Mr. Speaker, I have rapidly and hastily reviewed the history of pension legislation from the beginning of the war until now. It has not been altogether a pleasant task. I have dealt with facts; but facts are not always pleasant things. For the facts I am not responsible. The necessity for pensions is a sad one; but for that necessity we upon this side of the House are not responsible.

I would that there were neither sectional nor party lines on the pension questions; but I do not suppose that it could be otherwise. The war was a sectional war, and the parties to it were divided largely upon party lines. I do not mention this by way of censure, but rather by way of history. . . .

But our path of duty is plain. It is to be true to the men who were true to union and liberty and law.

We dare not look into the bloody past, with its unequaled record of sacrifice and suffering, and do these men less than justice. We dare not look into the future, with all its thronging years, its crowding generations, and its momentous possibilities, and permit it to be truly said that the Republic has been ungrateful to its defenders.

The great Republican party, which placed Lincoln in the chair of state and stood around him while he called the volunteers from their homes and set their invincible battalions in the field, which sustained the hands of Grant from Donelson to Appamattox, will neither be unmindful of nor unfaithful to its duty. These men were our brothers, our kindred, our comrades.

It was our fight in which they fell. It was their valor and their sacrifice that preserved our country, that assured our future, that conquered our peace. It was while bearing their country's flag in the path of patriotic duty that they met disease, disaster, and death. Theirs was the sacrifice, ours is the fruition. It is easy in these times of blood-purchased peace to speak lightly of their service, their suffering, and their sacrifice.

But in that awful hour of our dire necessity, when the slippery slopes of Gettysburgh blazed with deadly fire and the fate of the great republic hung in the trembling scales of destiny, the great metropolitan journals had not yet learned to sneer at "the grand army of paupers and mendicants." Then they were patriots. Then they were heroes. Then they were worthy of all praise and reward. Then there was nothing that could be done or promised beyond their deserts. And while the millionaires and the speculators and journalists made merchandise of their heroism, these men bared their breasts to the storm and rolled back the crimson tide of war.

Mr. Speaker, I can respect the feeling of brave men still smarting under the stinging blows of defeat, who hesitate, out of their comparative poverty, to vote pensions to their late antagonists; but I have naught but unmixed and unspeakable contempt for those organs of the piled-up millions of the wealth of the North who have lost all sense of gratitude to the men who made their hoarded millions possible.

Mr. Speaker, others may act as they see fit, but as for myself I shall stand, without evasion, or shuffling, or apology, for generous justice to the men who redeemed the republic and kept "the jewel of liberty in the family of freedom."[7]

NOTES

6. Richardson, Volume XI, pp. 5134–5135, 5141.

7. *Congressional Record, Fiftieth Congress, First Session,* Volume XIX, Part I

(Washington, D.C.: Government Printing Office, 1888), Appendix to the Congressional Record, p. 324.

THE ISSUE: THE TARIFF

Common wisdom asserts that presidents—or, for that matter, any elected officials—seeking reelection should avoid taking strong stands on potentially controversial subjects shortly before voters head to the polls. Cleveland, however, flew in the face of convention when he took a stand for tariff reform before the election of 1888. Opposition was fierce, and the Republican candidate for the White House, Benjamin Harrison, forced the issue by taking an equally strong stand in favor of the protective tariff. Cleveland's position may have cost him the election, but it did not keep him out of the chief executive's chair for long.

Cleveland opposed the practice of protective tariffs, which taxed incoming goods from foreign markets in order to encourage buyers to purchase U.S. wares rather than international ones and to discourage overseas competitors from exporting too much to the United States. First, he argued, protectionism was meant to be a temporary measure to encourage fledgling national manufacturing and industry as they struggled to catch up to comparative production in older, more well-established countries. By the late nineteenth century, however, U.S. businesses had enjoyed a century of history. Just as the nation was no longer the newcomer on the world stage, neither were its business interests. In short, the baby had outgrown the pampering it had received when it was newborn and fragile, and it was now old enough to play on its own.

Second, Cleveland explained, the government policy meant to protect some sectors of the economy—and the expense to the taxpayer it cost to enforce such policy—invariably played favorites, benefiting some and ignoring others. He did not believe it was fair play in a democracy to use the power of the government to grant favors to some and deny such favors to others. Cleveland favored positions that treated all equally under the law, and the protective tariff did just the opposite. Ironically enough, Cleveland's stand set him against some big business interests, although soft money advocates declared him in bed with big business due to his support of the gold standard.

Pro-tariff voices such as Republican congressman Oscar L. Jackson of Pennsylvania suggested that Cleveland was secretly trying to push a free-trade agenda forward, although there was little covert in Cleveland's remarks. Sounding much like silver advocates, Cleveland's opponents also charged him with playing into the hands of foreign, particularly British, interests with his desire to open trade and competition on an international scale. They feared that no protectionism would mean that U.S. markets would be flooded with international goods that cost less due to the poor wages paid to overseas workers. Few made the connection that the influx of more affordable goods might actually help the U.S. consumers, the "little men" who suffered during economic crisis.

In 1888 Cleveland won the support of a majority of U.S. citizens who voted by a margin of approximately 100,000 thanks to his stand against the protective tariff. Republican Benjamin Harrison's campaign, however, received large contributions from many pro-tariff industrial powers with a vested interest in the issue, and carried the key states of Indiana and New York, and thus captured the electoral college vote to become president. The tariff issue became a crucial part of Harrison's presidential agenda; four years later, however, it was Cleveland, not Harrison, who returned to the White House.

The President's Position: Against a High Tariff

CLEVELAND'S ANNUAL ADDRESS
DECEMBER 3, 1888

A century has passed. Our cities are the abiding places of wealth and luxury; our manufactories yield fortunes never dreamed of by the fathers of the Republic; our business men are madly striving in the race for riches, and immense aggregations of capital outrun the imagination in the magnitude of their undertakings.

We view with pride and satisfaction this bright picture of our country's growth and prosperity, while only a closer scrutiny develops a somber shading. Upon more careful inspection we find the wealth and luxury of our cities mingled with poverty and wretchedness and unremunerative toil. A crowded and constantly increasing urban population suggests the impoverishment of rural sections and discontent with agricultural pursuits. The farmer's son, not satisfied with his father's simple and laborious life, joins the eager chase for easily acquired wealth.

We discover that the fortunes realized by our manufacturers are no longer solely the reward of sturdy industry and enlightened foresight, but that they result from the discriminating favor of the Government and are largely built upon undue exactions from the masses of our people. The gulf between employers and the employed is constantly widening, and classes are rapidly forming, one comprising the very rich and powerful, while in another are found the toiling poor.

As we view the achievements of aggregated capital, we discover the existence of trusts, combinations, and monopolies, while the citizen is struggling far in the rear or is trampled to death beneath an iron heel. Corporations, which should be the carefully restrained creatures of the law and the servants of the people, are fast becoming the people's masters.

Still congratulating ourselves upon the wealth and prosperity of our country and complacently contemplating every incident of change inseparable from these conditions, it is our duty as patriotic citizens to inquire at the present stage of our progress how the bond of the Government made with the people has been kept and performed.

Instead of limiting the tribute drawn from our citizens to the necessities of its economical administration, the Government persists in exacting from the substance of the people millions which, unapplied and useless, lie dormant in its Treasury. This flagrant injustice and this breach of faith and obligation add to extortion the danger attending the diversion of the currency of the country from the legitimate channels of business.

Under the same laws by which these results are produced the Government permits many millions more to be added to the cost of the living of our people and to be taken from our consumers, which unreasonably swell the profits of a small but powerful minority.

The people must still be taxed for the support of the Government under the operation of tariff laws. But to the extent that the mass of our citizens are inordinately burdened beyond any useful public purpose and for the benefit of a favored few, the Government, under pretext of an exercise of its taxing power, enters gratuitously into partnership with these favorites, to their advantage and to the injury of a vast majority of our people.

This is not equality before the law.

The existing situation is injurious to the health of our entire body politic. It stifles in those for whose benefit it is permitted all patriotic love of country, and substitutes in its place selfish greed and grasping avarice. Devotion to American citizenship for its own sake and for what it should accomplish as a motive to our nation's advancement and the happiness of all our people is displaced by the assumption that the Government, instead of being the embodiment of equality, is but an instrumentality through which especial and individual advantages are to be gained.

The arrogance of this assumption is unconcealed. It appears in the sordid disregard of all but personal interests, in the refusal to abate for the benefit of others one iota of selfish advantage, and in combinations to perpetuate such advantages through efforts to control legislation and improperly influence the suffrages of the people.

The grievances of those not included within the circle of these beneficiaries, when fully realized, will surely arouse irritation and discontent. Our farmers, long suffering and patient, struggling in the race of life with the hardest and most unremitting toil, will not fail to see, in spite of misrepresentations and misleading fallacies, that they are obliged to accept such prices for their products as are fixed in foreign markets where they compete with the farmers of the world; that their lands are declining in value while their debts increase, and that without compensating favor they are forced by the action of the Government to pay for the benefit of others such enhanced prices for the things they need that the scanty returns of their labor fail to furnish their support or leave no margin for accumulation. . . .

When to the selfishness of the beneficiaries of unjust discrimination under our laws there shall be added the discontent of those who suffer from such discrimination, we will realize the fact that the beneficent purposes of our Government, dependent upon the patriotism and contentment of our people, is endangered. . . .

A just and sensible revision of our tariff laws should be made for the relief of those of our countrymen who suffer under present conditions. Such a revision should receive the support of all who love that justice and equality due to American citizenship; of all who realize that in this justice and equality our Government finds its strength and its power to protect the citizen and his property; of all who believe that the contented competence and comfort of many accord better with the spirit of our institutions than colossal fortunes unfairly gathered in the hands of a few; of all who appreciate that the forbearance and fraternity among our people, which recognize the value of every American interest, are the surest guaranty of our national progress, and of all who desire to see the products of American skill and ingenuity in every market of the world, with a resulting restoration of American commerce.[8]

Against the President's Position: For a Protective Tariff

REPRESENTATIVE OSCAR L. JACKSON OF
PENNSYLVANIA
MAY 15, 1888

Mr. Chairman: At the beginning of the present session of Congress the President of the United States, in the performance of a constitutional duty which requires that he shall "give to the Congress information of the state of the Union and recommend to their consideration such measures as he shall judge necessary and expedient," communicated to the two Houses what may be called his annual message.

This paper is remarkable for the reasons that it refers to only a single subject-matter, and that in it the present occupant of the Executive office omitted to give full information of the state of the Union and the relations which our Government sustained with other nations of the world. No satisfactory reasons for this exception and extraordinary course were given by him, and up to this time no Senator or Representative in Congress has either seen fit or been able to explain or defend it.

No President preceding him has ever omitted in an annual message to give full information of the state of the Union. A long line of illustrious predecessors for a hundred years, in following as they thought the mandates of the Constitution, had never failed to communicate to Congress full information concerning all the Departments of the government and our relations as a nation with other nations of the earth. This was done alike in times of prosperity and commercial depression, during the many years of peace that blessed our land and in the darkest days of all our wars. But at almost the end of the third year of its existence this Administration has but one matter worthy of giving information about. The message to the present Congress refers alone "to the amount of money exacted" from those who import foreign goods into our country, and which is accumulating in the Treasury to an amount which exceeds the sum "necessary to meet the expenses of the government." . . .

We have, therefore, before us in considering this message the single question of protection by the imposition of tariff duties. I am not unmindful of the great importance of this question, and how intimately connected it is with the welfare of all our people and the prosperity of the whole country. But as the subject is not a new one and has been under discussion and consideration at almost every session of Congress from the administration of Washington to Arthur, I am the more surprised that the present Executive considered it the only question necessary to give information about.

We seek in vain for any condition of affairs, either in the commercial business of the country or in the national Treasury, to justify the singling out of this one question for a message. It is true there is a surplus in the Treasury beyond an amount needed for current expenditures. But the Government is still in debt and previous administrations, without any additional legislation, had made use of much larger sums in a most satisfactory manner in payment of the liabilities of the Government. Our tariff laws, under which the money is being paid into the Treasury, have been on the statute-book for many years, during which the country made great advances in wealth and population and the people enjoyed unusual prosperity and happiness.

Mr. Chairman, there is but one meaning to be taken from the President's message. He is opposed to our system of protection and desires to see it abandoned, and that we shall adopt in the place of it a system of free trade. It is plain that the leaders of the party that elected him have determined on this new departure in politics, and that he and they are in accord on this subject. . . .

We can all understand how a tariff passed at one period of time might greatly increase prior duties and thus be a tariff for protection, and the same rate of duty twenty or thirty years afterward might lower the then existing rates and be in the direction of free trade. You [Mr. McMillin] have avowed here the policy that you propose of cutting down duties. You say you are opposed to the whole theory of a tariff for protection. You expect eventually to dispose of all of it, I have no doubt. One of your leading speakers here, when interrogated on this point, said it would not do to go all the way now. Another said, if protectionists are not content with this bill, they will get one millions worse for them in another year. That is your purpose; you go now as far as you possibly can, and call it only a step in the right direction. [Applause on the Republican side.]

By this bill a distinct issue is made up that the people must finally determine. It is free trade against protection, and no amount of sophistry or declamations by the advocates of the Mills bill can change this. Let the Democratic party whose Presidential leaders have given us this measure stand up and meet the issue squarely. I know that in the debate on this floor advocates of the bill deny that it is a free-trade measure. This is done from motives of policy to reconcile the people to its passage, but such statements ought not to deceive any one. . . .

The animus and feeling of these gentlemen toward the American system of protection is well shown in the extreme and harsh language in which they are accustomed to speak of it, as "robbery, oppression, injustice;" "taxes wrung from the poor," and such like expressions.

Mr. Chairman, it is well known that England is the great champion of free trade, and has long desired that our tariff laws should be repealed that she might fill our markets with her goods, manufactured with her poorly paid labor. . . . There is no doubt that the President's message is hailed with delight in England, for the very reason that it threatens destruction to American industries; and if English manufacturers had the power the Mills bill would soon become a law.[9]

NOTES

8. Watts and Israel, pp. 166–169.

9. *Congressional Record, Fiftieth Congress, First Session,* Volume XIX, Part I (Washington, D.C.: Government Printing Office, 1888), Appendix to the Congressional Record, pp. 98–99.

RECOMMENDED READINGS

Borden, Morton, ed. *America's Ten Greatest Presidents.* Chicago: Rand McNally, 1961.

Brodsky, Alyn. *Grover Cleveland: A Study in Character.* New York: St. Martin's Press, 2000.

Cleveland, Grover. *Letters of Grover Cleveland, 1850–1908.* Boston: Houghton Mifflin, 1933.

Graff, Henry F. *Grover Cleveland.* New York: Times Books, 2002.

Hollingsworth, J. Rogers. *The Whirligig of Politics: The Democracy of Cleveland and Bryan.* Chicago: University of Chicago Press, 1963.

Jeffers, H. Paul. *An Honest President: The Life and Presidencies of Grover Cleveland.* New York: W. Morrow, 2000.

Tugwell, Rexford G. *Grover Cleveland.* New York: Macmillan, 1968.

Welch, Richard E., Jr. *The Presidencies of Grover Cleveland.* Lawrence: University Press of Kansas, 1988.

5

BENJAMIN HARRISON

(1889–1893)

Benjamin Harrison's presidency was a surprise to many—including the majority of U.S. citizens, who had voted for Grover Cleveland, and Harrison himself, who only a year before failed to be reelected to the Senate—but, in fact, Harrison seemed born to be president. His grandfather was William Henry Harrison, the ninth president of the United States, and his great-grandfather was Benjamin Harrison (for whom he was named), who signed the Declaration of Independence. Considering his political family, it seemed natural that Harrison would pursue positions of leadership.

Born a farmer's son in 1833, Harrison studied law and established a practice in Indianapolis, where he became involved in the new Republican party. After service in the Union army during the Civil War—he was, in fact, the last Union general to serve as president—Harrison ran unsuccessfully for the governorship of Indiana before he was elected to the U.S. Senate in 1881. When he failed to win reelection he believed his political career was over; instead, his party nominated him as its candidate for president a year later.

Though he possessed strong and principled convictions, a powerful oratory ability, and a remarkable memory, Harrison was something of an eccentric, even weak, figure. As a senator he gained the reputation of being someone more likely to be respected than genuinely liked, in part due to his cold personal style, probably exacerbated by the fact he sometimes wore gloves to protect himself from others' germs. He was deeply religious, an elder of the Presbyterian Church for forty years, and led his family in prayers for half an hour a day, one part of a rigid and exact household schedule that continued even during his presidential administration. As with germs, electricity, which was installed in the White House during his term, caused him to worry; the family sometimes left lights on even at night for fear of being shocked by the electrical switches. In this unusual man, the Republican party saw a leader who could be led—some would say used—and who would be willing to allow congressional leaders, such as the outspoken Speaker of the House, Maine's Thomas B. Reed, to set the agenda for legislation and policy. This obviously contrasted with the leadership style of Grover Cleveland, who vetoed more laws than all other presidents before him combined.

Cleveland threw down the gauntlet in the 1888 campaign by opposing protectionism actively. The Harrison campaign responded by championing protectionism. Large contributions from big-business interests helped Harrison's bid for the White House, especially in key states such as Indiana and New York. In the end, Cleveland won the popular vote with 5,540,309 to Harrison's 5,444,337, but Harrison took 233 votes in the electoral college to Cleveland's 168.

Though his campaign sounded only one note, several things of interest occurred during the Harrison administration. With his secretary of state, James G. Blaine (who had served as Garfield's secretary of state and the Republican candidate for the presidency against Cleveland in 1884), Harrison saw U.S. influence expand abroad. Blaine presided over the First International Conference of American States, which created the International Union of American Republics for the exchange of scientific and cultural information. The United States secured treaties for commercial reciprocity with a number of nations, as well. Though Democrats blocked the treaty of annexation Harrison supported for Hawaii, annexation followed only a few years later.

Three key laws passed during the administration: the Sherman Anti-Trust Act, the Sherman Silver Purchase Act, and the McKinley Tariff Act. The Sherman Anti-Trust Act outlawed any conspiracy or collusion that restrained U.S. or international trade. This law responded to growing popular fears of monopolies and their control of key markets and industries. Although some business leaders fought to win public opinion to their side, the act reflected a wide national consensus and received Harrison's blessing. The Sherman Silver Purchase Act superseded the Bland-Allison Act by requiring the U.S. government to purchase more silver bullion per month for minting silver coins. Although Harrison was not a gold standard advocate, he was only cautiously optimistic about gold, and he favored gradual and careful change to the country's monetary policy. The act appeared more conservative, however, when compared to ideas such as the subtreasury plan proposed by disgruntled agrarian activists, which called for unlimited silver coinage and a complete reorganization of the U.S. Treasury system. Harrison passively accepted the Sherman Silver Purchase Act, then, as the lesser of two evils, and as a means of winning Western support for protectionism.

The third act, the McKinley Tariff Act, made good on Harrison's campaign platform by raising duties on most imports. Despite the fact that the act incorporated several specific provisions to appeal to farming interests, the simultaneous increase in the price of common goods due to the tariff and the economic depression in the West fueled agrarian discontent. The Republicans lost many seats in the midterm elections as a result.

Not only did Harrison's central issue backfire, but the U.S. public began to link him with the nation's elite and with government waste. The latter resulted from the fact that Harrison allowed Congress to take the lead, thus causing the legislature to allow spending unheard-of sums on various expenditures, exhausting the nation's treasury surplus and earning the name "Billion-Dollar Congress." These problems, and the rise of labor violence toward the end of his term, made a second Harrison term unlikely although the Republican party did nominate him for reelection. During the election, Harrison's childhood sweetheart and wife of decades became ill and died, removing him from active campaigning. It came as no surprise when Cleveland won the 1892 election and returned to the White House.

Cleveland's powerful personal approach to leadership soon placed the executive at the nation's head once again. Harrison's single term might have appeared to be only a momentary, soon-forgotten detour between Cleveland's two administrations, but Harrison became a sought-after speaker on the national lecture circuit and he even published a memoir in 1901 called *Views of an Ex-President*. His continued activity did not lessen Cleveland's popularity, but it did ensure Harrison a place in U.S. memory.

THE ISSUE: ANTI-TRUST

Although Harrison had won the election against a relatively popular incumbent president, he did not gain significant power for himself. Instead, the influential party leaders who had chosen him, and the ranking Republican legislators with whom they coordinated, set the agenda for the Harrison administration. In effect, Congress led the executive. Although the Republican leadership was strong, the party's control over both houses was tenuous according to the numbers, so it was important for them to select policies when possible to mirror public demand and reflect the opinion of the majority of U.S. citizens. One case that illustrates this strategy was the Sherman Anti-Trust Act.

Harrison was a friend of business; after all, it was the significant contributions from business leaders that helped him win the White House. The climate of public opinion, however, was increasingly against the powerful rich, the so-called "robber barons" of the steel, railroad, and other industries, and the monopolies that cornered and controlled markets during the previous decade. Industry giants such as Andrew Carnegie sought to lessen citizens' fear and resentment in articles such as "Wealth," which argued how the concentration of money in the hands of the few was a "much more potent force for the elevation of our race" than equal distribution of wealth, because those few could create new jobs, invest in new ventures, and administer the funds for the common good—an early articulation of the "trickle-down" theory of economics. Carnegie argued that good fortune brought with it great responsibility, and went so far as to advocate heavy taxes on inheritance, a plan that would both encourage the wealthy to use rather than hoard their money, and redistribute large sums to the populace when this did not occur. In an era of economic depression and uncertainty, coupled with the vocal activism of agrarians and labor, this argument carried little weight with many. Despite the efforts of Carnegie and others, most mainstream citizens distrusted the wealthy in general and trusts in particular. Harrison followed this lead and condemned trusts as well.

In 1890, Congress passed the Sherman Anti-Trust Act, declaring all combinations that restrained trade between states or foreign countries illegal. Harrison's blessing was somewhat passive, but present. Over a decade passed, however, before the act was truly used, and even then it failed to inhibit any serious growth of trusts. In fact, the 1894 use of the act was against a striking railroad union, which, according to some definitions, formed a combination intending to restrain interstate trade. Perhaps the most important aspect of the Sherman Anti-Trust Act was that it, like the Interstate Commerce Act three years earlier, marked a shift in the way citizens sought solutions to economic problems. Rather than going to their individual states, or pursuing grievances privately through the courts, the public turned increasingly to national regulation as an answer to concerns. Harrison and his fellow Republicans helped make this shift possible. The Sherman Anti-Trust Act was also one of three significant pieces of legislation that passed in 1890, followed by laws concerning the silver question and the tariff issue.

The President's Position: Against Trusts

HARRISON'S INAUGURAL ADDRESS
MARCH 4, 1889

It is the duty of the Executive to administer and enforce in the methods and by the instrumentalities pointed out and provided by the Constitution all the laws enacted by Congress. These laws are general and their administration should be uniform and equal. As a citizen may not elect what laws he will obey, neither may the Executive eject which he will enforce. The duty to obey and to execute embraces the Constitution in its entirety and the whole code of laws enacted under it. The evil example of permitting individuals, corporations, or communities to nullify the laws because they cross some selfish or local interest or prejudices is full of danger, not only to the nation at large, but much more to those who use this pernicious expedient to escape their just obligations or to obtain an unjust advantage over others. They will presently themselves be compelled to appeal to the law for protection, and those who would use the law as a defense must not deny that use of it to others.

If our great corporations would more scrupulously observe their legal limitations and duties, they would have less cause to complain of the unlawful limitations of their rights or of violent interference with their operations. The community that by concert, open or secret, among its citizens denies to a portion of its members their plain rights under the law has severed the only safe bond of social order and prosperity. The evil works from a bad center both ways. It demoralizes those who practice it and destroys the faith of those who suffer by it in the efficiency of the law as a safe protector. The man in whose breast that faith has been darkened is naturally the subject of dangerous and uncanny suggestions. Those who use unlawful methods, if moved by no higher motive than the selfishness that prompted them, may well stop and inquire what is to be the end of this.

An unlawful expedient can not become a permanent condition of government. If the educated and influential classes in a community either practice or connive at the systematic violation of laws that seem to them to cross their convenience, what can they expect when the lesson that convenience or a supposed class interest is a sufficient cause for lawlessness has been well learned by the ignorant classes? A community where law is the rule of conduct and where courts, not mobs, execute its penalties is the only attractive field for business investments and honest labor.[1]

HARRISON'S ANNUAL MESSAGE TO CONGRESS
DECEMBER 3, 1889

Earnest attention should be given by Congress to a consideration of the question how far the restraint of those combinations of capital commonly called "trusts" is a matter of Federal jurisdiction. When organized, as they often are, to crush out all healthy competition and to monopolize the production or sale of an article of commerce and general necessity, they are dangerous conspiracies against the public good, and should be made the subject of prohibitory and even penal legislation.[2]

Against the President's Position: In Favor of Concentrated Wealth

ANDREW CARNEGIE
"WEALTH"
NORTH AMERICAN REVIEW, JUNE 1889

The problem of our age is the administration of wealth, so that the ties of brotherhood may still bind together the rich and poor in harmonious relationship. The conditions of human life have not only been changed, but revolutionized, within the past few hundred years. In former days there was little difference between the dwelling, dress, food, and environment of the chief and those of his retainers. . . . The contrast between the palace of the millionaire and the cottage of the laborer with us today measures the change which has come with civilization.

This change, however, is not to be deplored, but welcomed as highly beneficial. It is well, nay, essential for the progress of the race, that the houses of some should be homes for all that is highest and best in literature and the arts, and for all the refinements of civilization, rather than that none should be so. Much better this great irregularity than universal squalor. Without wealth there can be no Maecenas [Note: a rich Roman patron of the arts]. The "good old times" were not good old times. Neither master nor servant was as well situated then as to day. A relapse to old conditions would be disastrous to both-not the least so to him who serves-and would sweep away civilization with it. . . .

. . .

We start, then, with a condition of affairs under which the best interests of the race are promoted, but which inevitably gives wealth to the few. Thus far, accepting conditions as they exist, the situation can be surveyed and pronounced good. The question then arises-and, if the foregoing be correct, it is the only question with which we have to deal-What is the proper mode of administering wealth after the laws upon which civilization is founded have thrown it into the hands of the few? And it is of this great question that I believe I offer the true solution. It will be understood that fortunes are here spoken of, not moderate sums saved by many years of effort, the returns from which are required for the comfortable maintenance and education of families. This is not wealth, but only competence, which it should be the aim of all to acquire.

There are but three modes in which surplus wealth can be disposed of. It can be left to the families of the decedents; or it can be bequeathed for public purposes; or, finally, it can be administered during their lives by its possessors. Under the first and second modes most of the wealth of the world that has reached the few has hitherto been applied. Let us in turn consider each of these modes. The first is the most injudicious. In monarchial countries, the estates and the greatest portion of the wealth are left to the first son, that the vanity of the parent may be gratified by the thought that his name and title are to descend to succeeding generations unimpaired. The condition of this class in Europe today teaches the futility of such hopes or ambitions. The successors have become impoverished through their follies or from the fall in the value of land. . . . Why should men leave great fortunes to their children? If this is done from affection, is it not misguided affection? Observation teaches that, generally speaking, it is not well for the children that they should be so burdened. Neither is it well for the state. Beyond providing for the wife and daughters moderate sources of income, and very moderate allowances indeed, if any, for the sons, men may well hesitate, for it is no longer questionable that great sums bequeathed oftener work more for the injury than for the good of the recipients. Wise men will soon con-

clude that, for the best interests of the members of their families and of
the state, such bequests are an improper use of their means.

. . .

As to the second mode, that of leaving wealth at death for public uses,
it may be said that this is only a means for the disposal of wealth, provided a man is content to wait until he is dead before it becomes of
much good in the world. . . . The cases are not few in which the real
object sought by the testator is not attained, nor are they few in which
his real wishes are thwarted. . . .

The growing disposition to tax more and more heavily large estates
left at death is a cheering indication of the growth of a salutary change
in public opinion. . . . Of all forms of taxation, this seems the wisest. Men
who continue hoarding great sums all their lives, the proper use of which
for public ends would work good to the community, should be made to
feel that the community, in the form of the state, cannot thus be deprived
of its proper share. By taxing estates heavily at death, the state marks
its condemnation of the selfish millionaire's unworthy life.

. . . This policy would work powerfully to induce the rich man to attend to the administration of wealth during his life, which is the end
that society should always have in view, as being that by far most fruitful
for the people. . . .

There remains, then, only one mode of using great fortunes: but in
this way we have the true antidote for the temporary unequal distribution of wealth, the reconciliation of the rich and the poor—a reign of
harmony—another ideal, differing, indeed from that of the Communist
in requiring only the further evolution of existing conditions, not the
total overthrow of our civilization. It is founded upon the present most
intense individualism, and the race is prepared to put it in practice by
degrees whenever it pleases. Under its sway we shall have an ideal state,
in which the surplus wealth of the few will become, in the best sense,
the property of the many, because administered for the common good,
and this wealth, passing through the hands of the few, can be made a
much more potent force for the elevation of our race than if it had been
distributed in small sums to the people themselves. Even the poorest can
be made to see this, and to agree that great sums gathered by some of
their fellow citizens and spent for public purposes, from which the
masses reap the principal benefit, are more valuable to them than if scattered among them through the course of many years in trifling amounts.[3]

NOTES

1. The Avalon Project at Yale Law School, *Inaugural Addresses of the Presidents*, www.yale.edu/lawweb/avalon/presiden/inaug/harris.htm (accessed November 5, 2002).

2. Benjamin Harrison, *Public Papers and Addresses of Benjamin Harrison, Twenty-third President of the United States: March 4, 1889, to March 4, 1893* (Washington, D.C.: Government Printing Office, 1893), p. 48.

3. Fordham University web site, www.fordham.edu/halsall/mod/1889 carnegie.html (accessed November 22, 2002).

THE ISSUE: SILVER

As with the anti-trust issue, Harrison did not take the lead on the question of silver, but rather acquiesced to the direction taken by Congress in response to popular demands for action. In fact, Harrison was even more guarded and low key in his response to the silver question than to the anti-trust debate. The Free Silver movement, spurred on by growing economic depression in the South and West, called for an increasingly bimetallic standard in the hopes that an increase in the amount of money—particularly silver money—in circulation would make it easier to repay debts and sell crops at increased prices.

Harrison was in no way a staunch gold standard disciple in the image of Grover Cleveland. His enthusiasm for silver, however, was cautious. He admitted that the increase in the production of silver coins required by the Bland-Allison Act did not have the dire consequences hard money advocates had predicted; in fact, the coins were used little, he said, compared to their paper substitutes—silver certificates—and gold and silver had maintained something of an equal value. This did not mean that the situation could not change, however, and Harrison warned against dramatic change in the amount of bullion purchased or coins minted. His view of silver remained guardedly optimistic.

When the price of silver began to fall, concerned mine owners added their voice to inflation-seeking Western farmers. The result was the Sherman Silver Purchase Act, which required the Treasury to buy 4,500,000 ounces of silver at market price each month, an increase of more than 50 percent of the purchase previously mandated by the Bland-Allison Act, which it superseded. This policy did not fit Harrison's ideal vision of currency reform. It was, however, less drastic than other suggested plans.

One radical alternative was presented by an agrarian activist group called the Southern Alliance and was know as the subtreasury plan. Outlined in the "Report of the Committee on the Monetary System," it presented the free silver agenda through a blueprint for an overhauled, reformed monetary system. First, the plan called for free and unlimited coinage of silver based on an equally unlimited supply of silver bullion. Second, the plan demanded that the existing system of selecting certain banks as federal depositories be abandoned. In its place, the plan continued, the U.S. government would create a subtreasury office in every county in the nation whose yearly agricultural produce met a certain quota. These offices would store this produce, judge it for quality, and offer an 80 percent advance of the produce's worth on interest. The subtreasury plan re-created the U.S. economic system in the sole image of agrarian interests, and seemed both costly and reckless to enact. Nevertheless, with unrest growing along with demand for action, something had to be done.

In the end, Harrison and his party chose what they considered to be the lesser of two evils—the Sherman Silver Purchase Act over the subtreasury plan—and advocated, or rather failed to block, its passage. Harrison translated his original guarded optimism about silver into lukewarm support for the act for another reason, as well; by giving Western voters what they wanted with regard to silver, he could count on their reciprocal support on an issue that mattered to him greatly: the protective tariff. The following Cleveland administration forced the act's repeal.

The President's Position: Careful Change

HARRISON'S ANNUAL MESSAGE TO CONGRESS
DECEMBER 3, 1889

During the fiscal year there were applied to the purchase of bonds, in addition to those for the sinking fund, $90,456,172.35, and during the first quarter of the current year the sum of $37,838,937.77, all of which were credited to the sinking fund. The revenues for the fiscal year ending June 30, 1891, are estimated by the Treasury Department at $385,000,000, and the expenditures of the same period, including the sinking fund, at $341,430,477.70. This shows an estimated surplus for that year of

$43,569,522.30, which is more likely to be increased than reduced when the actual transactions are written up.

The existence of so large an actual and anticipated surplus should have the immediate attention of Congress, with a view to reducing the receipts of the Treasury to the needs of the Government as closely as may be. The collection of moneys not needed for public uses imposes an unnecessary burden upon our people, and the presence of so large a surplus in the public vaults is a disturbing element in the conduct of private business. It has called into use expedients for putting it into circulation of very questionable propriety. We should not collect revenue for the purpose of anticipating our bonds, beyond the requirements of the sinking fund, but any unappropriated surplus in the Treasury should be so used, as there is no other lawful way of returning the money to circulation, and the profit realized by the Government offers a substantial advantage. . . .

A table presented by the Secretary of the Treasury, showing the amount of money of all kinds in circulation each year from 1878 to the present time, is of interest. It appears that the amount of national-bank notes in circulation has decreased during that period $114,109,729, of which $37,799,229 is chargeable to the last year. The withdrawal of bank circulation will necessarily continue under existing conditions. It is probable that the adoption of the suggestions made by the Comptroller of the Currency, viz, that the minimum deposit of bonds for the establishment of bonds be reduced, and that an issue of notes to the par value of bonds be allowed, would help to maintain the bank circulation. But, while this withdrawal of bank notes has been going on, there has been a large increase in the amount of gold and silver coin in circulation and in the issues of gold and silver certificates.

The total amount of money of all kinds in circulation on March 1, 1878, was $805,793,807, while on October 1, 1889, the total was $1,405,018,000. There was an increase of $293,417,552 in gold coin, of $57,554,100 in standard silver dollars, of $72,311,249 in gold certificates, of $276,619,715 in silver certificates, and of $14,073,787 in United States notes, making a total of $713,976,403. There was during the same period a decrease of $114,109,729 in bank circulation, and of $642,481 in subsidiary silver. The net increase was $599,224,193. The circulation per capita has increased about $5 during the time . . . referred to.

The total coinage of silver dollars was, on November 1, 1889, $343,638,001, of which $283,539,521 were in the Treasury vaults and $60,098,480 were in circulation. Of the amount in the vaults, $277,319,944 were represented by outstanding silver certificates, leaving $6,219,577 not in circulation and not represented by certificates.

The law requiring the purchase, by the Treasury, of $2,000,000 worth of silver bullion each month, to be coined into silver dollars of 412 1/2 grains, has been observed by the Department; but neither the present Secretary nor any of his predecessors has deemed it safe to exercise the discretion given by law to increase the monthly purchases to $4,000,000. When the law was enacted (February 28, 1878) the price of silver in the market was $1.20 4/10 per ounce, making the bullion value of the dollar 93 cents. Since that time the price has fallen as low as 91.2 cents per ounce, reducing the bullion value of the dollar to 70.6 cents. Within the last few months the market price has somewhat advanced, and on the 1st day of November last the bullion value of the silver dollar was 72 cents.

The evil anticipations which have accompanied the coinage and use of the silver dollar have not been realized. As a coin it has not had general use, and the public Treasury has been compelled to store it. But this is manifestly owing to the fact that its paper representative is more convenient. The general acceptance and use of the silver certificate show that silver has not been otherwise discredited. Some favorable conditions have contributed to maintain this practical equality, in their commercial use, between the gold and silver dollars. But some of these are trade conditions that statutory enactments do not control and of the continuance of which we can not be certain.

I think it is clear that if we should make the coinage of silver at the present ratio free, we must expect that the difference in the bullion values of the gold and silver dollars will be taken account of in commercial transactions, and I fear the same result would follow any considerable increase of the present rate of coinage. Such a result would be discreditable to our financial management and disastrous edge of such a peril. And, indeed, nothing more harmful could happen to the silver interests. Any safe legislation upon this subject must secure the equality of the two coins in their commercial interests. . . . To the plan which will be presented by the Secretary of the Treasury for the issuance of notes or certificates upon the deposit of silver bullion at its market value, I have been able to give only a hasty examination . . . but the general plan suggested by him seems to satisfy the purpose—to continue the use of silver in connection with our currency, and at the same time to obviate the danger of which I have spoken.[4]

Against the President's Position: Radical Change

"REPORT OF THE COMMITTEE ON THE MONETARY SYSTEM" APPROVED BY THE ST. LOUIS CONVENTION OF THE SOUTHERN ALLIANCE, 1889

The financial policy of the general government seems to-day to be peculiarly adapted to further the interests of the speculative class at the expense and to the manifest detriment of the productive class, and while there are many forms of relief offered, there has up to the present time been no true remedy presented which has secured a support universal enough to render its adoption probable. Neither of the political parties offers a remedy adequate to our necessities, and the two parties that have been in power since the war have pursued practically the same financial policy. The situation is this: The most desirable and necessary reform is one that will adjust the financial system of the general government so that its provisions cannot be utilized by a class, which thereby becomes privileged, and is consequence contrary to the genius of our government, and which is to-day the principal cause of the depressed condition of agriculture. Regardless of all this, the political parties utterly ignore these great evils and refuse to remove their cause, and the importunities of the privileged class have, no doubt, often led the executive and legislative branches of the government to believe that the masses were passive and reconciled to the existence of this system whereby a privileged class can, by means of the power of money to oppress, exact from labor all that it produces except a bare subsistence. Since, then, it is the most necessary of all reforms, and receives no attention from any of the prominent political parties, it is highly appropriate and important that our efforts be concentrated to secure the needed reform in this direction, provided all can agree upon such measures. Such action will in no wise connect this movement to any partisan effort, as it can be applied to the party to which each member belongs. . . .

The government and the people of this country realize that the amount of gold and silver, and the certificates based on these metals, do not comprise a volume of money sufficient to supply the wants of the country, and in order to increase the volume, the government allows individuals to associate themselves into a body corporate, and deposit with the government bonds which represent national indebtedness, which the government holds in trust and issues to such corporation paper money equal to 90 per cent of the value of the bonds, and charges said corporation interest at the rate of 1 per cent per annum for the use of said paper money. This allows the issue of paper money to increase the volume of the circulating medium on a perfectly safe basis, because the margin is a guarantee that the banks will redeem the bonds before they mature. But now we find that the circulation secured by this method is still not adequate; or to tale a very conservative position, if we admit that it is adequate on the average, we know that the fact of its being entirely inadequate for half the year makes its inflexibility an engine of oppression, because a season in which it is inadequate must be followed by one of superabundance in order to bring about the average, and such a range in volume means great fluctuations in prices which cut against the producer, both in buying and selling, because he must sell at a season when produce is low, and buy when commodities are high. The system, now in vogue by the United States government of supplementing its circulating medium by a safe and redeemable paper money, should be pushed a little further and conducted in such a manner as to secure a certain augmentation of supply at the season of the year in which the agricultural additions to the wealth of the nation demand money, and a diminution in such supply of money as said agricultural products are consumed. It is not an average adequate amount that is needed, because under it the greatest abuses may prevail, but a certain adequate amount that adjusts itself to the wants of the country at all seasons. For this purpose let us demand that the United States government modify its present financial system:

1. So as to allow the free and unlimited coinage or the issue of the silver certificates against an unlimited deposit of bullion.

2. That the system of using certain banks as United States depositories be abolished, and in its place of said system establish in every county in each of the States that offers for sale during the year five hundred thousand dollars worth of farm products, including wheat, corn, oats, barley, rye, rice, tobacco, cotton, wool and sugar, all together, a sub-treasury office, which shall have in connection with it such warehouses or elevators as are necessary for carefully storing and preserving such agricultural products as are offered it for storage; and it should be the duty

of such sub-treasury department to receive such agricultural products as are offered for storage and make a careful examination of such products and class same as to quality and give a certificate of the deposit showing the amount and quality, and that United States legal tender paper money equal to 80 per cent of the local current value of the products deposited has been advanced on same on interest at the rate of 1 per cent per annum, on the condition that the agricultural product within twelve months from the date of the certificate, or the trustees will sell same at public auction to the highest bidder for the purpose of satisfying the debt. . . .

Our forefathers fought in the revolutionary war, making sacrifices that will forever perpetuate their names in history, to emancipate productive labor from the power of the monarch to oppress. Their battle cry was "liberty." Our monarch is a false, unjust, and statutory power given to money, which calls for a conflict on our part to emancipate productive labor from the power of money to oppress. Let the watch word again be, "Liberty!"[5]

NOTES

4. Benjamin Harrison, *Public Papers and Addresses of Benjamin Harrison, Twenty-third President of the United States: March 4, 1889, to March 4, 1893* (Washington, D.C.: Government Printing Office, 1893), pp. 42–46.

5. C. W. Macune, "Report of the Committee on the Monetary System," in George Brown Tindall, ed. *A Populist Reader: Selections from the Works of American Populist Leaders* (New York: Harper & Row, 1966), pp. 80–81, 83–84, 87.

THE ISSUE: THE TARIFF

Pro-tariff Harrison had accepted the challenge posed by anti-tariff Cleveland when Cleveland took a strong stand against protectionism near the end of his term. The issue became the central focus of the 1888 campaign, and it won the electoral college vote and White House, if not the general election, for Harrison. Nevertheless, Harrison's advocacy of a protectionist tariff during his term in office proved to be a political disaster.

The McKinley Tariff Act passed Congress with Harrison's backing in 1890, a month before the year's midterm elections. The act increased tariffs on imported items, including products of general consumption, thus making it less expensive to buy U.S. products for their actual price than to buy international items at their price plus the tariff. In essence, the tariff tried to manipulate the buying habits of the public. Many business leaders appreciated such a favor to domestic industry. Due to the climate of the times, both economically and politically, however, Harrison and fellow Republicans felt it important to reach out to the agrarian interests as well. Some agricultural products were added to the list of protected items, giving a special advantage to U.S. farmers over international farmers. Other agricultural items were not so protected. In the case of sugar, which was an important and vocal agricultural industry, the act required the U.S. government to subsidize sugar planters with payments of two cents per pound.

The strategy to woo agricultural support for the tariff backfired. The prices fetched by U.S. produce continued to decrease despite the tariff, and yet thanks to the tariff, some everyday items farmers purchased became more costly. The resentment of the West and South grew and bled into the 1890 elections. The resulting Republican defeats were substantial. The party lost half of its number in the U.S. House, for example. This loss not only upset the current balance of power but promised future difficulty in Harrison's reelection campaign. In subsequent speeches, Harrison did his best at damage control, arguing that many problems attributed to the tariff were not its fault and asking for patience until the real effects of the tariff could be seen and studied. His efforts at placating critics were for the most part unsuccessful.

Midwestern orator, silver advocate, and eventual presidential candidate of the Populist and Democratic parties both, William Jennings Bryan was one of many leaders sympathetic to the plight of farmers, debtors, workers, and other representatives of the "little man" who suffered during economic crisis. Bryan attacked protectionism in speeches and works such as his 1893 article in the *North American Review*. His arguments mirrored many given previously by Cleveland against the tariff: protectionism benefited some over others with clearly unfair favoritism, using public power to secure private gain; it was meant to be only a temporary measure until industries could be established and then compete on their own; and the ones most hurt by increased prices were those least able to afford the added financial strain.

In the end, the tariff issue helped to build the political careers of some, like Bryan, while it helped end the careers of others and dramatically shift the balance of power away from Republicans in Washington. Harrison, who had run essentially on one issue, faced the problem of maintaining his administration in the absence—and failure—of that issue.

The President's Position: Pro-Tariff

HARRISON'S ANNUAL MESSAGE TO CONGRESS
DECEMBER 8, 1889

I recommend a revision of our tariff law, both in its administrative features and in the schedules. The need of the former is generally conceded and an agreement upon the evils and inconveniences to be remedied and the best methods for their correction will probably not be difficult. Uniformity of valuation at all our ports is essential, and effective measures should be taken to secure it. It is equally desirable that questions affecting rates and classifications should be promptly decided.

The preparation of a new schedule of customs duties is a matter of great delicacy because of its direct effect upon the business of the country, and of great difficulty by reason of the wide divergence of opinion as to the objects that may properly be promoted by such legislation. Some disturbance of business may perhaps result from the consideration of this subject by Congress, but this temporary ill effect will be reduced to the minimum by prompt action and by the assurance which the country already enjoys that any necessary changes will be so made as not to impair the just and reasonable protection of our home industries. The inequalities of the law should be adjusted, but the protective principle should be maintained and fairly applied to the products of our farms as well as of our shops. These duties necessarily have relation to other things besides the public revenues. We can not limit their effects by fixing our eyes on the public treasury alone. They have a direct relation to home production, to work, to wages, and to the commercial independence of our country, and the wise and patriotic legislator should enlarge the field of his vision to include all of these.[6]

HARRISON'S ANNUAL MESSAGE TO CONGRESS
DECEMBER 1, 1890

The general tariff act has only partially gone into operation, some of its important provisions being limited to take effect at dates yet in the future. The general provisions of the law have been in force less than sixty days. Its permanent effects upon trade and prices still largely stand in conjecture. It is curious to note that the advance in the prices of articles wholly unaffected by the tariff act was by many hastily ascribed to that act. Notice was not taken of the fact that the general tendency of markets was upward from influences wholly apart from the recent tariff legislation. The enlargement of our currency by the silver bill undoubtedly gave an upward tendency to trade and had a marked effect on prices; but this natural and desired effect of the silver legislation was by many erroneously attributed to the tariff act.

There is neither wisdom nor justice in the suggestion that the subject of tariff revision shall again be opened before this law has had a fair trial. It is quite true that every tariff schedule is subject to objections. No bill was ever framed, I suppose, that in all its rates and classifications had the full approval even of a party caucus. Such legislation is always and necessarily the product of compromise as to details, and the present law is no exception. But in its general scope and effect I think it will justify the support of those who believe that American legislation should conserve and defend American trade and the wages of American workmen. . . .

There is no disposition among any of our people to promote prohibitory or retaliatory legislation. Our policies are adopted not to the hurt of others, but to secure for ourselves those advantages of government, with its incident of universal suffrage, makes it imperative that we shall save our working people from the agitations and distresses which scant work and wages that have no margin for comfort always beget. But after all this is done it will be found that our markets are open to friendly commercial exchanges of enormous value to the other great powers.

From the time of my induction into office the duty of using every power and influence given by law to the Executive Department for the development of larger markets for our products, especially our farm products, has been kept constantly in mind, and no effort has been or will be spared to promote that end. We are under no disadvantage in any foreign market, except that we pay our workmen and workwomen better wages than are paid elsewhere—better abstractly, better relatively to the cost of the necessaries of life. I do not doubt that a very largely increased foreign trade is accessible to us without bartering for it either our home market for such products of the farm and shop as our own people can supply or the wages of our working people.[7]

HARRISON'S ANNUAL MESSAGE TO CONGRESS
DECEMBER 9, 1891

There is certainly nothing in the condition of trade, foreign or domestic, there is certainly nothing in the condition of our people of any class, to suggest that the existing tariff and revenue legislation bears oppressively upon the people or retards the commercial development of the nation. It may be argued that our condition would be better if tariff legislation were upon a free-trade basis; but it can not be denied that all the conditions of prosperity and of general contentment are present in a larger degree than ever before in our history, and that, too, just when it was prophesied they would be in the worst state. Agitation for radical changes in tariff and financial legislation can not help, but may seriously impede, business, to the prosperity of which some degree of stability in legislation is essential.

I think there are conclusive evidences that the new tariff has created several great industries which will, within a few years, give employment to several hundred thousand American working men and women. In view of the somewhat overcrowded condition of the labor market of the United States every patriotic citizen should rejoice at such a result.[8]

Against the President's Position: Against the Tariff

WILLIAM JENNINGS BRYAN
NORTH AMERICAN REVIEW
1893

In the early days of the Republic the main argument made in favor of a protective tariff was that it would encourage the establishment of new industries and guard them from competition with older foreign rivals until they become firmly rooted. Such a tariff was intended to be temporary only. Mr. Hamilton said in his report on manufactures in 1791:

The continuance of bounties on manufactures long established must always be of questionable policy, because a presumption would arise in every such case that there were natural and inherent impediments to success.

Mr. Clay said in 1833:

> The theory of protection supposes, too, that after a certain time the
> protected arts will have acquired such strength and perfection as
> will enable them subsequently, unaided, to stand against foreign
> competition.

And again in 1840:

> No one, Mr. President, in the commencement of the protective pol-
> icy, ever supposed that it was to be perpetual.

Time, however, exhausted that argument. The child becomes ashamed
to nurse as it grows older, but the industrial infant is not separated from
the breast by any such sentimental reason. It is as scantily endowed with
modesty as it is plentifully supplied with appetite, but, as the industry
could no longer conceal its corpulent body and its extending limbs in
childhood's attire, it sought some new excuse for continued public support, while it changed its attitude from that of a temporary ward of the
nation to that of a permanent charge upon all profitable industries. The
contention now is that we are not able to compete upon even terms in
foreign lands and that the government must make good the difference
either directly by a bounty, as in the case of sugar production, or indirectly by a protective tariff, as in the case of wool.

Mr. Lawrence, of Ohio, in addressing the wool growers in a speech made
about two years ago, said:

> And these are the existing conditions. In Australia merino wool can
> be and is produced at a less cost that it can be in the United States,
> because (1) pasturage can be had there for a few cents an acre, and
> (2) the climate there is such that substantially no winter feeding is
> required. The same is true of South America.

As protectionists do not claim that their system will reduce the price of
pasturage or moderate the climate so as to make winter feeding unnecessary, they must defend the wool tariff as a perpetual tax. The same is
true of other industries where the tariff is maintained for the ostensible
purpose of paying higher wages than are paid abroad. As it is not con-
tended that protection will finally reduce wages and thus enable us to
reduce the tariff, protection in these cases must be justified as a perma-

nent system by which the price of certain goods shall be increased by operation of law for the immediate benefit of those who produce the goods and for the pretended benefit ultimately of every one else. . . .

If it is difficult to defend the principle of transferring one man's money to another man's pocket by law, it is equally difficult to defend the policy of such a system. Whenever a legislative body announces that it has opened up business for that purpose, it is at once besieged by those who seek to use the taxing power for private gain.[9]

NOTES

6. Benjamin Harrison, *Public Papers and Addresses of Benjamin Harrison, Twenty-third President of the United States: March 4, 1889, to March 4, 1893* (Washington, D.C.: Government Printing Office, 1893), pp. 42–46.

7. Benjamin Harrison, *Public Papers and Addresses of Benjamin Harrison, Twenty-third President of the United States: March 4, 1889, to March 4, 1893* (Washington, D.C.: Government Printing Office, 1893), pp. 81–82.

8. Benjamin Harrison, *Public Papers and Addresses of Benjamin Harrison, Twenty-third President of the United States: March 4, 1889, to March 4, 1893* (Washington, D.C.: Government Printing Office, 1893), pp. 104–105.

9. William Jennings Bryan, "The North American Review," http://cdl.library. cornell.edu/cgi-bin/moa/moa-cgi?notisid\BQ7578–0157–64 (accessed November 22, 2002).

THE ISSUE: ANNEXATION OF HAWAII

The United States had intertwined its history with Hawaii's for some time. In the early nineteenth century, U.S., British, and French forces hovered around the strategically important islands, observing their development. Missionaries visited Hawaii as well and articulated political as well as religious messages to the natives. This Western influence had demonstrable results. Hawaii's ruler, Kamehameha III passed a Declaration of Rights (1839), Edict of Toleration (1839), and written constitution (1840) in a tradition familiar to U.S. onlookers. Although the United States followed such progressive steps with formal recognition of Hawaii's independence, U.S. officials continued to remain involved covertly in a match of diplomatic chess with France and Great Britain, using Hawaii as the gameboard. When Hawaii's monarchy fell in 1893, the United States helped to create a republic on the islands. Whether the U.S. government wished to admit the fact or not, it had been manipulating the political landscape of Hawaii for years, albeit with assistance from some native Hawaiian factions. The question in 1893 fell to the Harrison administration: What would be done with the new and vulnerable Hawaiian republic?

Harrison favored annexation of Hawaii in order to make it another state in the union. He denied U.S. involvement in the overthrow of Hawaii's Queen Liliuokalani, but admitted that the United States had several reasons to be interested in the Hawaiian situation. First, he argued, it was the duty of the United States to be certain the Hawaiian people enjoyed peace and adequate protection of their rights. In the instability following the demise of one government and the creation of another, he feared the best interests of the people of Hawaii would fall between the cracks. With a paternalism that hinted at no small amount of racial and ethnic stereotyping, Harrison voiced concern for the Hawaiian people and a willingness to intercede on their behalf.

Not only was Harrison concerned about the administration of the islands internally, but he was protective of U.S. business interests in Hawaii, as it served both as a market for U.S. goods, investment, and development, and as a strategic port for U.S. ships. Moreover, Harrison noted that it was against U.S. security interests to allow any other foreign power, such as Great Britain or France, to move in and dominate the islands. The solution, he believed, was for the United States itself to control them. He mentioned the options of making Hawaii either a protectorate or a state, but he believed statehood offered the greater benefit for both Hawaii and the United States.

Harrison was unsuccessful with his desire to annex Hawaii, however. Opposition came from two directions. First, the overthrown Queen Liliuokalani protested the unconstitutional rebellion that toppled her legitimate government and erected a new one in its place. She blamed the United States for this and called upon the nation to restore her to power. Likewise, the reelected Grover Cleveland, whose term followed Harrison's, also blamed the United States for unconscionable meddling in the affairs of Hawaii. He argued that the Hawaiians had the same freedom and right to self-rule as U.S. citizens, and that annexation would be unjust because the United States would have acquired Hawaii by illegal and unethical means. For the time, the arguments against annexation held. Harrison's position shortly prevailed, however. Congress passed a joint annexation resolution regarding Hawaii in 1898. The islands became a territory two years later and a state in 1959.

The President's Position: For Annexation

To the Senate:

I transmit herewith, with a view to its ratification, a treaty of annexation concluded on the 14th day of February, 1893, between John W. Foster, Secretary of State, who was duly empowered to act in that behalf on the part of the United States, and Lorrin A. Thurston, W. R. Castle, W. C. Wilder, C. L. Carter, and Joseph Marsden, the commissioners on the part of the Government of the Hawaiian Islands. The provisional treaty, it will be observed, does not attempt to deal in detail with the questions that grow out of the annexation of the Hawaiian Islands to the United States. The commissioners representing the Hawaiian Government have consented to leave to the future and to the just and benevolent purposes of the United States the adjustment of all such questions.

I do not deem it necessary to discuss at any length the conditions which have resulted in this decisive action. It has been the policy of the administration not only to respect but to encourage the continuance of an independent government in the Hawaiian Islands so long as it afforded suitable guaranties for the protection of life and property, and maintained a stability and strength that gave adequate security against the domination of any other power. The moral support of this Government has continually manifested itself in the most friendly diplomatic relations and in many acts of courtesy to the Hawaiian rulers.

The overthrow of the monarchy was not in any way promoted by this Government, but had its origin in what seems to have been a reactionary and revolutionary policy on the part of Queen Liliuokalani which put in serious peril not only the large and preponderating interests of the United States in the islands, but all foreign interests, and indeed the decent administration of civil affairs and the peace of the islands. It is quite evident that the monarchy had become effete and the Queen's government so weak and inadequate as to be the prey of designing and unscrupulous persons. The restoration of Queen Liliuokalani to her throne is undesirable, if not impossible, and unless actively supported by the United States would be accompanied by serious disaster and the disorganizations of all business interests. The influence and interest of the United States in the islands must be increased and not diminished.

Only two courses are now open—one the establishment of a protectorate by the United States, and the other annexation full and complete.

I think the latter course, which has been adopted in the treaty, will be highly promotive of the best interests of the Hawaiian people, and is the only one that will adequately secure the interests of the United States. These interests are not wholly selfish. It is essential that none of the other great powers shall secure these islands. Such a possession would not consist with our safety and with the peace of the world. This view of the situation is so apparent and conclusive that no protest has been heard from any government against proceedings looking to annexation. Every foreign representative at Honolulu promptly acknowledged the Provisional Government, and I think there is a general concurrence in the opinion that the deposed Queen ought not be restored.

Prompt action upon this treaty is very desirable. If it meets the approval of the Senate, peace and good order will be secured in the islands under existing laws until such time as Congress can provide by legislation a permanent form of government for the islands. This legislation should be, and I do not doubt will be, not only just to the natives and all other residents and citizens of the islands, but should be characterized by great liberality and a high regard to the rights of all people and of all foreigners domiciled there. The correspondence which accompanies the treaty will put the Senate in possession of all the facts known to the Executive.

Benj. Harrison
Executive Mansion,
February 15, 1893[10]

Against the President's Position: Against Annexation

STATEMENT OF QUEEN LILI'UOKALANI
JANUARY 17, 1893

I, Lili'uokalani, by the grace of God and under the constitution of the Hawaiian kingdom Queen, do hereby solemnly protest against any and all acts done against myself and the constitutional government of the Hawaiian kingdom by certain persons claiming to have established a Provisional Government of and for this kingdom. . . .

Now, to avoid any collision of armed forces, and perhaps the loss of life, I do, under this protest and impelled by said forces, yield my authority until such time as the Government of the United States shall, upon the facts being presented to it, undo the action of its representative, and reinstate me in the authority which I claim as the constitutional sovereign of the Hawaiian Islands.[11]

PRESIDENT CLEVELAND'S MESSAGE
DECEMBER 18, 1893

When the present Administration entered upon its duties the Senate had under consideration a treaty providing for the annexation of the Hawaiian Islands to the territory of the United States.

... While naturally sympathizing with every effort to establish a republican form of government, it has been the settled policy of the United States to concede to people of foreign countries the same freedom and independence in the management of their domestic affairs that we have always claimed for ourselves; and it has been our practice to recognize revolutionary governments as soon as it became apparent that they were supported by the people. For illustration of this rule I need only to refer to the revolution in Brazil in 1889, when our Minister was instructed to recognize the Republic "so soon as a majority of the people of Brazil should have signified their assent to its establishment and maintenance"; to the revolution in Chile in 1891, when our Minister was directed to recognize the new government "if it was accepted by the people"; and to the revolution in Venezuela in 1892, when our recognition was accorded on condition that the new government was "fully established, in possession of the power of the nation, and accepted by the people."

As I apprehend the situation, we are brought face to face with the following conditions:

The lawful Government of Hawaii was overthrown without the drawing of a sword or the firing of a shot by a process every step of which, it may be safely asserted, is directly traceable to and dependent for its success upon the agency of the United States acting through its diplomatic and naval representatives.

But for the notorious predilections of the United States Minister for annexation, the Committee of Safety, which should be called the Committee of Annexation, would never have existed.

But for the landing of the United States forces upon false pretexts respecting the danger to life and property the committee would never have exposed themselves to the pains and penalties of treason by undertaking the subversion of the Queen's Government.

But for the presence of the United States forces in the immediate vicinity and in position to afford all needed protection and support the committee would not have proclaimed the provisional government from the steps of the Government building.

And finally, but for the lawless occupation of Honolulu under false pretexts by the United States forces, and but for Minister Stevens' recognition of the provisional government when the United States forces were its sole support and constituted its only military strength, the Queen and her Government would never have yielded to the provisional government, even for a time and for the sole purpose of submitting her case to the enlightened justice of the United States.

Believing, therefore, that the United States could not, under the circumstances disclosed, annex the islands without justly incurring the imputation of acquiring them by unjustifiable methods, I shall not again submit the treaty of annexation to the Senate for its consideration, and in the instructions to Minister Willis, a copy of which accompanies this message, I have directed him to so inform the provisional government. But in the present instance our duty does not, in my opinion, end with refusing to consummate this questionable transaction. It has been the boast of our government that it seeks to do justice in all things without regard to the strength or weakness of those with whom it deals. I mistake the American people if they favor the odious doctrine that there is no such thing as international morality, that there is one law for a strong nation and another for a weak one, and that even by indirection a strong power may with impunity despoil a weak one of its territory.

By an act of war, committed with the participation of a diplomatic representative of the United States and without authority of Congress, the Government of a feeble but friendly and confiding people has been overthrown. A substantial wrong has thus been done which a due regard for our national character as well as the rights of the injured people requires we should endeavor to repair. The provisional government has not assumed a republican or other constitutional form, but has remained a mere executive council or oligarchy, set up without the assent of the people. It has not sought to find a permanent basis of popular support and has given no evidence of an intention to do so. Indeed, the representatives of that government assert that the people of Hawaii are unfit for popular government and frankly avow that they can be best ruled by arbitrary or despotic power.

The law of nations is founded upon reason and justice, and the rules of conduct governing individual relations between citizens or subjects of a civilized state are equally applicable as between enlightened nations. . . . On that ground the United States can not properly be put in the position of countenancing a wrong after its commission any more than in that of consenting to it in advance. On that ground it can not allow itself to refuse to redress an injury inflicted through an abuse of power by officers clothed with its authority and wearing its uniform; and on the same ground, if a feeble but friendly state is in danger of being robbed of its independence and its sovereignty by a misuse of the name and power of the United States, the United States can not fail to vindicate its honor and its sense of justice by an earnest effort to make all possible reparation.[12]

NOTES

10. Benjamin Harrison, *Public Papers and Addresses of Benjamin Harrison, Twenty-third President of the United States: March 4, 1889, to March 4, 1893* (Washington, D.C.: Government Printing Office, 1893), pp. 214–215.

11. The Hawaiian Sovereignty Movement, www.hookele.com/non-hawaiians/chapter3.html (accessed November 22, 2002).

12. The Hawaiian Sovereignty Movement, www.hookele.com/non-hawaiians/cleveland.html (accessed November 22, 2002).

RECOMMENDED READINGS

Campbell, Ballard C. *The Growth of American Government: Governance from the Cleveland Era to the Present.* Bloomington: Indiana University Press, 1995.

Harrison, Benjamin. *Speeches of Benjamin Harrison.* Charles Hedges, ed. Reprint Edition. New York: Kennikat Press, 1971.

Sievers, Harry Joseph. *Benjamin Harrison, Hoosier President: The White House and After.* Indianapolis: Bobbs-Merrill Co., 1968.

Volwiler, Albert T., ed. *The Correspondence Between Benjamin Harrison and James G. Blaine, 1882–1893.* Philadelphia: The American Philosophical Society, 1940.

Wicker, Elmus. *Banking Panics of the Gilded Age.* Cambridge: Cambridge University Press, 2000.

6

GROVER CLEVELAND

(1893–1897)

During Harrison's term, Cleveland practiced law in New York City and established a home with the wife he married during his first term. Frances Cleveland was twenty-seven years his junior and had been a beloved First Lady. Together they watched and waited as the Harrison administration became its own worst enemy. First, Harrison's willingness to cede power to Congress led to unprecedented and exorbitant legislative spending, and in a very short time, the Treasury surplus Cleveland had bequeathed to Harrison had vanished. Second, Harrison's strong support of the high McKinley Tariff backfired, alienating interests in the South and West and further disrupting the economy. Cleveland won the 1892 Democratic nomination—his candidacy never seemed in doubt, since the Harrison years seemed to offer a case study in support of Cleveland's policies—and easily defeated both Harrison and the Populist party candidate to win the White House. Never before had a president been elected to two discontinuous terms.

The tide of popularity Cleveland rode into his second term did not last, however. The labor unrest that plagued Harrison's final days in office erupted into the most violent strike yet during Cleveland's second term. The Pullman Strike caused Cleveland to deploy federal troops to Chicago against the wishes of the Illinois governor in order to end the strike. The president's decision to meet violence with violence, and then to pursue union leaders as obstacles to trade under the Sherman Anti-Trust Act, ended any support labor might have given Cleveland.

Things could get worse, and they did. As Cleveland reentered the

White House the nation suffered from a severe economic setback, the Panic of 1893. The shockwaves lasted for at least three years and closed the doors of hundreds of banks and thousands of businesses, sending the unemployment rate skyrocketing. Cleveland blamed the depression on the dwindling gold reserve in the Treasury, and he was at least partially correct in his assessment. His response, though arguably necessary, alienated free-silver populists in the same way his handling of the Pullman Strike alienated labor populists.

First, Cleveland worked with banking leaders to acquire more silver for the U.S. Treasury. This worked, but it also played into populist conspiracy theories of collusion between government and big business to oppress the "little men," the working, farming debtors, of the United States. Second, Cleveland managed to choreograph the repeal of the Sherman Silver Purchase Act. Though this move, too, made economic sense, it added insult to injury for the free-silver advocates who had campaigned for the act years earlier.

Unlike his first term, much of Cleveland's second term involved questions of international rather than domestic policy. When Venezuela encountered a border dispute with Great Britain over land contested between Venezuela and British Guiana, Cleveland intervened. He reasoned that the Monroe Doctrine made Venezuelan business United States business, especially since a European power was involved in the Western Hemisphere. Cleveland used U.S. influence to force Great Britain to accept arbitration, and the conflict ended. The policy precedent set in the Venezuelan incident by Cleveland and his former attorney general turned secretary of state Richard Olney—who was perhaps the closest thing the independent Cleveland had to a trusted adviser—became known as the Olney Corollary to the Monroe Doctrine.

If the conclusion of the Venezuelan dispute seemed anticlimactic, it nevertheless drew concern from populist leaders such as William Jennings Bryan. These critics feared that expanding the Monroe Doctrine, and thereby the influence and involvement of the United States in the Western Hemisphere, was another step toward imperialism. Control and domination of other lands, they argued, was not compatible with U.S. principles of liberty and democracy. The outcry over Venezuela, however, was mild compared to the controversy surrounding Cleveland's handling of the Cuban rebellion against Spain.

If opponents feared Cleveland's Venezuelan policy contradicted U.S. ideals, they were certain that Cleveland's Cuban policy abandoned the very foundation of the U.S. system. When the Cubans revolted against the Spanish colonial power that controlled the Caribbean island (and mismanaged it into severe economic depression), many U.S. citizens and leaders believed the Cubans were reenacting the North American colonies' War of Independence from Great Britain. These sympathizers believed it was the duty of the United States to support the Cuban rebellion. Cleveland, however, followed his perception of U.S. national interests by seeking a return of Spanish authority in Cuba, albeit with some concessions to placate the Cuban people. Cleveland's mixed messages to Spain and unwillingness to intercede on behalf of the Cubans left the situation unresolved in a violent and controversial limbo for the next presidential administration.

Negative feelings about the Cuban situation, combined with what seemed to be the never-ending argument between gold and silver advocates, made the outcome of the 1896 Democratic party convention anyone's guess. In the end, the fiery orator, populist leader, and vocal critic of Cleveland's international policy and gold standard position, William Jennings Bryan, secured the party's nomination. The Democrats repudiated Cleveland, who became the first and only president so renounced by his party. Bryan went on to lose the White House to Republican William McKinley. Though Bryan ran twice more, he was never successful in his bid to become chief executive.

The country's economic problem seemed the topic with the most emotional attachment for most citizens, and as the gold standard debate became less heated and financial prosperity returned, Cleveland's reputation improved. He became a trustee and lecturer at Princeton University, an ex-president remembered with fondness rather than frustration. The shift from Cleveland to Bryan as the Democratic presidential candidate marked a watershed moment for the party. Cleveland was the last limited-government, pro-business, economically conservative Democrat to become president; the Democrats of the twentieth century reflected different policies and political agendas. Cleveland's forthright honesty, stubborn attachment to his positions, and willingness to be unpopular when necessary—truly a unique attribute in any politician— marked him as a different breed of leader, and brought him the admiration of generations of presidential historians, who mark him as the most successful, and perhaps the greatest, president of the post-Lincoln nineteenth century.

THE ISSUE: THE PULLMAN STRIKE

Populism, an agrarian backlash against industrialism, fed on the economic problems of the era and created new urgency in labor activism.

Toward the end of the Harrison administration, growing labor discontent led to several strikes, including a violent steel strike in Homestead, Pennsylvania, in July of 1892. Cleveland inherited the challenge of maintaining peace in a time when the patience and endurance of both labor and management were under severe strain. His leadership was especially tested during the Pullman Strike of 1894.

Financial crisis and severe economic depression, known in short as the Panic of 1893, placed hardship on industries that already faced significant problems over the last two decades. The Pullman Palace Car Company, which serviced the railroad industry, cut wages by nearly one fourth. Employees who lived in the company-controlled town of Pullman, outside of Chicago, found that rent and other expenses did not decrease in relation to incomes, however, so families spent the same although they earned far less than they had earlier. Members of the American Railway Union in Pullman went on strike in Pullman on May 11, 1894, to protest the situation. The company president, George M. Pullman, refused to discuss the matter or seek arbitration of the dispute. In response to Pullman's unwillingness to compromise, the union's national council president, Eugene V. Debs, called for a national boycott of Pullman cars. The spark ignited a wildfire: soon sympathy strikes broke out in twenty-seven different U.S. states and territories. Chicago in particular became the center of unprecedented violent demonstrations.

Despite the bloodshed, the governor of Illinois, John P. Altgeld, refused to call the militia to impose order, because he was sympathetic to the strikers and the difficulties they faced. The U.S. attorney general, Richard Olney, had no such qualms. He secured an injunction against the strikers for impeding mail service and interstate commerce through their actions. Cleveland backed this with force, ordering 2,500 federal troops to Chicago on July 4 despite Governor Altgeld's wishes. Within a week the strike ended and by July 20, Cleveland felt satisfied that order was restored and withdrew the troops. Union national president Debs was convicted of contempt of court and conspiring against interstate commerce, proving that the Sherman Anti-Trust Act could be used against union officials and activity as well as industry leaders and practices.

Debs continued to pen letters and treatises from prison, arguing on behalf of labor concerns and attacking the decision to turn U.S. troops against strikers. Cleveland, however, was satisfied that he had done the right thing by ending violence and putting down the "riotous mob." Debs viewed the workers as the victims of management's greed and the economy's downturn; Cleveland saw the bystanding people of Chicago who encountered the violence created by the strike situation as the innocents. If Cleveland's hard money, pro-gold standard position already suggested to populists that he sympathized with business over labor, the president's actions regarding the Pullman Strike confirmed this assessment. Cleveland's choice earned the gratitude of industry leaders but severed any final links he might have had with labor.

The President's Position: Against the Strike

PRESIDENT CLEVELAND'S DECISION TO SEND TROOPS TO CHICAGO TO COUNTER THE PULLMAN STRIKE
JULY 8, 1894

On the eighth day of July, in view of the apparently near approach of a crisis which the Government had attempted to avoid, the following Executive Proclamation was issued and at once published in the city of Chicago:

Whereas, by reason of unlawful obstruction, combinations and assemblages of persons, it has become impracticable, in the judgment of the President, to enforce, by the ordinary course of judicial proceedings, the laws of the United States within the State of Illinois, and especially in the city of Chicago within said State; and

Whereas, for the purpose of enforcing the faithful execution of the laws of the United States and protecting its property and removing obstructions to the United States mails in the State and city aforesaid, the President has employed a part of the military forces of the United States:

Now, therefore, I, Grover Cleveland, President of the United States, do hereby admonish all good citizens, and all persons who may be or may come within the City and State aforesaid, against aiding, countenancing, encouraging, or taking any part in such unlawful obstructions, combinations, and assemblages; and I hereby warn all persons engaged in or in any way connected with such unlawful obstructions, combinations, and assemblages to disperse and retire peaceably to their respective abodes on or before twelve o'clock noon of the 9th day of July instant.

Those who disregard this warning and persist in taking part with a riotous mob in forcibly resisting and obstructing the execution of the laws of the United States, or interfering with the functions of the Government, or destroying or attempting to destroy the property belonging to the United States or under its protection, cannot be regarded otherwise than as public enemies.

Troops employed against such a riotous mob will act with all the moderation and forbearance consistent with the accomplishment of the desired end; but the stern necessities that confront them will not with certainty permit discrimination between guilty participants and those who are mingling with them from curiosity and without criminal intent. The only safe course, therefore, for those not actually participating, is to abide at their homes, or at least not to be found in the neighborhood of riotous assemblages.

While there will be no vacillation in the decisive treatment of the guilty, this warning is especially intended to protect and save the innocent.[1]

Against the President's Position: For the Strike

"LABOR OMNIA VINCIT"
BY EUGENE V. DEBS
AUGUST 5, 1895

I would hail the day upon which it could be truthfully said, "Labor conquers everything," with inexpressible gratification. Such a day would stand first in Labor's Millennium, that prophesied era when Christ shall begin in reign on the earth to continue a thousand years.

The old Latin fathers did a large business in manufacturing maxims, and the one I have selected for a caption of this article has been required to play shibboleth since, like "a thing of beauty and a joy forever," it came forth from its ancient laboratory.

It is one of those happy expressions which embodies quite as much fancy as fact.

The time has arrived for thoughtful men identified with labor—by which I mean the laboring classes—to inquire, what does labor conquer? or what has it conquered in all the ages? or what is it now conquering?

If by the term conquer is meant that labor, and only labor, removes obstacles to physical progress—levels down mountains or tunnels them—builds railroads and spans rivers and chasms with bridges—hews down the forests—digs canals, transforms deserts into gardens of fruitfulness—plows and sows and reaps, delves in the mines for coal and all the precious metals—if it is meant that labor builds all the forges and factories, and all the railroads that girdle the world and all the ships that cleave the waves, and mans them, builds all the cities and every monument in all lands—I say if such things are meant when we vauntingly exclaim, "labor conquers everything," no one will controvert the declaration—no one will demur—with one acclaim the averments will stand confessed.

But with all these grand achievements to the credit of labor, how stands labor itself? Having subdued every obstacle to physical progress, what is its condition? The answer is humiliating beyond the power of exaggeration and the aphorism, *"Labor Omnia Vincit,"* becomes the most conspicuous delusion that ever had a votary since time began.

It will be well for labor on Labor Day to concentrate its vision on the United States of America. The field is sufficiently broad and there are enough object lessons in full view to engage the attention of the most critical, and it will be strange indeed if the inquiry is not made. What has labor conquered up to date in the United States? The inquiry is fruitful of thought. What is the testimony of the labor press of the country, corroborated by statistics which defy contradiction? It is this, that the land is cursed with wage slavery—with the condition that labor, which, according to the proverb, "conquers everything," is itself conquered and lies prostrate and manacled beneath the iron hoofs of a despotism as cruel as ever cursed the world.

To hew and dig, to build and repair, to toil and starve, is not conquering in any proper sense of the term. Conquerors are not clothed in rags. Conquerors do not starve. The homes of conquerors are not huts, dark and dismal, where wives and children moan like the night winds and sob like the rain. Conquerors are not clubbed as if they were thieves, shot down as if they were vagabond dogs, nor imprisoned as if they were felons, by the decrees of despots. No! Conquerors rule—their word is law. Labor is not in the condition of a conqueror in the United States.

Go to the coal mines, go to the New England factories, go to Homestead and Pullman, go to the sweat shops, go to any place in all of the broad land where anvils ring, where shuttles fly, where toilers earn their bread in the sweat of their faces, and exclaim, *"Labor Omnia Vincit,"* and you will be laughed to scorn.

Why is it that labor does not conquer anything? Why does it not assert its mighty power? Why does it not rule in Congress, in legislatures and

courts? I answer because it is factionized, because it will not unify, because, for some inscrutable reason, it prefers division, weakness and
slavery, rather than unity, strength and victory.

Will it always be thus unmindful of its power and prerogatives? I do
not think so. Will it always tamely submit to degradation? I protest that
it will not. Labor has the ballot. It has redeeming power. I write from
behind prison bars, the victim of a petty tyrant. My crime was that I
sought to rescue Pullman slaves from the grasp of a monster of greed
and rapacity.

I think a day is coming when *"Labor Omnia Vincit"* will change conditions. I hear the slogan of the clans of organized labor. It cheers me. I
believe with the poet that

> A labor day is coming when our starry flag shall wave,
> Above a land where famine no longer digs a grave,
> Where money is not master, nor the workingman a slave—
> For the right is marching on.

Eugene V. Debs
McHenry County Jail, Woodstock, Ill., August 5, 1895.[2]

NOTES

1. Watts and Israel, pp. 175–176.
2. Eugene V. Debs, "Labor Omnia Vincit," in *Writings and Speeches of Eugene
V. Debs* (New York: Hermitage Press, 1948), pp. 4–6.

THE ISSUE: THE GOLD STANDARD

Although the currency controversy had faced presidents for decades,
the Panic of 1893, with its subsequent severe depression, brought new
urgency to the question during Cleveland's second term. The crisis had
some roots in Europe: problems in both Paris and London disturbed
international markets, and as an increasing flow of gold made its way
to Europe, the U.S. Treasury gold reserve dwindled. Other domestic factors also conspired to wreak economic havoc. The nation's banking system had not evolved at the same rate as the burgeoning industrial
economy, and consequently could not keep pace. Some industries also
expanded beyond the demand for their goods. Moreover, many in the

agricultural sector had experienced depression for two decades running with little or no relief.

The panic had a number of almost immediate results. Hundreds of state and national banks closed as depositors rushed to withdraw their funds, and other banks called in loans and refused to extend further credit. Seven major railroads went bankrupt, and some fifteen thousand other businesses also failed. "Industrial Black Friday" saw stock prices plummet. At its peak, the unemployment rate reached 20 percent of the U.S. workforce.

Needless to say, monetary policy became a hotly contested issue once again. Cleveland's interpretation of events had some validity. He believed that the dwindling gold reserve in the U.S. Treasury was the primary culprit. Not only was it poor business practice to allow this to happen, but it bred uncertainty; private businessmen then feared that the U.S. government would be unable to back all greenbacks, treasury notes, and silver certificates with gold as promised, and they made decisions about their own companies and economic positions. Determined to increase the U.S. Treasury's gold reserve, Cleveland negotiated with banking leaders such as John Pierpont Morgan to sell government bonds for gold overseas. He also called for a repeal of the Sherman Silver Purchase Act of 1890, which required the government to purchase 4.5 million ounces of silver monthly and, Cleveland believed, helped erode confidence in and devalue silver coins.

Cleveland's policies provoked outrage from populists who saw his cooperation with bankers as a conspiracy of the elite against the impoverished, and who believed his defense of the gold standard was a means of pleasing international leaders while punishing domestic debtors further. Activists such as William H. Harvey wrote tracts denouncing the nation's governmental and business leaders and calling for free silver coinage as a means of helping debtors and others injured by depression. Harvey's "Coin's Financial School" drew a picture of a pro-silver, bimetallist lecturer explaining the situation in an economics classroom. The work played into the familiar populist conspiracy theories, viewing Great Britain as a puppetmaster pulling the strings of U.S. leaders in order to follow British self-interest. According to Harvey and others like him, the U.S. elite in Washington and New York, including Cleveland, were trusts, robbers, and vampires who were out of touch with the U.S. mainstream and its financial suffering.

Despite such dramatic protests, Cleveland managed not only to replenish the gold reserve but also to repeal the Sherman Silver Purchase Act. The effects of the panic, however, lingered into 1896.

The President's Position: For the Gold Standard

PRESIDENT GROVER CLEVELAND'S DEFENSE OF THE GOLD STANDARD
JANUARY 28, 1895

With natural resources unlimited in variety and productive strength and with a people whose activity and enterprise seek only a fair opportunity to achieve national success and greatness, our progress should not be checked by a false financial policy and a heedless disregard of sound monetary laws, nor should the timidity and fear which they engender stand in the way of our prosperity.

It is hardly disputed that this predicament confronts us today. Therefore no one in any degree responsible for the making and execution of our laws should fail to see a patriotic duty in honestly and sincerely attempting to relieve the situation. Manifestly this effort will not succeed unless it is made untrammeled by the prejudice of partisanship and with a steadfast determination to resist the temptation to accomplish party advantage. We may well remember that if we are threatened with financial difficulties all our people in every station of life are concerned; and surely those who suffer will not receive the promotion of party interests as an excuse for permitting our present troubles to advance to a disastrous conclusion. It is also of the utmost importance that we approach the student of the problems presented as free as possible from the tyranny of preconceived opinions, to the end that in common danger we may be able to seek with unclouded vision a safe and reasonable protection.

The real trouble which confronts us consists in a lack of confidence, widespread and constantly increasing, in the continuing ability or disposition of the Government to pay its obligations in gold. This lack of confidence grows to some extent out of the palpable and apparent embarrassment attending the efforts of the Government under existing laws to procure gold and to a greater extent out of the impossibility of either keeping it in the Treasury or canceling obligations by its expenditure after it is obtained. . . .

It will hardly do to say that a simple increase of revenue will cure our troubles. The apprehension now existing and constantly increasing as to our financial ability does not rest upon a calculation of our revenue. The time has passed when the eyes of investors abroad and our people at home were fixed upon the revenues of the Government. Changed conditions have attracted their attention to the gold of the Government. There need be no fear that we can not pay our current expenses with such money as we have. There is now in the Treasury a comfortable surplus of more than $63,000,000, but it is not in gold, and therefore does not meet our difficulty.

I can not see that differences of opinion concerning the extent to which silver ought to be coined or used in our currency should interfere with the counsels of those whose duty it is to rectify evils now apparent in our financial situation. They have to consider the question of national credit and the consequences that will follow from its collapse. Whatever ideas may be insisted upon as to silver or bimetallism, a proper solution of the question now pressing upon us only requires a recognition of gold as well as silver and a concession of its importance, rightfully or wrongfully acquired, as a basis of national credit, a necessity in the honorable discharge of our obligations payable in gold, and a badge of solvency. I do not understand that the real friends of silver desire a condition that might follow inaction or neglect to appreciate the meaning of the present exigency if it should result in the entire banishment of gold from our financial and currency arrangements. . . .

While I am not unfriendly to silver and while I desire to see it recognized to such an extent as is consistent with financial safety and the preservation of national honor and credit, I am not willing to see gold entirely banished from our currency and finances. To avert such a consequence I believe thorough and radical remedial legislation should be promptly passed. I therefore beg the Congress to give the subject immediate attention.

In my opinion the Secretary of the Treasury should be authorized to issue bonds of the Government for the purpose of procuring and maintaining a sufficient gold reserve and the redemption and cancellation of the United States legal-tender notes and the Treasury notes issued for the purchase of silver under the law of 14 July 1890. We should be relieved from the humiliating process of issuing bonds to procure gold to be immediately and repeatedly drawn out on these obligations for purposes not related to the benefit of our Government or our people. The principal and interest of these bonds should be payable on their face in gold, because they should be sold only for gold or its representative, and because there would now probably be difficulty in favorably disposing of bonds not containing this stipulation. I suggest that the bonds be issued in denominations of twenty and fifty dollars and their multiples and that they bear interest at a rate not exceeding 3 per cent per annum. I do not see why they should not be payable fifty years from their date. We of the present generation have large amounts to pay if we meet our obligations, and long bonds are most salable. The Secretary of the Treasury might well be permitted at his discretion to receive on the sale of bonds the legal-tender and Treasury notes to be retired, and of course when they are thus retired or redeemed in gold they should be canceled. . . .

In conclusion I desire to frankly confess my reluctance to issuing [sic] more bonds in present circumstances and with no better results than have lately followed that course. I can not, however, refrain from adding to an assurance of my anxiety to cooperate with the present Congress in any reasonable measure of relief an expression of my determination to leave nothing undone which furnishes a hope for improving the situation or checking a suspicion of our disinclination or disability to meet with the strictest honor every national obligation.[3]

Against the President's Position: Bimetallism

"COIN'S FINANCIAL SCHOOL"
BY WILLIAM H. HARVEY

So much uncertainty prevailing about the many facts connect with the monetary question, very few are able to intelligently understand the subject.

Hard times are with us; the country is distracted; very few things are marketable at a price above the cost of production; tens of thousands are out of employment; the jails, penitentiaries, workhouses and insane asylums are full; the gold reserve at Washington is sinking; the government is running at a loss with a deficit in every department; a huge debt hangs like an appalling cloud over the country; taxes have assumed the importance of a mortgage, and 50 per cent of the public revenues are likely to go delinquent; hungered and half-starved men are banding into armies and marching toward Washington; the cry of distress is heard on every hand; business is paralyzed; commerce is at a standstill; riots and strikes prevail throughout the land; schemes to remedy our ills when put into execution are smashed like boxcars in a railroad wreck, and Wall street looks in vain for an excuse to account for the failure of prosperity to return since the repeal of the silver purchase act. . . .

"In the impending struggle for the mastery of the commerce of the world, the financial combat between England and the United States cannot be avoided if we are to retain our self-respect, and our people their freedom and prosperity. [Applause] . . .

"To wait on England is purile and unnecessary. Her interests are not our interests. 'But,' you ask me, 'how are we to do it?' It will work itself. We have been frightened at a shadow. We have been as much deceived in this respect as we have been about other matters connected with this subject.

"Free coinage in the United States will at once establish a parity between the two metals. Any nation that is big enough to take all the silver in the world, and give back merchandise and products in payment for it, will at once establish the parity between it and gold. [Applause] . . .

"When it is considered that we are giving two dollars worth of property now, in payment for one dollar in gold, you will realize that we are now paying 100 per cent premium on hold. [Applause]

"And this applies not only to our foreign business, but to our home business.

"With silver remonitized, and a just and equitable standard of values, we can, if necessary, by act of Congress, reduce the number of grains in a gold dollar till it is of the same value as the silver dollar. [Applause] We can legislate the premium out of gold. [Applause] Who will say that this is not an effective remedy? I pause for a reply!"

Coin waited for a reply. No one answering him, he continued.

"Until an answer that will commend itself to an unbiased mind is given to this remedy, that guarantees a parity between the metals, write upon the character of every 'international bimetallist' the words *gold monometallist.*' "

Pausing for a moment, as if still waiting for his position to be attacked, he proceeded:

"Give the people back their favored primary money! Give us two arms with which to transact business! Silver the right arm and gold the left arm! Silver the money of the people, and gold the money of the rich.

"Citizens! the integrity of the government has been violated. A Financial Trust has control of your money, and with it, is robbing you of your property. Vampires feed upon your commercial blood. The money in the banks is subject to the check of the money lenders. They expect you to quietly submit, and leave your fellow citizens at their mercy. Through the instrumentality of law they have committed a crime that overshadows all other crimes. And yet they appeal to law for their protection. If the starving workingman commits the crime of trespass, they appeal to the law they have contaminated, for his punishment. Drive these money-changers from our temples. Let them discover by your aspect, their masters—the people. [Applause]

"The United States commands the situation, and can dictate bimetallism to the world at the ration she is inclined to fix.

"Our foreign ministers sailing out of New York harbor past the statue of 'Liberty Enlightening the World' should go with instructions to educate the nations of the earth upon the American Financial Policy. We should negative the self-interested influence of England, and speak for industrial prosperity.

"We are now the ally of England in the most cruel and unjust persecution against the weak and defenseless people of the world that was ever waged by tyrants since the dawn of history. [Applause]

"Our people are losing each year hundreds of millions of dollars; incalculable suffering exists throughout the land; we have begun the work of cutting each others throats; poor men crazed with hunger are daily shot down by the officers of the law; want, distress and anxiety pervades the entire Union.

"If we are to act let us act quickly.

"It has been truthfully said:

"'It is at once the result and security of oppression that its victim soon becomes incapable of resistance. Submission to its first encroachments is followed by the fatal lethargy that destroys every noble ambition, and converts the people into cowardly poltroons and fawning sycophants, who hug their chains and lick the hand that smites them!'

"Oppression now seeks to enslave this fair land. Its name is greed. Surrounded by the comforts of life, it is unconscious of the conditions of others. Despotism, whether in Russia marching its helpless victims to an eternal night of sorrow, or in Ireland where its humiliating influences are ever before the human eye, or elsewhere; it is the same.

"It is already with us. It has come in the same form that it has come everywhere—by regarding the interests of property as paramount to the interests of humanity. That influence extends from the highest to the lowest. The deputy sheriff regards the $4 he gets as more important to him than the life or cause of the workmen he shoots down.[4]

NOTES

3. Watts and Israel, pp. 177–181.

4. William H. Harvey, "Coin's Financial School," in George Brown Tindall, ed., *A Populist Reader: Selections from the Works of American Populist Leaders* (New York: Harper & Row, 1966), pp. 129, 143–146.

THE ISSUE: VENEZUELA

During Cleveland's second term, a boundary dispute developed in South America between Venezuela and Great Britain. The area in question stretched along the border between Venezuela and British Guiana. Although it was merely an uninhabited wilderness, gold had been discovered there in 1877, making it a most attractive territory to both nations. The Venezuelan and British governments traded claims and counterclaims, each professing ownership of the area. Great Britain refused to refer the dispute to arbitration, and in 1887 Venezuela suspended diplomatic relations with the European nation. The contest of wills was decidedly imbalanced, however, as one party was a powerful and wealthy empire while the other was a modest country recently delivered from political chaos and economic instability.

In 1885, Cleveland involved the United States in the matter. His interference had precedent: it was known as the Monroe Doctrine. In 1823, President James Monroe articulated a new approach to U.S. foreign policy, and his vision had guided U.S. actions since. Four ideas constituted the Monroe Doctrine: (1) the United States would remain uninvolved in the internal affairs of or disputes between European powers; (2) the United States recognized and respected existing European colonies and dependencies in the Western Hemisphere; (3) the United States would allow no further colonization in the Western Hemisphere; and (4) the United States would view a European attempt to control or oppress any nation in the Western Hemisphere as a hostile act against the United States itself. These guidelines created a distinct separation between the Eastern and Western Hemispheres, one that Cleveland believed Great Britain had crossed when it began the border dispute with Venezuela. In fact, Cleveland feared that Great Britain intended to extend its influence aggressively in South America and engage Venezuela in war. Cleveland proved willing to step between the two and brave U.S. war with Great Britain on behalf of U.S. interests in Venezuela and the entire South

American continent. His policy that the United States reserved the right to intervene in any international disputes in the Western Hemisphere, articulated by Cleveland's former attorney general turned secretary of state Richard Olney, became known as the Olney Corollary to the Monroe Doctrine.

Though many applauded Cleveland's bold foreign policy, others feared the trend it might begin. Populist leaders, such as William Jennings Bryan, favored a government that focused on its own internal issues and remained uninvolved with international agreements. Bryan and those who agreed with him believed that there was a fine line between watching out for neighboring countries and interfering with their business—even when U.S. motivation was to help the other nation—and becoming a dominating, imperial power that wished to expand its own interest and territory. Bryan spoke and wrote about his concern that the temptation to become imperialistic, to become a nation with its own colonies and dependencies and ever-growing sphere of influence, would be too hard to resist, and imperialism and democracy, he noted, did not mix.

In the end, the conclusion of the heated conflict seemed anticlimactic. Cleveland's position eventually convinced Great Britain to accept arbitration, and in 1899 the arbitral panel released its findings. Both Venezuela and Great Britain received portions of the disputed territory. Though populist fears of U.S. imperialism did not seem warranted, Cleveland's bold use of the Monroe Doctrine led to more U.S. involvement in international disputes, and eventually to war.

The President's Position: The Monroe Doctrine

PRESIDENT GROVER CLEVELAND'S THREAT OF WAR WITH ENGLAND
DECEMBER 17, 1895

... If a European power, by an extension of its boundaries, takes possession of the territory of one of our neighboring Republics against its will and in derogation of its rights, it is difficult to see why to that extent such European power does not thereby attempt to extend its system of government to that portion of this continent which is thus taken. This is the precise action which President Monroe declared to be "dangerous to our peace and safety," and it can make no difference whether the European system is extended by an advance of frontier or otherwise.

It is also suggested in the British reply that we should not seek to apply the Monroe doctrine to the pending dispute because it does not embody any principle of international law which "is founded on the general consent of nations," and that "no statesman, however eminent, and no nation, however powerful, are competent to insert into the code of international law a novel principle which was never recognized before, and which has not since been accepted by the Government of any other country."

Practically the principle for which we contend has peculiar if not exclusive relation to the United States. It may not have been admitted in so many words to the code of international law, but since in international councils every nation is entitled to the rights belonging to it, if the enforcement of the Monroe doctrine is something we may justly claim it has its place in the code of international law as certainly and as securely as if it were specifically mentioned, and where the United States is a suitor before the high tribunal that administers international law the question to be determined is whether or not we present claims which the justice of that code of law can find to be right and valid.

The Monroe doctrine finds its recognition in those principles of international law which are based upon the theory that every nation shall have its rights protected and its just claims enforced. . . .

In the belief that the doctrine for which we contend was clear and definite, that it was founded upon substantial considerations and involved our safety and welfare, that it was fully applicable to our present conditions and to the state of the world's progress and that it was directly related to the pending controversy and without any conviction as to the final merits of the dispute, but anxious to learn in a satisfactory and conclusive manner whether Great Britain sought, under a claim of boundary, to extend her possessions on this continent without right, or whether she merely sought possession of territory fairly included within her lines of ownership, this Government proposed to the Government of Great Britain a resort to arbitration as the proper means of settling the question to the end that a vexatious boundary dispute between the two contestants might be determined and our exact standing and relation in respect to the controversy might be made clear.

It will be seen from the correspondence herewith submitted that this proposition has been declined by the British Government, upon grounds which in the circumstances seem to me to be far from satisfactory. It is deeply disappointing that such an appeal actuated by the most friendly feelings towards both nations directly concerned, addressed to the sense of justice and to the magnanimity of one of the great powers of the world and touching its relations to one comparatively weak and small, should have produced no better results.

The course to be pursued by this Government in view of the present condition does not appear to admit of serious doubt. Having labored faithfully for many years to induce Great Britain to submit this dispute to impartial arbitration, and having been now finally apprized of her refusal to do so, nothing remains but to accept the situation, to recognize its plain requirements and deal with it accordingly. Great Britain's present proposition has never thus far been regarded as admissible by Venezuela, though any adjustment of the boundary which that country may deem for her advantage and may enter into of her own free will cannot of course be objected to by the United States.

Assuming, however, that the attitude of Venezuela will remain unchanged, the dispute has reached such a stage as to make it now incumbent upon the United States to take measures to determine with sufficient certainty for its justification what is the true divisional line between the Republic of Venezuela and British Guiana. The inquiry to that end should of course be conducted carefully and judicially and due weight should be given to all available evidence records and facts in support of the claims of both parties.

In order that such an examination should be prosecuted in a thorough and satisfactory manner I suggest that the Congress make an adequate appropriation for the expenses of a Commission, to be appointed by the Executive, who shall make the necessary investigation and report upon the matter with the least possible delay. When such report is made and accepted it will in my opinion be the duty of the United States to resist by every means in its power as a willful aggression upon its rights and interests the appropriation by Great Britain of any lands or the exercise of governmental jurisdiction over any territory which after investigation we have determined of right belongs to Venezuela.

In making these recommendations I am fully alive to the responsibility incurred, and keenly realize all the consequences that may follow.

I am nevertheless firm in my conviction that while it is a grievous thing to contemplate the two great English-speaking peoples of the world as being otherwise than friendly competitors in the onward march of civilization, and strenuous and worthy rivals in all the arts of peace, there is no calamity which a great nation can invite which equals that which follows a supine submission to wrong and injustice and the consequent loss of national self respect and honor beneath which are shielded and defended a people's safety and greatness.[5]

Against the President's Position: Anti-Interventionism

"AMERICA'S MISSION"
BY WILLIAM JENNINGS BRYAN

[Extract from speech delivered at Washington Day banquet given by the Virginia Democratic Association at Washington, D.C., February 22, 1899.]

When the advocates of imperialism find it impossible to reconcile a colonial policy with the principles of our government or with the canons of morality; when they are unable to defend it upon the ground of religious duty or pecuniary profit, they fall back in helpless despair upon the assertion that it is destiny. "Suppose it does violate the constitution," they say; "suppose it does break all the commandments; suppose it does entail upon the nation an incalculable expenditure of blood and money; it is destiny and we must submit."

The people have not voted for imperialism; no national convention has declared for it; no Congress has passed upon it. To whom, then, has the future been revealed? Whence this voice of authority? We can all prophesy, but our prophesies are merely guesses, colored by our hopes and our surroundings. Man's opinion of what is to be is half wish and half environment. Avarice paints destiny with a dollar mark before it, militarism equips it with a sword.

He is the best prophet who, recognizing the omnipotence of truth, comprehends most clearly the great forces which are working out the progress, not of one party, not of one nation, but of the human race.

History is replete with predictions which once wore the hue of destiny, but which failed of fulfillment because those who uttered them saw too small an arc of the circle of events. When Pharaoh pursued the fleeing Israelites to the edge of the Red Sea he was confident that their bondage would be renewed and that they would again make bricks without straw, but destiny was not revealed until Moses and his followers reached the farther shore dry shod and the waves rolled over the horses and chariots of the Egyptians. When Belshazzar, on the last night of his reign, led his thousand lords into the Babylonian banquet hall and sat down to a table glittering with vessels of silver and gold he felt sure of his kingdom for many years to come, but destiny was not revealed until the hand wrote upon the wall those awe-inspiring words, "Mene, Mene, Tekel Upharsin." When Abderrahman swept northward with his conquering hosts his imagination saw the Crescent triumphant throughout the world, but destiny was not revealed until Charles Martel raised the cross above the battlefield of Tours and saved Europe from the sword of Mohammedanism. When Napoleon emerged victorious from Marengo, from Ulm and from Austerlitz he thought himself the child of destiny, but destiny was not revealed until Blucher's forces joined the army of Wellington and the vanquished Corsican began his melancholy march toward St. Helena. When the redcoats of George the Third routed the New Englanders at Lexington and Bunker Hill there arose before the British sovereign visions of colonies taxed without representation and drained of their wealth by foreign-made laws, but destiny was not revealed until the surrender of Cornwallis completed the work begun at Independence Hall and ushered into existence a government deriving its just powers from the consent of the governed.

We have reached another crisis. The ancient doctrine of imperialism, banished from our land more than a century ago, has recrossed the Atlantic and challenged democracy to mortal combat upon American soil. . . .

If we embark upon a career of conquest no one can tell how many islands we may be able to seize, or how many races we may be able to subjugate; neither can any one estimate the cost, immediate and remote, to the nation's purse and to the nation's character, but whether we shall enter upon such a career is a question which the people have a right to decide for themselves.

Unexpected events may retard or advance the nation's growth, but the nation's purpose determines its destiny.

What is the nation's purpose?

The main purpose of the founders of our government was to secure for themselves and for posterity the blessings of liberty, and that purpose has been faithfully followed up to this time. Our statesmen have opposed each other upon economic questions, but they have agreed in defending self-government as the controlling national idea. They have quarreled among themselves over tariff and finance, but they have been united in their opposition to an entangling alliance with any European power.

Under this policy our nation has grown in numbers and in strength. Under this policy its beneficent influence has encircled the globe. Under this policy the taxpayers have been spared the burden and the menace of a large military establishment and the young men have been taught the arts of peace rather than the science of war. On each returning Fourth of July our people have met to celebrate the signing of the Declaration of Independence; their hearts have renewed their vows to free institutions and their voices have praised the forefathers whose wisdom and courage and patriotism made it possible for each succeeding generation to repeat the words,

> "My country, 'tis of thee,
> Sweet land of liberty,
> Of thee I sing."

. . . If I mistake not the sentiment of the American people they will spurn the bribe of imperialism, and, by resisting temptation, win such a victory as has not been won since the battle of Yorktown. Let it be written of the United States: Behold a republic that took up arms to aid a neighboring people, struggling to be free; a republic that, in the progress of the war, helped distant races whose wrongs were not in contemplation when hostilities began; a republic that, when peace was restored, turned a deaf ear to the clamorous voice of greed and to those borne down by the weight of a foreign yoke, spoke the welcome words, Stand up; be free—let this be the record made on history's page and the silent example of this republic, true to its principles in the hour of trial, will do more to extend the area of self-government and civilization than could be done by all the wars of conquest that we could wage in a generation. . . . [6]

NOTES

5. Watts and Israel, pp. 182–184.

6. Anti-imperialism in the United States, 1898–1935, www.boondocksnet. com/ai/ailtexts/bryan990222.html (accessed November 22, 2002).

THE ISSUE: CUBA

Cleveland was ready and willing to intervene on behalf of Venezuela—or, more appropriately, U.S. interests in Venezuela—against Great Britain. He was not so eager to intervene for Cuba against Spain. His Cuban policy was not as contradictory as it first seemed, however. Part of his position followed from what he perceived to be in the best interest of the United States. Part also followed from a consistent fear of European involvement in the Western Hemisphere. Cleveland's initiative in Venezuela brought a civil, even anticlimactic, end to the dispute; however, Cleveland's actions or lack of actions in Cuba left the issue open for his successor to handle with war.

Cuba was important to the United States. The Spanish Caribbean island imported 40 percent of its goods from the United States and exported 90 percent of its goods to the United States. When severe economic depression hit Cuba, thanks in part to Spanish mismanagement of the economy, insurrection erupted against Spain. The rebellion evolved into bloody guerilla warfare with atrocities committed on both sides. Cubans fought for independence, and the Spanish fought for control.

The U.S. press focused on inhumane Spanish actions, including the detainment of Cuban civilians in holding areas so rebels could not recruit new soldiers. These Spanish-run camps claimed many lives with disease and starvation. Some U.S. citizens, including many members of Congress, saw the Cuban insurrectionists as freedom fighters in the tradition of those who fought in the War of Independence against Great Britain. Leaders such as Democratic senator John T. Morgan of Alabama claimed in their congressional speeches that it was the United States' duty as an example to the world to support those seeking liberty. It was a humiliating disgrace, he continued, for the nation to stand by idly while Cubans lost their lives struggling for independence. These leaders tried to wrest away control of foreign policy from the executive branch and recognize the belligerency, and therefore legitimacy, of the Cuban revolutionaries.

Cleveland disagreed for two key reasons. First, he did not trust the Cubans—a position based largely on ethnic and racial bias—and he believed the economic and security interests of the United States would be best served by Spanish rule over Cuba, albeit with some Spanish concessions, such as economic reforms and a limited measure of autonomy to pacify the Cuban nationals. Second, and more importantly, he feared that independence would leave Cuba in the hands of those not ready to govern it. Anarchy might erupt, he reasoned, and European intervention might follow. Cleveland did not want to give any European power the excuse of interfering in the Western Hemisphere. The best he could devise was to proclaim neutrality and work behind the scenes for a speedy resolution to the conflict.

A speedy resolution was not forthcoming. Through Secretary of State Olney, Cleveland expressed to Spain his lack of empathy with the revolutionaries and his disappointment that Spain had been unable to crush the rebellion. He then warned that Spain would be unable to control Cuba if war raged much longer, and he urged the nation to make a few concessions to the Cubans in order to pacify them and restore order and control swiftly. This did not happen. In the end, Cleveland left the problem unresolved to await his successor to the White House, Republican William McKinley. Cleveland's position on Cuba proved quite unpopular, and the stigma followed him into the election. The Democrats repudiated him, making him the only sitting president so renounced by his own party; rather than nominating Cleveland for another term, they nominated William Jennings Bryan as the Democratic presidential candidate in 1896.

The President's Position: Not Support the Cuban Rebels

SECRETARY OF STATE RICHARD OLNEY TO SPANISH MINISTER TO THE UNITED STATES DUPUY DE LÔME APRIL 4, 1896

It might well be deemed a dereliction of duty to the Government of the United States, as well as a censurable want of candor to that of Spain, if I were longer to defer official expression as well of the anxiety with which the President regards the existing situation in Cuba as of his earnest desire for the prompt and permanent pacification of that island. Any plan giving reasonable assurance of that result and not inconsistent with the just rights and reasonable demands of all concerned would be earnestly promoted by all means which the Constitution and laws of this country place at his disposal.

It is now some nine or ten months since the nature and prospects of the insurrection were first discussed between us. In explanation of its rapid and, up to that time, quite unopposed growth and progress, you called attention to the rainy season which from May or June until November renders regular military operations impracticable. Spain was pouring such numbers of troops into Cuba that your theory and opinion that, when they could be used in an active campaign, the insurrection would be almost instantly suppressed, seemed reasonable and probable. In this particular you believed, and sincerely believed, that the present insurrection would offer a most marked contrast to that which began in

1868, and which, being feebly encountered with comparatively small forces, prolonged its life for upward of ten years.

It is impossible to deny that the expectations thus entertained by you in the summer and fall of 1895, and shared not merely by all Spaniards but by most disinterested observers as well, have been completely disappointed. . . .

The object of the present communication, however, is not to discuss intervention, nor to propose intervention, nor to pave the way for intervention. The purpose is exactly the reverse—to suggest whether a solution of present troubles can not be found which will prevent all thought of intervention by rendering it unnecessary. What the United States desires to do, if the way can be pointed out, is to cooperate with Spain in the immediate pacification of the island on such a plan as, leaving Spain her rights of sovereignty, shall yet secure to the people of the island all such rights and powers of local self-government as they can reasonably ask. To that end the United States offers and will use her good offices at such time and in such manner as may be deemed most advisable. Its mediation, it is believed, should not be rejected in any quarter, since none could misconceive or mistrust its purpose.

Spain could not, because our respect for her sovereignty and our determination to do nothing to impair it have been maintained for many years at great cost and in spite of many temptations. The insurgents could not, because anything assented to by this Government which did not satisfy the reasonable demands and aspirations of Cuba would arouse the indignation of our whole people. It only remains to suggest that, if anything can be done in the direction indication, it should be done at once and on the initiative of Spain.

The more the contest is prolonged, the more bitter and more irreconcilable is the antagonism created, while there is danger that concessions may be so delayed as to be chargeable to weakness and fear of the issue of the contest, and thus be infinitely less acceptable and persuasive than if made while the result still hangs in the balance, and they could be properly credited in some degree at least to a sense of right and justice. Thus far Spain has faced the insurrection sword in hand, and has made no sign to show that surrender and submission would be followed by anything but a return to the old order of things. Would it not be wise to modify that policy and to accompany the application of military force with an authentic declaration of the organic changes that are meditated in the administration of the island with a view to remove all just grounds of complaint?

It is for Spain to consider and determine what those changes would be. But should they be such that the United States could urge their adoption, as substantially removing well-founded grievances, its influence would be exerted for their acceptance, and it can hardly be doubted, would be most potential for the termination of hostilities and the restoration of peace and order to the island. One result of the course of proceeding outlined, if no other, would be sure to follow, namely, that the rebellion would lose largely, if not altogether, the moral countenance and support it now enjoys from the people of the United States.

In closing this communication it is hardly necessary to repeat that it is prompted by the friendliest feelings toward Spain and the Spanish people. To attribute to the United States any hostile or hidden purposes would be a grave and most lamentable error. The United States has no designs upon Cuba and no designs against the sovereignty of Spain. Neither is it actuated by any spirit of meddlesomeness nor by any desire to force its will upon another nation. Its geographical proximity and all the considerations above detailed compel it to be interested in the solution of the Cuban problem whether it will or no. Its only anxiety is that the solution should be speedy, and, by being founded on truth and justice, should also be permanent.

To aid in that solution it offers the suggestions herein contained. They will be totally misapprehended unless the United States be credited with entertaining no other purpose toward Spain than that of lending its assistance to such termination of a fratricidal contest as will leave her honor and dignity unimpaired at the same time that it promotes and conserves the true interests of all parties concerned.[7]

Against the President's Position: Support the Cuban Rebels

SENATOR JOHN T. MORGAN OF ALABAMA
UNITED STATES SENATE
APRIL 6, 1897

A question of war or peace between this country and any foreign country, or a question of the existence of a war in any foreign country, is a matter of such grave importance to all the people of the United States that its consideration should always be entered upon with the utmost degree of deliberation and solemnity, and, as far as possible, it should be free from all the exasperations of feeling that we of course have when quarrels occur between us and other powers. It is in this view, and in this sense, and with this purpose, and only this, that I approach the subject this morning.

I do not wish to create a ferment in the United States about it. It is not necessary to do that, Mr. President, if I were disposed to get up some public excitement, because the mind of the people of the United States is agitated and all their hearts are full of this subject. We are in the midst of a very trying situation that has never heretofore existed as it exists now. All the aggravations that surround us at this moment and the same sense of indignation have never heretofore existed, even in the various and frequent irritations that have occurred between Spain and the United States on the subject of her government in Cuba. We have tried so to feel, we have tried to so believe, and we have so conformed our conduct that it is a matter of indifference to us whether Spain shall persecute her own subjects in Cuba or not. I say we have tried to feel it and we have tried to believe it. At the same time the history of Spanish occupation in Cuba from the beginning of this century, and, indeed, far back of that period of time—but I will say from the beginning of this century, because our Government became concerned in it about that time—the history of Spanish occupation in Cuba has been so full of that absolute and heartless spirit of tyranny toward her own subjects as that it is not to be expected that a country organized as ours is, upon the basis of self-government and of the respect that is due from the Government to the citizen, should be free from very profound agitation, in view of the repeated and flagrant and very outrageous demonstrations of persecution that have been made by the Crown of Spain against her own subjects in the Island of Cuba. . . .

Our people have suffered in one respect a degree of mortification and humiliation as well as a degree of personal distress that it has always been within the power of our Government to prevent. If the Government of the United States had taken care of its own people in the island of Cuba according to the full measure of its duty, many a life would have been saved in the former struggles and in the present one, much property would have been spared from destruction, great anguish of feeling would have been spared to our people, both native born and adopted. But the Government of the United States has not taken proper care of her own people in Cuba, and it is time that we begin to do so.

The object of the introduction of the joint resolution which is before the Senate to-day is to put the Government of the United States in a proper legal attitude toward the Government of Spain in Cuba, and to enable us simply to take care of our own citizens. I have always declared that this was my leading motive, and in fact my exclusive motive, as a Senator of the United States, in whatever support I have given to measures here in respect of our controversies and difficulties with Spain in the Island of Cuba. I have kept my mind fixed firmly and exclusively upon the duty of the Government of the United States—and I hope the Executive will concur with us—a definition and statement of a legal status or situation which makes it possible for us, under the laws of nations, to protect the lives and property of our people in the Island of Cuba.

In accomplishing thus result, Mr. President, it may turn out—and I would be very glad that it should—that assistance will be given to the people of the Island of Cuba in the establishment of their independence, in freeing themselves from an abominable yoke, which, so far as they are concerned, has never resulted in any benefit to the people there at all, but has been imposed upon them and maintained over them for the mere purpose of leeching out of them their substance and of keeping them as serfs and feudatories to the Crown of Spain and to the nobility and gentry of that country. I should be very glad that a result of that sort should follow; but whether that result shall follow, or one still more disastrous to the people of Cuba, nevertheless it is a duty that we can not abdicate to take care, as far as in us lies, of our people in that island. . . .

Now, can we afford to stand by here and see repeated, in a form that has become historic in Cuba, these wrongs and outrages against our own people, trusting to the settlement of an account for damages after the wrong has been done? . . .

Does war now exist in Cuba? Mr. President, that is a proposition that is absolutely so undebatable, so far beyond the domain of discussion, that I can not see how any sensible man can take it up for consideration when the answer lies immediately before him in every act that has occurred in the Island of Cuba within the past two years, and for a period much longer than that. . . . It is so palpable that no man in his senses, it seems to me, can possibly deny it.[8]

NOTES

7. Fred L. Israel, ed., *Major Presidential Decisions* (New York: Chelsea House, 1980), pp. 2–3, 6–8.

8. Israel, pp. 19–23.

RECOMMENDED READINGS

Borden, Morton, ed. *America's Ten Greatest Presidents.* Chicago: Rand McNally, 1961.

Brodsky, Alyn. *Grover Cleveland: A Study in Character.* New York: St. Martin's Press, 2000.

Cleveland, Grover. *Letters of Grover Cleveland, 1850–1908.* Boston: Houghton Mifflin, 1933.

Graff, Henry F. *Grover Cleveland.* New York: Times Books, 2002.

Hollingsworth, J. Rogers. *The Whirligig of Politics; the Democracy of Cleveland and Bryan.* Chicago: University of Chicago Press, 1963.

Jeffers, H. Paul. *An Honest President: The Life and Presidencies of Grover Cleveland.* New York: W. Morrow, 2000.

Tugwell, Rexford G. *Grover Cleveland.* New York: Macmillan, 1968.

Welch, Richard E., Jr. *The Presidencies of Grover Cleveland.* Lawrence: University Press of Kansas, 1988.

7

WILLIAM MCKINLEY

(1897–1901)

William McKinley's rise to political power was not an unusual tale. When he was born in 1843, his father managed a charcoal furnace and also worked as an iron founder. McKinley was only eighteen when the Civil War began, and he enlisted in an Ohio regiment led by future president Rutherford B. Hayes and received a promotion for valor at the bloody Battle of Antietam. After the war he studied law, passed the bar, and opened a law office in Canton, Ohio.

A Republican party member, McKinley supported his former commander Hayes for governor in 1867 and Grant for president in 1868. After several years of serving as Stark County's prosecuting attorney, McKinley was elected to the U.S. House of Representatives in 1877, where he remained until 1891, failing to win reelection only twice during the years. While chairman of the House Ways and Means Committee, the pro-protectionist McKinley sponsored the McKinley Tariff Act of 1890, which raised duties to their highest in history and ultimately ended both Harrison's term as president and McKinley's career as a congressman. (McKinley remained committed to protectionism, however, and supported the Dingley Tariff Act during his administration, which set duties even higher than the McKinley Tariff Act had.)

Mark Hanna, a wealthy Ohio businessman, Republican party leader, and close friend of McKinley, suggested that the former congressman run for the Ohio governorship. With Hanna's help, McKinley won two gubernatorial terms and then the Republican presidential nomination in 1896. McKinley's opposition was the young William Jennings Bryan, who secured the nomination of both the Democratic and Populist parties. Bryan traveled thousands of miles delivering speeches about silver coinage and the plight of debtors. McKinley, on the other hand, remained in Canton, receiving visiting groups of Republicans and issuing statements in favor of the gold standard from his front porch. Hanna coordinated other strategic speeches by Republican party leaders nationwide about McKinley, his platform, and his promise as a leader, as well as Bryan's frightening radicalism and the dire consequences in store if the populist were elected to the White House. The strategy succeeded. McKinley became the first president in twenty-four years to earn a popular majority of the vote.

McKinley brought an overt kindness to the White House unseen in the eccentric Harrison or stubborn Cleveland. His care for his First Lady and wife of twenty-five years, Ida Saxton McKinley, proved his compassion and gentleness. Two years after the McKinleys married, Ida McKinley watched both her mother and two daughters die, and the shock left her an invalid, suffering frequent seizures and nervous disorders for the rest of her life. McKinley's devotion and attentiveness to her brought him much admiration from U.S. leaders and the public at large.

McKinley's main domestic concerns were the gold standard, which he maintained, and the protective tariff, which he reinstated. Riding the wave of economic recovery and prosperity originally created by the policies of Grover Cleveland, McKinley faced down the usual critics of his positions with success. His gaze was turned outward, however, focusing on expanding the role of the United States on the world stage.

Hawaii's annexation, an issue inherited from the administrations of Benjamin Harrison and Grover Cleveland, became a ripe question during McKinley's term. He supported annexation and eventual statehood for Hawaii, the former of which was accomplished during his administration, and the latter of which followed later. McKinley also inherited the complex situation of Cuban rebellion from Cleveland's second term. At first, McKinley tried to negotiate a settlement between the Cuban revolutionaries in the Caribbean and the Spanish colonial power they wished to overthrow, despite calls from U.S. congressional leaders to recognize Cuba's independence and assist in the fight against Spain. The interception of a letter from the Spanish minister to the United States—certainly uncomplimentary about McKinley if not openly threatening—and the loss of the U.S. battleship *Maine* in a Cuban harbor led McKinley to intervene in the conflict. The quick and successful Spanish-American War followed. Despite criticisms from those who feared the United States was becoming just like the imperial, dominating Spain, McKinley enjoyed mainstream popularity for his decisive and winning action.

Victory against Spain left Cuba independent and the United States in control of Guam, Puerto Rico, and the Philippines. The Philippines became McKinley's next problem. The Filipinos, who had declared independence during the Spanish-American conflict, refused to accept U.S. domination and rebelled against U.S. administration of the Pacific Ocean islands. Military conflict followed and eventually subdued the Philippines and prepared it for the governance McKinley's committees devised. Opponents warned that imperialism and democracy did not mix, and that the United States was becoming what it had always hated and fought. Nevertheless, McKinley took the nation even one step closer to becoming an empire by initiating the Open Door Policy with regard to equal trade in China and the "spheres of influence" other nations had developed there. Anti-imperialists once again protested and once again were in the minority. McKinley won reelection by an even larger margin than his first presidential victory.

Scarce months into McKinley's second term, on September 6, 1901, he was shot in the stomach by Leon Czolgosz while shaking hands with visitors at the Pan-American Exposition in Buffalo, New York. A former millworker, Czolgosz had suffered a mental breakdown and then flirted with the anarcho-communist form of anarchism advocated by activists such as the outspoken Emma Goldman, but he grew deeply frustrated when the political groups he approached turned him away. Though he had fatally wounded McKinley, the dying president instructed his secretary to see to it that Czolgosz was not hurt, because he was just "some poor misguided fellow."[1] McKinley lingered for eight days and then succumbed to his injury.

McKinley's legacy is somewhat difficult to pinpoint. He was remembered with fondness, but not with the same duration as, for instance, the plainspoken Grover Cleveland, or McKinley's successor, the colorful Teddy Roosevelt. He inherited a nation in financial upheaval and left a nation with new prosperity, though he could not claim credit for much of that economic recovery. His personal compassion seemed in conflict with his will to build a U.S. empire. McKinley undeniably left his mark on the nation, especially in how the country's influence was felt across the world, from the Pacific to the Caribbean, from South America to Asia. His tragic death marked an end to the bloody era of assassinations, and his leadership ushered the United States into the twentieth century.

NOTES

1. Lewis L. Gould, *The Presidency of William McKinley* (Lawrence: University Press of Kansas, 1980), p. 251.

THE ISSUE: THE GOLD STANDARD

When the Democratic party renounced incumbent Grover Cleveland and gave its presidential nomination to populist William Jennings Bryan, in large part due to the strength of his stirring pro-silver "Cross of Gold" speech, they ensured that monetary policy would be the centerpiece of the 1896 campaign. And it was. Republican candidate William McKinley ran on a gold standard platform against Bryan. While Bryan courted farming and labor interests, McKinley courted big business backers and oversaw a choreographed lineup of Republican speakers who spoke nationwide about Bryan's radicalism and McKinley's commitment to financial prosperity. McKinley won handily, becoming the first president since 1872 to garner a popular majority in the polls. The people seemed to have spoken, and their voice favored the gold standard. In this sense, Cleveland had accomplished one of his goals, namely convincing U.S. citizens that the Panic of 1893 was caused and could be repeated by the depletion of gold in the national Treasury. McKinley built on this conservative economic foundation and thus made his way to the White House.

During the McKinley administration, the United States rebounded from its depression (to be fair, a process already underway by the end of Cleveland's term, though McKinley received much of the credit). McKinley's main contribution was holding off impatient calls for increased silver coinage by populists and shifting policy to alleviate the strain of gold redemption on the government in order to maintain higher gold reserves in the Treasury. In short, McKinley's position was a continuance of the one Cleveland had put in place. The gold standard position, coupled with his return to high protective tariffs through the 1897 Dingley Tariff Act, were his primary forays into domestic policy, as most of McKinley's attention during his administration was turned to international relations.

Despite its failure either to get Bryan elected president or to change U.S. economic policy in the short term, the importance of Bryan's historic "Cross of Gold" speech can hardly be overestimated. First, it launched on a truly national scale the career of the young—in 1896, only thirty-six years old—Bryan, whose career eventually influenced such reforms and measures as the income tax, women's suffrage, prohibition, the Department of Labor, and the popular election of senators. He won the presidential nomination of a remarkable three different political parties, namely the Democratic, Populist, and National Silver parties. He later served as President Woodrow Wilson's secretary of state and the prosecuting attorney for the Scopes Trial in which a teacher was found guilty and fined for teaching Darwin's theory of evolution rather than the Judeo-Christian story of creation. The Scopes Trial, in fact, served as a fitting metaphor for Bryan, who seemed throughout his life to wage war on behalf of populist traditionalism and fundamentalism against the rising tide of modernity.

McKinley's acceptance of conservative Democrat Cleveland's monetary policy served him well as the nineteenth century drew to a close and the U.S. economy rebounded. The gold standard as McKinley and Cleveland understood it, however, would not survive the Great Depression of the 1930s.

The President's Position: For the Gold Standard

MCKINLEY'S FIRST ANNUAL MESSAGE
DECEMBER 6, 1897

With the great resources of the Government, and with the honorable example of the past before us, we ought not to hesitate to enter upon a currency revision which will make our demand obligations less onerous to the Government and relieve our financial laws from ambiguity and doubt.

The brief review of what was accomplished from the close of the war to 1983, makes unreasonable and groundless any distrust either of our financial ability or soundness; while the situation from 1893 to 1897 must admonish Congress of the immediate necessity of so legislating as to make the return of the conditions then prevailing impossible.

There are many plans proposed as a remedy for the evil. Before we can find the true remedy we must appreciate the real evil. It is not that our currency of every kind is not good, for every dollar of it is good; good because the Government's pledge is out to keep it so, and that pledge will not be broken. However, the guaranty of our purpose to keep the pledge will be best shown by advancing toward its fulfillment.

The evil of the present system is found in the great cost to the Government of maintaining the parity of our different forms of money, that is, keeping all of them at par with gold. We surely cannot be longer heedless of the burden this imposes on the people, even under fairly prosperous conditions, while the past four years have demonstrated that it is not only an expensive charge upon the Government, but a dangerous menace to the National credit.

It is manifest that we must devise some plan to protect the Government against bond issues for repeated redemptions. We must either curtail the opportunity for speculation, made easy by the multiplied redemptions of our demand obligations, or increase the gold reserve for their redemption. We have $900,000,000 of currency which the Government by solemn enactment has undertaken to keep at par with gold. Nobody is obliged to redeem in gold but the Government. The banks are not required to redeem in gold. The Government is obliged to keep equal with gold all its outstanding currency and coin obligations, while its receipts are not required to be paid in gold. They are paid in every kind of money but gold, and the only means by which the Government can with certainty get gold is by borrowing. It can get it in no other way when it most needs it. The Government without any fixed gold revenue is pledged to maintain gold redemption, which it has steadily and faithfully done, and which, under the authority now given, it will continue to do.

The law which requires the Government, after having redeemed its United States notes, to pay them out again as current funds, demands a constant replenishment of the gold reserve. This is especially so in times of business panic and when the revenues are insufficient to meet the expenses of the Government. At such times the Government has no other way to supply its deficit and maintain the redemption but through the increase of its bonded debt, as during the Administration of my predecessor, when $262,315,400 of four-and-a-half per cent bonds were issued and sold and the proceeds used to pay the expenses of the Government in excess of the revenues and sustain the gold reserve. While it is true that the greater part of the proceeds of these bonds were used to supply deficient revenues, a considerable portion was required to maintain the gold reserve.

With our revenues equal to our expenses, there would be no deficit requiring the issuance of bonds. But if the gold reserve falls below $100,000,000, how will it be replenished except by selling more bonds? Is there any other way practicable under existing law? The serious question then is, Shall we continue the policy that has been pursued in the past; that is, when the gold reserve reaches the point of danger, issue more bonds and supply the needed gold, or shall we provide other means to prevent these recurring drains upon the gold reserve? If no further legislation is had and the policy of selling bonds is to be continued, then Congress should give the Secretary of the Treasury authority to sell bonds at long or short periods, bearing a less rate of interest than is now authorized by law.

I earnestly recommend, as soon as the receipts of the Government are quite sufficient to pay all the expenses of the Government, that when any of the United States notes are presented for redemption in gold and are redeemed in gold, such notes shall be kept and set apart, and only paid out in exchange for gold. This is an obvious duty. If the holder of the United States note prefers the gold and gets it from the Government, he should not receive back from the Government a United States note without paying gold in exchange for it. The reason for this is made all the more apparent when the Government issues an interest-bearing debt to provide gold for the redemption of United States notes—a non-interest-bearing debt. Surely it should not pay them out again except on demand and for gold. If they are put out in any other way, they may return again to be followed by another bond issue to redeem them—another interest-bearing debt to redeem a non-interest-bearing debt.

In my view, it is of the utmost importance that the Government should be relieved from the burden of providing all the gold required for exchanges and export. This responsibility is alone borne by the Government, without any of the usual and necessary banking powers to help itself. The banks do not feel the strain of gold redemption. The whole strain rests upon the Government, and the size of the gold reserve in the Treasury has come to be, with or without reason, the signal of danger or security. This ought to be stopped.[2]

Against the President's Position: Free Silver

"CROSS OF GOLD" SPEECH
BY WILLIAM JENNINGS BRYAN
JULY 9, 1896

Why is it that within three months such a change has come over the country? Three months ago when it was confidently asserted that those who believe in the gold standard would frame our platform and nominate our candidates, even the advocates of the gold standard did not think that we could elect a President. And they had good reason for their doubt, because there is scarcely a state here to-day asking for the gold standard which is not in the absolute control of the Republican party. But note the change. Mr. McKinley was nominated at St. Louis upon a platform which declared for the maintenance of the gold standard until it can be changed into bimetallism by international agreement. Mr. McKinley was the most popular man among the Republicans, and three months ago everybody in the Republican party prophesied his election. How is it to-day? Why, the man who was once pleased to think that he looked like Napoleon—that man shudders to-day when he remembers that he was nominated on the anniversary of the battle of Waterloo. Not only that, but as he listens he can hear with ever-increasing distinctness the sound of the waves as they beat upon the lonely shores of St. Helena.

Why this change? Ah, my friends, is not the reason for the change evident to any one who will look at the matter? No private character, however pure, no personal popularity, however great, can protect from the avenging wrath of an indignant people a man who will declare that he is in favor of fastening the gold standard upon this country, or who is willing to surrender the right of self-government and place the legislative control of our affairs in the hands of foreign potentates and powers.

We go forth confident that we shall win. Why? Because upon the paramount issue of this campaign there is not a spot of ground upon which the enemy will dare to challenge battle. If they tell us that the gold standard is a good thing, we shall point to their platform and tell them that their platform pledges the party to get rid of the gold standard and substitute bimetallism. If the gold standard is a good thing, why try to get rid of it? I call your attention to the fact that some of the very people who are in this Convention to-day and who tell us that we ought to declare in favor of international bimetallism—thereby declaring that the gold standard is wrong and that the principle of bimetallism is better— these very people four months ago were open and avowed advocates of the gold standard, and were then telling us that we could not legislate two metals together, even with the aid of all the world. If the gold standard is a good thing, we ought to declare in favor of its retention and not in favor of abandoning it; and if the gold standard is a bad thing why should we wait until other nations are willing to help us to let go? Here is the line of battle, and we care not upon which issue they force the fight; we are prepared to meet them on either issue or on both. If they tell us that the gold standard is the standard of civilization, we reply to them that this, the most enlightened of all the nations of the earth, has never declared for a gold standard and that both the great parties this year are declaring against it. If the gold standard is the standard of civilization, why, my friends, should we not have it? If they come to meet us on that issue we can present the history of our nation. More than that; we can tell them that they will search the pages of history in vain to find a single instance where the common people of any land have ever declared themselves in favor of the gold standard. They can find where the holders of fixed investments have declared for a gold standard, but not where the masses have.

Mr. Carlisle said in 1878 that this was a struggle between "the idle holders of idle capital" and "the struggling masses, who produce the wealth and pay the taxes of the country"; and, my friends, the question we are to decide is: Upon which side will the Democratic party fight; upon the side of "the idle holders of idle capital" or upon the side of "the struggling masses"? That is the question which the party must answer first, and then it must be answered by each individual hereafter. The sympathies of the Democratic party, as shown by the platform, are on the side of the struggling masses who have ever been the foundation of the Democratic party. There are two ideas of government. There are those who believe that, if you will only legislate to make the well-to-do prosperous, their prosperity will leak through on those below. The Democratic idea, however, has been that if you legislate to make the masses prosperous, their prosperity will find its way up through every class which rests upon them.

You come to us and tell us that the great cities are in favor of the gold standard; we reply that the great cities rest upon our broad and fertile prairies. Burn down your cities and leave our farms, and your cities will spring up again as if by magic; but destroy our farms and the grass will grow in the streets of every city in the country.

My friends, we declare that this nation is able to legislate for its own people on every question, without waiting for the aid or consent of any other nation on earth; and upon that issue we expect to carry every state in the Union. I shall not slander the inhabitants of the fair state of Massachusetts nor the inhabitants of the state of New York by saying that, when they are confronted with the proposition, they will declare that this nation is not able to attend to its own business. It is the issue of 1776 over again. Our ancestors, when but three millions in number had the courage to declare their political independence of every other nation; shall we, their descendants, when we have grown to seventy millions, declare that we are less independent than our forefathers?

No, my friends, that will never be the verdict of our people. Therefore, we care not upon what lines the battle is fought. If they say bimetallism is good, but that we cannot have it until other nations help us, we reply that, instead of having a gold standard because England has, we will restore bimetallism, and then let England have bimetallism because the United States has it. If they dare to come out in the open field and defend the gold standard as a good thing, we will fight them to the uttermost. Having behind us the producing masses of this nation and the world, supported by the commercial interests, the laboring interests and the toilers everywhere, we will answer their demand for a gold standard by saying to them: You shall not press down upon the brow of labor this crown of thorns, you shall not crucify mankind upon a cross of gold.[3]

NOTES

2. Richardson, Volume XIII, pp. 6252–6254.

3. Douglass: Archives of American Public Address, http://douglass.speech. nwu.edu/brya_a26.htm (accessed November 4, 2002).

THE ISSUE: THE CUBAN REVOLUTION

During Cleveland's second term, the president's unwillingness to involve the United States in the crisis caused by Cuban rebellion against Spanish control was a matter of great controversy. Many called on him to recognize the Cuban revolutionaries as freedom fighters against tyranny in the tradition of the United States and its revolt against Great Britain. Cleveland believed U.S. interests would be better served by Spanish domination of Cuba, though with some concessions to pacify the rebels, and he feared Cuban independence would lead first to anarchy on the Caribbean island and then to new European intervention in the Western Hemisphere. His efforts to influence Spain failed, leaving a challenge McKinley had to accept.

McKinley saw wisdom in Cleveland's refusal to recognize Cuba's belligerency, thus granting the rebels legitimacy and independence. His approach was somewhat more straightforward than Cleveland's, however. Through diplomatic channels, McKinley communicated to Spain U.S. concern about ongoing violence, civil rights abuses, and trade disruption in Cuba. He urged Spain to end the fighting and find a solution both acceptable to Spain and just for Cuba. The Spanish reply to McKinley's request seemed friendly and cooperative, agreeing to institute political reforms in Cuba to help ameliorate some of its worst conditions, though continuing the war to subdue the rebels. Spain recognized U.S. concerns and promised changes. McKinley was willing to give the colonial power the benefit of the doubt, especially if it meant keeping the United States out of bloody conflict with a European nation.

Many others were far less forgiving or patient. Since the Cuban rebellion had begun, public sympathy for the revolutionaries had grown. Sensationalistic journalists, such as William Randolph Hearst and Joseph Pulitzer, fueled pro-Cuban sentiments by focusing newspaper stories on Spanish atrocities and the brutal conditions faced even by innocent civilians in Cuba. Popular anti-Spanish opinion extended to Washington. Congressmen, such as Democratic representative John Williams of Mississippi, called in Congress for the United States to recognize the belligerency of the Cuban nationals, and in so doing admit that the conflict was, indeed, a war and not merely a private, internal Spanish matter. If the first step was recognizing Cuban belligerency, then the second was recognizing Cuba's independence from Spain, Williams and his colleagues believed. Opponents of the president's position believed that the violence would end only when the Cubans were free; moreover, they argued Cuban independence would stabilize the Cuban economy and allow the United States to resume trade with Cuba, a major factor in both country's economies. Most importantly, Cuban supporters said, helping fellow individuals fight against tyranny and for freedom was one of the United States' duties and responsibilities.

McKinley nevertheless was willing to wait, at least for a time. Then two events took place in February 1898. First, the Spanish minister to Washington wrote a letter that was intercepted and published in U.S. newspapers. In the document the minister described McKinley as a weak man, overeager for public adulation. Six days later, the U.S. battleship *Maine*, which was anchored in Cuba's Havana harbor with 266 U.S. enlisted men and officers aboard, exploded and sank. Though later proven an internal explosion, the tragedy at first appeared to be a direct attack on U.S. forces. McKinley could wait no longer. Everything changed.

The President's Position: For Diplomatic Solution to Crisis

MCKINLEY'S STATE OF THE UNION MESSAGE
DECEMBER 6, 1897

The instructions given to our new minister to Spain before his departure for his post directed him to impress upon that Government the sincere wish of the United States to lend its aid toward the ending of the war in Cuba by reaching a peaceful and lasting result, just and honorable alike to Spain and to the Cuban people. These instructions recited the character and duration of the contest, the widespread losses it entails, the burdens and restraints it imposes upon us, with constant disturbance of national interests, and the injury resulting from an indefinite continuance of this state of things. It was stated that at this juncture our Government was constrained to seriously inquire if the time was not ripe when Spain of her own volition, moved by her own interests and every sentiment of humanity, should put a stop to this destructive war and make proposals of settlement honorable to herself and just to her Cuban colony. It was urged that as a neighboring nation, with large interests in Cuba, we could be required to wait only a reasonable time for the mother country to establish its authority and restore peace and order within the borders of the island; that we could not contemplate an indefinite period for the accomplishment of this result.

No solution was proposed to which the slightest idea of humiliation to Spain could attach, and, indeed, precise proposals were withheld to avoid embarrassment to that Government. All that was asked or expected was that some safe way might be speedily provided and permanent peace restored. It so chanced that the consideration of this offer, addressed to the same Spanish administrator which had declined the tenders of my predecessor, and which for more than two years had poured men and treasure into Cuba in the fruitless effort to suppress the revolt, fell to others. Between the departure of General Woodford, the new envoy, and his arrival in Spain the statesman who had shaped the policy of his country fell by the hand of an assassin, and although the cabinet of the late premier still held office and received from our envoy the proposals he bore, that cabinet gave place within a few days thereafter to a new administration, under the leadership of Sagasta.

The reply to our note was received on the 23rd day of October. It is in the direction of a better understanding. It appreciated the friendly

purposes of this Government. It admits that our country is deeply affected by the war in Cuba and that its desires for peace are just. It declares that the present Spanish government is bound by every
consideration to a change of policy that should satisfy the United States
and pacify Cuba within a reasonable time. To this end Spain has decided
to put into effect the political reforms heretofore advocated by the present premier, without halting for any consideration in the path which in
its judgment leads to peace. The military operations, it is said, will continue, but will be humane and conducted with all regard for private
rights, being accompanied by political action leading to the autonomy of
Cuba while guarding Spanish sovereignty. This, it is claimed, will result
in investing Cuba with a distinct personality, the island to be governed
by an executive and by a local council or chamber, reserving to Spain
the control of foreign relations, the army and navy, and the judicial administration. To accomplish this the present government proposes to
modify existing legislation by decree, leaving the Spanish Cortes, with
the aid of Cuban senators and deputies, to solve the economic problem
and properly distribute the existing debt.

In the absence of a declaration of the measures that this Government
proposes to take in carrying out its proffer of good offices, it suggests
that Spain be left free to conduct military operations and grant political
reforms, while the United States for its part shall enforce its neutral obligations and cut off the assistance which it is asserted the insurgents
receive from this country. The supposition of an indefinite prolongation
of the war is denied. It is asserted that the western provinces are already
well-nigh reclaimed, that the planting of cane and tobacco therein has
been resumed, and that by force of arms and new and ample reforms
very early and complete pacification is hoped for.

The immediate amelioration of existing conditions under the new administration of Cuban affairs is predicted, and therewithal the disturbance and all occasion for any change of attitude on the part of the
United States. Discussion of the question of the international duties and
responsibilities of the United States as Spain understands them is presented, with an apparent disposition to charge us with failure in this
regard. This charge is without any basis in fact. It could not have been
made if Spain had been cognizant of the constant efforts this Government
has made, at the cost of millions and by the employment of the administrative machinery of the nation at command, to perform its full duty
according to the law of nations. That it has successfully prevented the
departure of a single military expedition or armed vessel from our shores

in violation of our laws would seem to be a sufficient answer. But of this aspect of the Spanish note it is not necessary to speak further now. Firm in the conviction of a wholly performed obligation, due response to this charge has been made in diplomatic course. . . .

It is honestly due to Spain and to our friendly relations with Spain that she should be given a reasonable chance to realize her expectations and to prove the asserted efficacy of the new order of things to which she stands irrevocably committed.[4]

Against the President's Position: For Recognizing Cuban Belligerency and Independence

REPRESENTATIVE JOHN WILLIAMS OF MISSISSIPPI
U.S. HOUSE OF REPRESENTATIVES
JANUARY 20, 1898

Now, I feel like giving a brief bit of history; and I want to mention a few of the rather inconsistent positions taken by the [Republican] chairman of our [foreign affairs] committee. The first was that there was no "public war" in the Island of Cuba, because all international law writers agree that wherever a state of public war exists it is a matter of right on our part and of justice to belligerents to recognize the fact, and that *the recognition of the fact of the existence of public war is a recognition of belligerency.* There is no mystery about it.

In the next breath he praised the McKinley Administration because it had stopped the "cruel warfare" that had been waged by one Weyler, and that this war was being now waged by Spain in a civilized manner. It must be, then, that this is not a public war, but just a private affair, between Cubans and Spain, touching no one else, and with which the balance of the world has nothing to do! That is not exactly the definition of "private war" in the intendment of the books on international law, but it must be in the intendment of the gentleman!

Now, the next position taken by the gentleman from Illinois is that we can not now recognize that a state of public war exists in Cuba—in other words, recognize her belligerency—because rights of belligerents would not do the Cubans any good. Shades of history, of all people who have ever rebelled against their mother countries, what an important piece of information this is! What a great pity that George Washington, Nathanael Greene, and Thomas Jefferson, during the Revolution, when seeking recognition of belligerency at the hands of the powers of Europe, did not know that recognition of belligerency was of no advantage to America!

When the gentleman comes to his third position, he enters upon a very open field of diplomacy. He throws out one of those diplomatic "hints" practiced by Lord Beaconsfield, a hint thrown out into the atmosphere. He hints that the time may come—the time may be nearer than we think—when the McKinley Administration will brace itself up, not for the purpose of recognizing the belligerency, but for the purpose of recognizing and enforcing the independence of Cuba! What a great thing a hint is when thrown out by a diplomat! Ordinarily you would believe it better that men should make plain, explicit statements, leaving as little as can be to the imagination. That is true of ordinary mortals. But when it comes to diplomats like my colleague from Mississippi [Mr. Allen], myself, and the gentleman from Illinois, we do things high-handedly by hints. If Cuba shall ever obtain freedom from the Republican Administration, I imagine she will be "hinted" into it!

Now, a little bit of history, gentlemen, for the record. A little over two years ago, in the last Congress, you told the people, and howled until you were hoarse, about the cowardice of Mr. Cleveland's Administration in not recognizing Cuban belligerency. With our aid you passed through this House a concurrent resolution favoring belligerency. In the last campaign you made the air resonant with a repetition of your war cries and appeals in behalf of "humanity and bleeding Cuba." When your convention met, you promised that you would try to give "peace and independence" to Cuba.

Now, I tell you, you are faced with a situation out of which you can not wriggle when we go before the people. Look at it! The Senate sent to the Committee on Foreign Affairs of this House a recognition of belligerency. It is sleeping there because you want it to sleep. When this bill now pending came into this House, we offered certain amendments, some recognizing belligerency and some independence. To them points of order were made by the Republican chairman of the Foreign Affairs Committee with the knowledge and approval of your Speaker and all your leaders. These amendments were perhaps obnoxious to the point of order. We will not rehash that straw. But the point of order *need* not have been raised. It *would* not have been raised, if the Republican party had been willing to help Cuba. This evening we will move to recommit with instructions, against which motion the point of order can not justly lie. There is no doubt about that. Then we will have a yea-and-nay vote in this House, I trust, and put you upon record.

Then, if the point of order is made and it is held that it lies against the motion to recommit, we will appeal from the decision of the Speaker and get a yea-and-nay vote on that.

Then we have already sent to your Foreign Affairs Committee two bills recognizing the independence of Cuba. If you do not take them up and pass them, if you do not bring them to the attention of this House, you can not go to the people afterwards and say, as so many of you have said, that while you have the warmest love for the struggling patriots and I wish to see liberty enthroned in Cuba, you have defeated our efforts in that direction because—and only because—we have not tried to consummate our aim in the right way.

Now, Mr. Chairman, I am no "jingo." I am the farthest from it. I am not arguing for Cuban annexation; this is not a question of annexation; it is a question at most of independence. . . . This is not a jingo question; it is a question of justice. All international law says that if there is a "state of public war" in the Island of Cuba to-day we have the right and we should, as a matter of justice to the Cubans, recognize the existence of that fact. The recognition of the existence of the fact is a recognition of belligerency. Nobody would have a right to complain, if in our discretion we exercised our right.[5]

NOTES

4. Israel, pp. 69–72.
5. Israel, pp. 91–94.

THE ISSUE: THE SPANISH-AMERICAN WAR

In March 1898, after the publication of the Spanish minister's letter and the explosion and sinking of the *Maine*, McKinley gave Spain an ultimatum demanding, among other things, negotiations aimed at securing independence for the Cuban people. Spain, however, proved unwilling to part with its colony. On April 11, McKinley outlined four reasons intervention against Spain and for Cuban independence was necessary: (1) the barbaric conditions and bloodshed in Cuba had to be alleviated for humanitarian reasons; (2) U.S. citizens in Cuba deserved to have their lives and property defended; (3) U.S. commerce and trade, which were hurt by the conflict, needed to be protected; and (4) the conflict threatened U.S. peace and economic security. On April 20, Congress authorized the president to use armed force to gain independence for Cuba; on April 25, Congress declared war against Spain, making the declaration retroactive (April 21) to predate Spain's April 24 declaration of war against the United States.

McKinley assumed personal control of the war effort, organizing U.S. forces and managing military movements with an eye to every detail. The conflict proved little challenge for the commander in chief, however. As one senator put it, "Was there ever before such a war with such great results, so short in duration, such wonderful results, with no reverses?"[6] The United States struck Spanish forces in Puerto Rico and the Philippines as well as Cuba. Spain had not marshaled its army or navy to fight a major power so far from its home soil. For example, it cost U.S. forces only one morning and seven wounded to destroy the Spanish fleet anchored in Manila Bay in the Philippines. When U.S. forces led by General William Shafter—including future president Teddy Roosevelt and his famous "Rough Riders" 1st Volunteer Cavalry—secured the surrender of the Spanish in the Cuban town of Santiago on July 17, the war was effectively over.

In the resulting Treaty of Paris signed in December, Spain ceded Puerto Rico, Guam, and the Philippines to the United States and recognized Cuba as independent. McKinley was thrilled with the United States' new status on the world stage; not only was the Cuban situation solved, but the United States had territories of its own like a real world power. Many in Congress and elsewhere were less thrilled, however, that the United States had become an empire with its own acquisitions of new people and places. In articles such as "The Conquest of the United States by Spain," William Graham Sumner, a U.S. sociologist and economist, argued that Spain, not the United States, had won the war, because Spain had managed to remake the United States in its own greedy, controlling, imperial image. Just as some had argued that it was incompatible for a nation built on liberty and democracy to stand idle as others fought against tyranny for their own freedom, they now argued that becoming the tyrant, however benevolent the tyranny might be, was incompatible for a nation built on a foundation such as that of the United States. The anti-imperialist argument made the vote for ratifying the Treaty of Paris very close. Had two votes changed, the treaty would have failed. McKinley's position pulled through in the eleventh hour, however, and left the United States not only a victor in war but also a new empire.

The President's Position: For Intervention

MCKINLEY'S DECISION TO WAGE WAR ON THE SPANISH EMPIRE
APRIL 11, 1898

... The forcible intervention of the United States as a neutral to stop the war, according to the large dictates of humanity and following many historical precedents where neighboring States have interfered to check the hopeless sacrifices of life by internecine conflicts beyond their borders, is justifiable on rational grounds. It involves, however, hostile constraint upon both the parties to the contest as well to enforce a truce as to guide the eventual settlement.

The grounds for such intervention may be briefly summarized as follows:

First. In the cause of humanity and to put an end to the barbarities, bloodshed, starvation, and horrible miseries now existing there, and which the parties to the conflict are either unable or unwilling to stop or mitigate. It is no answer to say this is all in another country, belonging to another nation, and is therefore none of our business. It is specially our duty, for it is right at our door.

Second. We owe it to our citizens in Cuba to afford them that protection and indemnity for life and property which no government there can or will afford, and to that end to terminate the conditions that deprive them of legal protection.

Third. The right to intervene may be justified by the very serious injury to the commerce, trade, and business of our people, and by the wanton destruction of property and devastation of the island.

Fourth, and which is of the utmost importance. The present condition of affairs in Cuba is a constant menace to our peace, and entails upon this Government an enormous expense. With such a conflict waged for years in an island so near us and with which our people have such trade and business relations; when the lives and liberty of our citizens are in constant danger and their property destroyed and themselves ruined; where our trading vessels are liable to seizure and are seized at our very door by war ships of a foreign nation, the expeditions of filibustering that we are powerless to prevent altogether, and the irritating questions and entanglements thus arising—all these and others that I need not mention, with the resulting strained relations, are a constant menace to our peace, and compel us to keep on a semiwar footing with a nation with which we are at peace.

These elements of danger and disorder already pointed out have been strikingly illustrated by a tragic event which has deeply and justly moved the American people. I have already transmitted to Congress the report of the naval court of inquiry on the destruction of the battle ship *Maine* in the harbor of Havana during the night of the 15th of February. The destruction of that noble vessel has filled the national heart with inexpressible horror. Two hundred and fifty-eight brave sailors and marines and two officers of our Navy, reposing in the fancied security of a friendly harbor, have been hurled to death, grief, and want brought to their homes, and sorrow to the nation.

The naval court of inquiry, which, it is needless to say, commands the unqualified confidence of the Government, was unanimous in its conclusion that the destruction of the *Maine* was caused by an exterior explosion, that of a submarine mine. It did not assume to place the responsibility. That remains to be fixed.

In any event the destruction of the *Maine,* by whatever exterior cause, is a patent and impressive proof of a state of things in Cuba that is intolerable. That condition is thus shown to be such that the Spanish Government can not assure safety and security to a vessel of the American Navy in the harbor of Havana on a mission of peace, and rightfully there.

Further referring in this connection to recent diplomatic correspondence, a dispatch from our minister to Spain, of the 26th ultimo, contained the statement that the Spanish minister for foreign affairs assured him positively that Spain will do all the highest honor and justice require in the matter of the *Maine*. . . .

The long trial has proved that the object for which Spain has waged the war can not be attained. The fire of insurrection may flame or may smolder with varying seasons, but it has not been and it is plain that it can not be extinguished by present methods. The only hope of relief and repose from a condition which can no longer be endured is the enforced pacification of Cuba. In the name of humanity, in the name of civilization, in behalf of endangered American interests which give us the right and the duty to speak and to act, the war in Cuba must stop.

In view of these facts and of these considerations, I ask the Congress to authorize and empower the President to take measures to secure a full and final termination of hostilities between the Government of Spain and the people of Cuba, and to secure in the island the establishment of a stable government, capable of maintaining order and observing its international obligations, insuring peace and tranquility and the security of its citizens as well as our own, and to use the military and naval forces of the United States as may be necessary for these purposes.

And in the interest of humanity and to aid in preserving the lives of the starving people of the island I recommend that the distribution of food and supplies be continued, and that an appropriation be made out of the public Treasury to supplement the charity of our citizens.

The issue is now with the Congress. It is a solemn responsibility. I have exhausted every effort to relieve the intolerable condition of affairs which is at our doors. Prepared to execute every obligation imposed upon me by the Constitution and the law, I await your action.[7]

Against the President's Position: Anti-imperialism

"THE CONQUEST OF THE UNITED STATES BY SPAIN"
(1898)
BY WILLIAM GRAHAM SUMNER

Spain was the first, for a long time the greatest, of the modern imperialist states. The United States, by its historical origin, its traditions, and its principles, is the chief representative of the revolt and reaction against that kind of state. I intend to show that, by the line of action now proposed to us, which we call expansion and imperialism, we are throwing away some of the most important elements of the American symbol and are adopting some of the most important elements of the Spanish symbol.

We have beaten Spain in a military conflict, but we are submitting to be conquered by her on the field of ideas and policies. Expansionism and imperialism are nothing but the old philosophies of national prosperity which have brought Spain to where she now is. Those philosophies appeal to national vanity and national cupidity. They are seductive, especially upon the first view and the most superficial judgment, and therefore it cannot be denied that they are very strong for popular effect.

They are delusions, and they will lead us to ruin unless we are hardheaded enough to resist them. . . .

Now what will hasten the day when our present advantages will wear out and when we shall come down to the conditions of the older and densely populated nations? The answer is: war, debt, taxation, diplomacy, a grand governmental system, pomp, glory, a big army and navy, lavish expenditures, political jobbery—in a word, imperialism.

In the old days the democratic masses of this country, who knew little about our modern doctrines of social philosophy, had a sound instinct on these matters, and it is no small ground of political disquietude to see it decline. They resisted every appeal to their vanity in the way of pomp and glory which they knew must be paid for. They dreaded a public debt . . . and went too far with these notions, but they were, at least, right, if they wanted to strengthen democracy. . . .

Expansion and imperialism are at war with the best traditions, principles, and interests of the American people . . . and they will plunge us into a network of difficult problems and political perils, which we might have avoided, while they offer us no corresponding advantage in return. . . .

And yet this scheme of a republic which our fathers formed was a glorious dream which demands more than a word of respect and affection before it passes away. Indeed, it is not fair to call it a dream or even an ideal; it was a possibility which was within our reach if we had been wise enough to grasp and hold it. . . .

There would be no armies except a militia, which would have no functions but those of police. . . . They would have no public debt. They repudiated with scorn the notion that a public debt is a public blessing; if debt was incurred in war it was to be paid in peace and not entailed on posterity. There was to be no grand diplomacy, because they intended to mind their own business and not be involved in any of the intrigues to which European statesmen were accustomed. . . .

Our fathers would have an economical government, even if grand people called it a parsimonious one, and taxes should be no greater than were absolutely necessary to pay for such a government. The citizen was to keep all the rest of his earnings and use them as he thought best for the happiness of himself and his family; he was, above all, to be insured peace and quiet while he pursued his honest industry and obeyed the laws.

No adventurous policies of conquest or ambition, such as, in the belief of our fathers, kings and nobles had forced, for their own advantage, on European states, would ever be undertaken by a free democratic republic. Therefore the citizen here would never be forced to leave his family or to give his sons to shed blood for glory and to leave widows and orphans in misery for nothing.

Justice and law were to reign in the midst of simplicity, and a government which had little to do was to offer little field for ambition. In a society where industry, frugality, and prudence were honored, it was believed that the vices of wealth would never flourish. . . .

There are people who are boasting of their patriotism, because they say that we have taken our place now amongst the nations of the earth by virtue of this war. My patriotism is of the kind which is outraged by the notion that the United States never was a great nation until in a petty three months' campaign it knocked to pieces a poor, decrepit, bankrupt old state like Spain. To hold such an opinion is to abandon all American standards, to put shame and scorn on all that our ancestors tried to build up here, and to go over to the standards of which Spain is a representative.[8]

NOTES

6. Senator Redfield Proctor, quoted in Lewis L. Gould, *The Presidency of William McKinley* (Lawrence: University Press of Kansas, 1980), p. 91.

7. Watts and Israel, pp. 191–193.

8. Future of Freedom Foundation, www.fff.org/freedom/1101i.asp (accessed November 4, 2002).

THE ISSUE: ANNEXATION OF HAWAII

The U.S. reach continued to expand across the globe. Since Hawaii's kingdom had been overthrown with U.S. help in 1893 and a republic erected in its place, the status of Hawaii with regard to the United States had been unclear. Benjamin Harrison had sought to annex Hawaii as a first step toward Hawaii statehood, but Grover Cleveland opposed this due to the unseemly and aggressive role the United States had played in Hawaii's internal politics. In short, the U.S. part played in Hawaii looked uncomfortably close to conquest in Cleveland's opinion. McKinley had no such qualms. He believed the Hawaiian people genuinely wanted statehood; moreover, he felt that the current "peculiar status" limbo Hawaii occupied posed problems for the islands' civil infrastructure. Law and order would be more easily provided for the Hawaiian people and U.S. interests in the islands, he believed, if Hawaii's status were to be clarified. With McKinley's support, Congress passed a joint annexation resolution in 1898. Hawaii became a U.S. territory the following year, and a state in 1959.

Hawaii's annexation and eventual statehood might have appeared inevitable to some, but others harbored serious concerns. Democratic representative James Hamilton Lewis of Washington articulated some of these when he spoke in the U.S. House of Representatives. First, Lewis questioned whether or not something as serious and nation changing as annexation should be decided without a better way to determine what the U.S. citizenry thought of the matter. In other words, Lewis wanted to understand public opinion on Hawaii before committing to the annexation question.

Second, Lewis questioned the pro-annexation argument that Hawaii was necessary to provide a stop for U.S. commercial traffic in the Pacific Ocean. He pointed out that the United States had managed well enough with its commercial traffic before using Hawaii as a port and base; furthermore, the United States already had secured rights to Hawaii's Pearl Harbor by treaty, so annexation was not necessary in order to have a stop in the islands. Anticipating the arguments of other anti-imperialists, Lewis also noted that no colonial power would dare to swoop in and claim Hawaii if the United States failed to annex the islands, since the expanded meaning of the Monroe Doctrine committed U.S. forces to deflect any attempt at international encroachment in the Western Hemisphere. Lewis likewise found the argument that Hawaii was necessary for U.S. military interests unconvincing. If anything, he believed that Hawaii would be a military liability. Just as Spain had found it difficult to defend possessions thousands of miles away in the Spanish-American War, he explained, the United States would find Hawaii a challenge to protect against aggressors.

Despite concern about the practical and philosophical implications of annexing Hawaii, however, the McKinley administration managed to do just that. Adding Guam, Puerto Rico, and the Philippines to the list of U.S. holdings expanded the nation's reach across the globe even further. Some argued that the methods the country used to acquire these lands, and the fact that it refused to release them to complete self-rule, meant that the United States had become the very thing it had fought against in its own War of Independence.

The President's Position: For Annexation

MCKINLEY SPEECH AT OTTUMWA, IOWA
OCTOBER 13, 1898

. . . We have been settling a great many things in the past few months. We have been settling some foreign complications. We settled the question as to whether the American flag shall float over Hawaii [great applause], and the flag is floating there to-day, in all its glory, over a happy and contented people, who wanted to be annexed to the United States because they loved our institutions. . . .[9]

MCKINLEY'S THIRD ANNUAL MESSAGE
DECEMBER 5, 1899

Some embarrassment in administration has occurred by reason of the peculiar status which the Hawaiian Islands at present occupy under the joint resolution of annexation approved July 7, 1898. While by that resolution the Republic of Hawaii as an independent nation was extinguished, its separate sovereignty destroyed, and its property and possessions vested in the United States, yet a complete establishment for its government under our system was not effected. While the municipal laws of the islands not enacted for the fulfillment of treaties and not inconsistent with the joint resolution or contrary to the Constitution of the United States or any of its treaties remain in force, yet these laws relate only to the social and internal affairs of the islands, and do not touch many subjects of importance which are of a broader national character. For example, the Hawaiian Republic was divested of all title to the public lands to settlers desiring to take up homestead sites, but is without power to give complete title in cases where lands have been entered upon under lease or other conditions which carry with them the right to the purchase, lessee, or settler to have a full title granted to him upon compliance with the conditions prescribed by law or by his particular agreement of entry.

Questions of doubt and difficulty have also arisen with reference to the collection of tonnage tax on vessels coming from Hawaiian ports; with reference to the status of Chinese in the islands, their entrance and exit therefrom; as to patents and copyrights; as to the register of vessels under the navigation laws; as to the necessity of holding elections in accordance with the provisions of the Hawaiian statutes for the choice of various officers, and as to several other matters of detail touching the interests both of the island and of the Federal Government.

By the resolution of the annexation the President was directed to appoint five commissioners to recommend to Congress such legislation concerning the islands as they should deem necessary or proper. These commissioners were duly appointed and after a careful investigation and study of the system of laws and government prevailing in the islands, and of the conditions existing there, they prepared a bill to provide a government under the title of "The Territory of Hawaii." The report of the Commission, with the bill which they prepared, was transmitted by me to Congress on December 6, 1898, but the bill still awaits final action.

The people of these islands are entitled to the benefits and privileges of our Constitution, but in the absence of any act of Congress providing for the Federal courts in the islands, and for a procedure by which appeals, writs of error, and other judicial proceedings necessary for the enforcement of civil rights may be prosecuted, they are powerless to secure their enforcement by the judgment of the courts of the United States. It is manifestly important, therefore, that an act shall be passed as speedily as possible erecting these islands into a judicial district, providing for the appointment of a judge and other proper officers and methods of procedure in appellate proceedings, and that the government of this newly acquired territory under the Federal Constitution shall be fully defined and provided for.[10]

Against the President's Position: Against Annexation

REPRESENTATIVE JAMES HAMILTON LEWIS OF WASHINGTON
U.S. HOUSE OF REPRESENTATIVES
JUNE 11, 1898

Mr Speaker: Whether it were wise, expedient, or profitable to annex Hawaii is not the subject of my observations. I have personal fears as well as my zealous hopes growing out of our action in this connection. Whatever my personal sentiments may have been previous to the Spanish-American war, before the fall of Manila, do not concern me now or interest the House. The late events have decided many questions for us. My State, her citizens, my constituents, have in various ways expressed their desires, wishes, and preferences upon the issue. Their expressions are my guide, their wishes my duty to execute, while I, as a faithful representative, must accept, as I do cheerfully, their orders and obey them. . . .

Here is where I complain. This is the subject of my plaint. It is that by the form of our organization and the plan of our form of legislation no opportunity is allowed the people to express their wishes. Whenever any questions, however important, arises within the two years between the Congressional elections, or between the Presidential elections, the Representative must enter upon conjecture, speculate upon chances.

Where is the opportunity for the wishes of the people to be expressed, their desires to be obtained? Beyond this, when the Representative does act, he may awake to discover that his act was not in accord with his constituents—was opposed to their welfare. No correction can be made. The act is complete; the evil or injury consummated. However zealous he may be to be a true and faithful Representative, however anxious never to transcend the limits of authority, he still is confused, as he has no guide or compass of direction but his last preceding platform. . . .

. . . But the annexation of Hawaii is urged, first, as a commercial necessity; that the commercial bird shall have a place midway the Pacific to rest its weary wing and take on additional supplies. The answer might be, we have progressed very well for a hundred years without these islands; but the answer is, taking the argument as sound, we already have such a place in Pearl Harbor on the islands—ours by treaty right. The bugbear that the annexationists seek to frighten us with—that if we do not annex these islands some foreign country will—is but a will-o'-the-wisp, because, under the Monroe doctrine as now enlarged and construed, we are as fully committed to resist the encroachment of any foreign country into the Western Hemisphere as if we owned the islands. But, secondly, it is urged as a military necessity, and a great deal of military authority is quoted in its support, much of it respectable and entitled to great weight, but some of it attracting attention only by reason of the high-sounding titles attached to the self-constituted Solomons.

This country has waged a number of wars successfully without these islands. Instead of being a source of strength, to own and be responsible for outlying islands 2,000 miles from our shores, it entails added responsibility and is a source of weakness, military experts to the contrary notwithstanding. This is well illustrated by the present war with Spain.

Have her islands been a source of strength or weakness to her? To ask the question suggests the negative answer to every sensible man. . . .

Spain is struggling—struggling, oh, how desperately—to hold islands thousands of miles from her shores which she has owned for many years! Shall we repeat the story? Shall we annex the Philippines and Hawaii, all thousands of miles from us? How easy, in case of war, for an enemy to attack those islands, hundreds in number, with its fleet? We might have the greatest navy in the world, but we need it all to defend our Atlantic and Pacific seacoasts, stretching thousands of miles. How easy for a foreign fleet to swoop down upon those distant possessions beyond the seas!

One of the strongest arguments in favor of the annexation of the Hawaiian islands is that being located in the Western Hemisphere we would not consent under the Monroe doctrine to allow any other country in the Eastern to annex them, and being responsible to some extent for them it might be better to annex them. This same argument, however, would apply to all the Central and South American so-called Republics, and no one has had the hardihood so far to claim they should be incorporated into our body politic. . . .

I shall vote against the pending resolutions for the annexation of Hawaii not because I can see no reason for the annexation, but because I consider the reasons against action at the present time outweigh those in favor of immediate action. This question should be postponed until this war is concluded, and the annexation of outlying islands and the embarkation upon a policy of colonial extension and expansion should be a matter of serious and careful deliberation, to be entered upon, if at all, by Congress only in time of peace and after the sense of the people is taken upon the subject.[11]

NOTES

9. William McKinley, *Speeches and Addresses of William McKinley: From March 1, 1897 to May 30, 1900* (New York: Doubleday & McClure Co., 1900), pp. 114–115.

10. Richardson, Volume XIII, pp. 6399–6400.

11. *Congressional Record: Containing the Proceedings and Debates of the Fifty-fifth Congress, Second Session*, Volume XXXI (Washington, D.C.: Government Printing Office, 1898), Appendix to the Congressional Record, pp. 531, 533.

THE ISSUE: OPEN DOOR POLICY

McKinley's expansion of the United States' influence did not stop with Hawaii, Guam, Puerto Rico, and the Philippines. Through Secretary of State John Hay, McKinley sent circular notes to Great Britain, France, Germany, Italy, Japan, and Russia articulating a new Open Door Policy, composed of two parts: the protection of equal privileges among nations trading with China, and the support of Chinese territorial and administrative integrity. The principles articulated in the Open Door notes served as the cornerstone of U.S. foreign policy in Asia for over forty years.

Since Great Britain signed two key treaties with China in 1842 and 1844, the European power had enforced a similar policy by ensuring that all countries had equal access to Chinese ports that were open to international trade. The Sino-Japanese war in 1894 and 1895 collapsed this tradition, however. European nations such as Great Britain, France, Germany, and Russia then scrambled to stake out "spheres of influence" in China, where each could claim exclusive rights to investment and significant advantages in trade. Leaders in the United States watched and worried that segmenting China into different economic parts controlled by different countries would lead to the oppression of the Chinese and the eventual division of China into multiple European colonies.

By McKinley's term, growing interest in foreign commerce led U.S. textile manufacturers to discover new markets for cotton goods in China. The president's sense of U.S. interests—in part, the desire to preserve open opportunities for U.S. commerce and, in part, the urge to cut out a position for U.S. power in China before all the other nations had staked their claim—led him to devise the Open Door Policy. Though the policy provided for free trading opportunities, it recognized the existing spheres of influence, providing that (1) each power maintain free access to a treaty port or any other vested interest in its particular sphere, (2) the Chinese government be the only power to tax trade, and (3) no nation with a sphere of influence be exempt from paying harbor dues or rail charges. Hay interpreted the responses he received to the new U.S. policy as acceptances. Over fifteen years passed before Japan became the first to violate the policy.

It seemed strange to some that the United States and other nations could devise policies for the way China should be divided and handled, considering that the decision should have been left to China itself. Anti-imperialist critics of McKinley, however, were not surprised, as they saw the Open Door Policy as simply the latest in a succession of moves to make the United States an imperial world power. This time, however, not even the name of the Monroe Doctrine could be invoked, since China could hardly have been considered the United States' "backyard." In "Jefferson versus Imperialism," William Jennings Bryan conjured up the image of Jefferson to use against McKinley, as if to remind him how far the United States had come from the beliefs of its founders to its modern age of conquest. Despite such protests, the Open Door Policy became a key feature of twentieth-century foreign relations.

The President's Position: For the Open Door Policy

MCKINLEY'S THIRD ANNUAL MESSAGE
DECEMBER 5, 1899

In view of disturbances in the populous provinces of northern China, where are many of our citizens, and of the imminence of disorder near the capital and toward the seaboard, a guard of marines was landed from the *Boston* and stationed during last winter in the legation compound at Peking. With the restoration of order this protection was withdrawn.

The interests of our citizens in that vast Empire have not been neglected during the past year. Adequate protection has been secured for our missionaries and some injuries to their property have been redressed.

American capital has sought and found various opportunities of competing to carry out the internal improvements which the Imperial Government is wisely encouraging, and to develop the natural resources of the Empire. Our trade with China has continued to grow, and our commercial rights under existing treaties have been everywhere maintained during the past year, as they will be in the future.

The extension of the area open to international foreign settlement at Shanghai and the opening of the ports of Nanking, Tsing-tao (Kiao chao), and Ta-lien-wan to foreign trade and settlement will doubtless afford American enterprise additional facilities and new fields, of which it will not be slow to take advantage.

In my message to Congress of December 5, 1898, I urged that the recommendation which had been made to the Speaker of the House of Representatives by the Secretary of the Treasury on the 14th of June, 1898, for an appropriation for a commission to study the commercial and industrial conditions in the Chinese Empire and report as to the opportunities for, and obstacles to, the enlargement of markets in China for the raw products and manufactures of the United States, should receive at your hands the consideration which its importance and timeliness merited, but the Congress failed to take action.

I now renew this recommendation, as the importance of the subject has steadily grown since it was first submitted to you, and no time should be lost in studying for ourselves the resources of this great field for American trade and enterprise. . . .

In this age of keen rivalry among nations for mastery in commerce, the doctrine of evolution and the rule of the survival of the fittest must be as inexorable in their operation as they are positive in the results they bring about. The place won in the struggle by an industrial people can only be held by unrelaxed endeavor and constant advance in achievement. The present extraordinary impetus in every line in American exportation and the astounding increase in the volume and value of our share in the world's markets may not be attributed to accidental conditions.

The reasons are not far to seek. They lie deep in our national character and find expression year by year in every branch of handicraft, in every new device whereby the materials we so abundantly produce are subdued to the artisan's will and made to yield the largest, most practical, and most beneficial return. The American exhibit at [next year's World's Exposition in] Paris should, and I am confident will, be an open volume, whose lessons of skillfully directed endeavor, unfaltering energy, and consummate performance may be read by all on every page, thus spreading abroad a clearer knowledge of the worth of our productions and the justice of our claim to an important place in the marts of the world.[12]

Against the President's Position: Anti-imperialism

"JEFFERSON VERSUS IMPERIALISM"
BY WILLIAM JENNINGS BRYAN
NEW YORK JOURNAL, DECEMBER 25, 1898

The advocates of imperialism have sought to support their position by appealing to the authority of Jefferson. Of all the statesmen who have ever lived, Jefferson was the one most hostile to the doctrines embodied in the demand for a European colonial policy.

Imperialism as it now presents itself embraces four distinct propositions:

1. That the acquisition of territory by conquest is right.
2. That the acquisition of remote territory is desirable.
3. That the doctrine that governments derive their just powers from the consent of the governed is unsound.
4. That people can be wisely governed by aliens.

To all these propositions Jefferson was emphatically opposed. In a letter to William Short, written in 1791, he said:

"If there be one principle more deeply written than any other in the mind of every American, it is that we should have nothing to do with conquest."

Could he be more explicit? Here we have a clear and strong denunciation of the doctrine that territory should be acquired by force. If it is said that we have outgrown the ideas of the fathers, it may be observed that the doctrine laid down by Jefferson was reiterated only a few years ago by no less a Republican than James G. Blaine. All remember the enthusiasm with which he entered into the work of bringing the republics of North and South America into close and cordial relations; some, however may have forgotten the resolutions introduced by him at the conference held in 1890, and approved by the commissioners present. They are as follows:

"First—That the principle of conquest, shall not, during the continuance of the treaty of arbitration, be recognized as admissible under American public law.

"Second—That all cessions of territory made during the continuance of the treaty of arbitration, shall be void if made under threats of war or in the presence of an armed force.

"Third—Any nation from which such cessions shall be exacted may demand that the validity of the cessions so made shall be submitted to arbitration.

"Fourth—Any renunciation of the right to arbitration made under the conditions named in the second section shall be null and void."

If the principle of conquest is right, why should it be denied a place in American public law? So objectionable is the theory of acquisition of territory by conquest that the nation which suffers such injustice can, according to the resolutions, recover by arbitration the land ceded in the presence of an armed force. So abhorrent is it, that a waiver of arbitration, made under such circumstances, is null and void. While the resolutions were only for the consideration of the American republics, the principle therein stated cannot be limited by latitude or longitude . . .

Jefferson has been called an expansionist, but our opponents will search in vain for a single instance where he advocated the acquisition of remote territory. . . . Thinking that some one might use the annexation of Cuba as a precedent for indefinite expansion, he said in a letter to President Madison, dated April 27, 1809:

"I would immediately erect a column on the southernmost limit of Cuba, and inscribe on it a ne plus ultra as to us in that direction."

It may be argued that Jefferson was wrong in asserting that we should confine our possessions to the North American continent, but certainly no one can truthfully quote him as an authority for excursions into the eastern hemisphere. If he was unwilling to go farther south than Cuba, even in the western hemisphere, would he be likely to look with favor upon colonies in the Orient?

If the authority of Jefferson cannot be invoked to support the acquisition of remote territory, much less can his great name be used to excuse a colonial policy which denies to the people the right to govern themselves. When he suggested an inscription for his monument he did not enumerate the honors which he had received, though no American had been more highly honored; he only asked to be remembered for what he had done, and he named the writing of the Declaration of Independence as the greatest of his deeds. In that memorable document he declared it a self-evident truth that governments derive their just powers from the consent of the governed. The defense and development of that doctrine was his special care. His writings abound with expressions showing his devotion to that doctrine and his solicitude for it. He preached it in the enthusiasm of his youth; he reiterated it when he reached the age of maturity; he crowned it with benedictions in his old age. Who will say that, if living, he would jeopardize it today by engrafting upon it the doctrine of government by external force?

Upon the fourth proposition Jefferson is no less explicit. Now, when some are suggesting the wisdom of a military government for the Philippines, or a colonial system such as England administers in India, it will not be out of place to refer to the manner in which Jefferson viewed the inability of aliens to prescribe laws and administer government. In 1817 a French society was formed for the purpose of settling upon a tract of land near the Tombigbee river. Jefferson was invited to formulate laws and regulations for the society. On the 16th of January of that year he wrote from Monticello expressing his high appreciation of the confidence expressed in him, but declining to undertake the task. The reasons he gave are well worth considering at this time. After wishing them great happiness in their undertaking he said.

> "The laws, however, which must effect this must flow from their own habits, their own feelings, and the resources of their own minds. No stranger to these could possibly propose regulations adapted to them. Every people have their own particular habits, ways of thinking, manners, etc., which have grown up with them from their infancy, are become a part of their nature, and to which the regulations which are to make them happy must be accommodated. No member of a foreign country can have a sufficient sympathy with these."

The alien may possess greater intelligence and greater strength, but he lacks the sympathy for, and the identification with, the people. We have only to recall the grievances enumerated in the Declaration of Independence to learn how an ocean may dilute justice and how the cry of the oppressed can be silenced by distance. And yet the inhabitants of the colonies were the descendants of Englishmen—blood of their blood and bone of their bone. Shall we be more considerate of subjects farther away from us, and differing from us in color, race and tongue, than the English were of their own offspring?[13]

NOTES

12. Richardson, Volume XIII, pp. 6367–6368.

13. Anti-imperialism in the United States, 1898–1935, www.boondocksnet. com/ai/ailtexts/bryan981225.html (accessed November 22, 2002).

THE ISSUE: THE PHILIPPINES

When the Treaty of Paris ended war with Spain in 1898, one of its provisions required Spain to cede its colony of the Philippines to the

United States. McKinley made it clear that the United States intended to administer the Philippines with an eye to the natives' best interests. The key word in McKinley's policy was "administer." The United States refused to consider or discuss Filipino independence. While the United States had battled Spain, Filipinos had declared independence, called a constitutional congress, devised a constitution, and elected a president. McKinley ignored these developments. Certainly racial and ethnic bias figured into the U.S. conviction that the Filipinos could not govern themselves. Also present, though, was a keen sense of the potential benefits the Philippines might bring to the United States.

Though McKinley insisted in his rhetoric that the transfer of sovereignty over the Philippines to the United States was the best thing for the Philippines and was actually desired by its people, this was not so. Filipino nationals had rejected Spanish control of the Pacific Ocean islands, and thus they rejected U.S. claims to domination, as well. In fact, McKinley sent Cornell University president Jacob J. Shurman to lead a five-man fact-finding mission to the Philippines in 1899, and the resulting report explained that the Filipinos wanted independence. U.S. policy, however, did not change, making conflict inevitable. For two years the United States fought a violent conflict against the Filipino Revolution and its goal of self-rule. Eventually the United States succeeded in crushing opposition to its control. By 1901, the second committee sent by McKinley, this one headed by future president William Howard Taft, had established a government for the Philippines. The islands did not gain independence until 1946.

Though McKinley's policy won the day and took the United States another step toward being an empire, it was not without its critics. One such opponent was the well-known U.S. sociologist and economist William Graham Sumner, best known for applying Darwinist theories of evolution to the social sciences. In "On Empire and the Philippines," Sumner mocked the conceit he saw in the U.S. belief that it knew better what was good for the Philippines than the Filipinos knew themselves. He questioned how the United States could fight against Spain and what it had done as an imperial aggressor, only to do the same thing Spain had done itself when given the opportunity. In particular, he attacked the form of self-delusion that allowed the United States to assume that its way was in fact the only way, and of course all other peoples would be happy and eager to adopt its way. Sumner feared what he saw the United States becoming. Not only did he worry for what the schizophrenic clash between democracy and imperialism would do to the

United States, but he also was concerned what the United States, while working through that tension, would do to the rest of the world.

McKinley was proud at the U.S. expansion wrought in his first term. Indeed, the new U.S. international presence and foreign policy lasted well into the twentieth century. McKinley did not have the opportunity to consider further U.S. opportunities on the global stage, however; after a successful reelection buoyed by popular satisfaction with the Spanish-American War victory and its aftermath, McKinley was assassinated by an anarchist gunman in 1901.

The President's Position: For the U.S. Administration of the Philippines

MCKINLEY'S THIRD ANNUAL MESSAGE
DECEMBER 5, 1899

On the 10th of December, 1898, the treaty of peace between the United States and Spain was signed. It provided, among other things, that Spain should cede to the United States the archipelago known as the Philippine Islands, that the United States should pay to Spain the sum of twenty millions of dollars, and that the civil rights and political status of the native inhabitants of the territories thus ceded to the United States should be determined by the Congress. The treaty was ratified by the Senate on the 6th of February, 1899, and by the Government of Spain on the 19th of March following. The ratifications were exchanged on the 11th of April and the treaty publicly proclaimed. On the 2d of March the Congress voted the sum contemplated by the treaty, and the amount was paid over to the Spanish Government on the 1st of May.

In this manner the Philippines came to the United States. The islands were ceded by the Government of Spain, which had been in undisputed possession of them for centuries. They were accepted not merely by our authorized commissioners in Paris, under the direction of the Executive, but by the constitutional and well-considered action of the representatives of the people of the United States in both Houses of Congress. I had every reason to believe, and I still believe that this transfer of sovereignty was in accordance with the wishes and the aspirations of the great mass of the Filipino people.

From the earliest moment no opportunity was lost of assuring the people of the islands of our ardent desire for their welfare and of the intention of this Government to do everything possible to advance their interests. In my order of the 19th of May, 1898, the commander of the military expedition dispatched to the Philippines was instructed to declare that we came not to make war upon the people of that country, "nor upon any party or faction among them, but to protect them in their homes, in their employments, and in their personal and religious rights." That there should be no doubt as to the paramount authority there, on the 17th of August it was directed that "there must be no joint occupation with the insurgents"; that the United States must preserve the peace and protect persons and property within the territory occupied by their military and naval forces; that the insurgents and all others must recognize the military occupation and authority of the United States. As early as December 4, before the cession, and in anticipation of that event, the commander in Manila was urged to restore peace and tranquility and to undertake the establishment of a beneficent government, which should afford the fullest security for life and property. . . .

But before their [the presidentially appointed commissioners'] arrival at Manila the sinister ambition of a few leaders of the Filipinos had created a situation full of embarrassment for us and most grievous in its consequences to themselves. The clear and impartial preliminary report of the Commissioners, which I transmit herewith, gives so lucid and comprehensive a history of the present insurrectionary movement that the story need not be here repeated. It is enough to say that the claim of the rebel leader that he was promised independence by an officer of the United States in return for his assistance has no foundation in fact and is categorically denied by the very witnesses who were called to prove it. The most the insurgent leader hoped for when he came back to Manila was the liberation of the islands from the Spanish control, which they had been laboring for years without success to throw off.

The prompt accomplishment of this work by the American Army and Navy gave him other ideas and ambitions, and insidious suggestions from various quarters perverted the purposes and intentions with which he had taken up arms. No sooner had our army captured Manila than the Filipino forces began to assume an attitude of suspicion and hostility which the utmost efforts of our officers and troops were unable to disarm or modify. Their kindness and forbearance were taken as proof of cowardice. The aggressions of the Filipinos continually increased until finally, just before the time set by the Senate of the United States for a vote upon the treaty, an attack, evidently prepared in advance, was made all along the American lines, which resulted in a terribly destructive and sanguinary repulse of the insurgents. . . .

This was the unhappy condition of affairs which confronted our Commissioners on their arrival in Manila. They had come with the hope and intention of co-operating with Admiral Dewey and Major-General Otis in establishing peace and order in the archipelago and the largest measure of self-government compatible with the true welfare of the people. What they actually found can best be set forth in their own words: "Deplorable as war is, the one in which we are now engaged was unavoidable by us. We were attacked by a bold, adventurous, and enthusiastic army. . . . "

The course thus clearly indicated has been unflinchingly pursued. The rebellion must be put down. Civil government cannot be thoroughly established until order is restored. With a devotion and gallantry worthy of its most brilliant history, the Army, ably and loyally assisted by the Navy, has carried on this unwelcome but most righteous campaign with richly deserved success. The noble self-sacrifice with which our soldiers and sailors whose terms of service had expired refused to avail themselves of their right to return home as long as they were needed at the front forms one of the brightest pages in our annals. Although their operations have been somewhat interrupted and checked by a rainy season of unusual violence and duration, they have gained ground steadily in every direction, and now look forward confidently to a speedy completion of their task.[14]

Against the President's Position: Against U.S. Administration of the Philippines

WILLIAM GRAHAM SUMNER
"ON EMPIRE AND THE PHILIPPINES" (1898)

There is not a civilized nation that does not talk about its civilizing mission just as grandly as we do. The English, who really have more to boast of it in this respect than anybody else, talk least about it, but the Phariseeism with which they correct and instruct other people has made them hated all over the globe. The French believe themselves the guardians of the highest and purest culture, and that the eyes of all mankind are fixed on Paris, whence they expect oracles of thought and taste. The

Germans regard themselves as charged with a mission, especially to us Americans, to save us from egoism and materialism. The Russians, in their books and newspapers, talk about the civilizing mission of Russian in language that might be translated from some of the finest paragraphs of our imperialistic newspapers.

The first principle of Mohammedanism is that we Christians are dogs and infidels, fit only to be enslaved or butchered by Moslems. It is a corollary that wherever Mohammedanism extends it carries, in the belief of its votaries, the highest blessings, and that the whole human race would be enormously elevated if Mohammedanism should supplant Christianity everywhere.

To come, last, to Spain, the Spaniards have, for centuries, considered themselves the most zealous and self-sacrificing Christians, especially charged by the Almighty, on this account, to spread the true religion and civilization over the globe. They think themselves free and noble, leaders in refinement and the sentiments of personal honor, and they despise us as sordid money-grabbers and heretics. I could bring you passages from peninsular authors of the first rank about the grand role of Spain and Portugal in spreading freedom and truth.

Now each nation laughs at all the others when it observes these man-ifestations of national vanity. You may rely upon it that they are all ridiculous by virtue of these pretensions, including ourselves. The point is that each of them repudiates the standards of the others, and the out-lying nations, which are to be civilized, hate all the standards of civilized men.

We assume that what we like and practice, and what we think better, must come as a welcome blessing to Spanish-Americans and Filipinos. This is grossly and obviously untrue. They hate our ways. They are hos-tile to our ideas. Our religion, language, institutions, and manners offend them. They like their own ways, and if we appear amongst them as rulers, there will be social discord in all the great departments of social interest. The most important thing which we shall inherit from the Span-iards will be the task of suppressing rebellions.

If the United States takes out of the hands of Spain her mission, on the ground that Spain is not executing it well, and if this nation in its turn attempts to be schoolmistress to others, it will shrivel up into the same vanity and self-conceit of which Spain now presents an example. To read our current literature one would think that we were already well on the way to it.

Now, the great reason why all these enterprises which begin by saying to somebody else, "We know what is good for you better than you know yourself and we are going to make you do it," are false and wrong is that they violate liberty; or, to turn the same statement into other words, the reason why liberty, of which we Americans talk so much, is a good thing is that it means leaving people to live out their own lives in their own way, while we do the same.

If we believe in liberty, as an American principle, why do we not stand by it? Why are we going to throw it away to enter upon a Spanish policy of dominion and regulation?[15]

NOTES

14. Richardson, Volume XIII, pp. 6391–6394.
15. Addison Wesley Longman, http://occawlonline.pearsoned.com/book bind/pubbooks/nash5e_awl/medialib/timeline/docs/sources/theme_primary sources_Military_2_5.html (accessed November 4, 2002).

RECOMMENDED READINGS

Brooks, Stewart M. *Our Murdered Presidents: The Medical Story*. New York: F. Fell, 1966.

Dobson, John M. *Reticent Expansionism: The Foreign Policy of William Mc-Kinley*. Pittsburgh: Dusquesne University Press, 1988.

Glad, Paul W. *McKinley, Bryan, and the People*. Philadelphia: Lippincott, 1964.

Gould, Lewis L. *The Presidency of William McKinley*. Lawrence: University Press of Kansas, 1980.

McKinley, William. *Speeches and Addresses of William McKinley: From March 1, 1897 to May 30, 1900*. New York: Doubleday & McClure Co., 1900.

Morgan, H. Wayne. *William McKinley and His America*. Syracuse, NY: Syracuse University Press, 1963.

Olcott, Charles S. *William McKinley*. New York: AMS Press, 1972.

Sposato, Jeffrey S. *William Thomas McKinley: A Bio-Bibliography*. Westport, CT: Greenwood Press, 1995.

BIBLIOGRAPHY

"Benjamin Harrison's Inaugural Address." *Inaugural Addresses of the Presidents*. The Avalon Project at Yale Law School.www.yale.edu/lawweb/avalon/presiden/inaug/harris.htm (accessed November 5, 2002).

Borden, Morton, ed. *America's Ten Greatest Presidents*. Chicago: Rand McNally, 1961.

Bryan, William Jennings. "America's Mission." *Anti-imperialism in the United States, 1898–1935*. www.boondocksnet.com/ai/ailtexts/bryan990222.html (accessed November 22, 2002).

———. "Jefferson versus Imperialism." *Anti-imperialism in the United States, 1898–1935*. www.boondocksnet.com/ai/ailtexts/bryan 981225.html (accessed November 22, 2002).

———. "The North American Review." http://cdl.library.cornell.edu/cgi-bin/moa/moa-cgi?notisid\BQ7578–0157–64 (accessed November 22, 2002).

Carnegie, Andrew. "Wealth." www.fordham.edu/halsall/mod/1889carnegie.html (accessed November 22, 2002).

Chief Joseph at his surrender in the Bear Paw Mountains, 1877. http://dkoch332.tripod.com/QuotesHTML/wisdom.htm (accessed November 22, 2002).

Congressional Record, Containing the Proceedings and Debates of the Forty-fourth Congress, First Session. Volume V, Part I; Volume V, Part III; Volume VII. Washington, D.C.: Government Printing Office, 1876.

Congressional Record, Containing the Proceedings and Debates of the Forty-fourth Congress, Second Session. Volume VII, Volume IX, Volume X. Washington, D.C.: Government Printing Office, 1878.

Congressional Record, Containing the Proceedings and Debates of the Forty-seventh Congress, First Session. Volume XIII. Washington, D.C.: Government Printing Office, 1882.

Congressional Record, Containing the Proceedings and Debates of the Forty-seventh Congress, Second Session. Volume XIII. Washington, D.C.: Government Printing Office, 1882.

Congressional Record, Containing the Proceedings and Debates of the Fiftieth Congress, First Session. Volume XIX, Part I. Washington, D.C.: Government Printing Office, 1888.

Congressional Record: Containing the Proceedings and Debates of the Fifty-fifth Congress, Second Session. Volume XXXI. Washington, D.C.: Government Printing Office, 1898.

Conkling, Alfred R. *The Life and Letters of Roscoe Conkling: Orator, Statesman, Advocate.* New York: Charles L. Webster and Company, 1889.

"The Dawes Act." www-personal.umich.edu/jamarcus/dawes.html (accessed November 11, 2002).

"The Dawes Severalty Act." *Statutes of the United States Concerning Native Americans.* The Avalon Project at Yale Law School. www.yale.edu/lawweb/avalon/statutes/native/dawes.htm (accessed November 11, 2002).

Debs, Eugene V. "Labor Omnia Vincit." In *Writings and Speeches of Eugene V. Debs.* New York: Hermitage Press, 1948.

Doenecke, Justus D. *The Presidencies of James A. Garfield and Chester A. Arthur.* Lawrence: University Press of Kansas, 1981.

Du Bois, W. E. B. "Strivings of the Negro People." http://eserver.org/race/strivings.txt (accessed November 22, 2002).

Emery, Sarah E. V. "Demonetization of Silver." In George Brown Tindall, ed. *A Populist Reader: Selections from the Works of American Populist Leaders,* pp. 52–59. New York: Harper & Row, 1966.

The Fieldston School United States History Survey. www.pinzler.com/ushistory/dawesactsupp.html (accessed November 11, 2002).

Garfield, James A. *The Diary of James A. Garfield.* Volume IV: 1878–1881. Harry James Brown and Frederick D. Williams, eds. Detroit: Michigan State University Press, 1981.

Gould, Lewis L. *The Presidency of William McKinley.* Lawrence: University Press of Kansas, 1980.

Greenback-Labor Party Platform 1880. www.geocities.com/CollegePark/
    Quad/6460/doct/880glp.html (accessed November 22, 2002).
"Grover Cleveland's First Inaugural Address." *Inaugural Addresses of the
    Presidents.* The Avalon Project at Yale Law School. www.yale.
    edu/lawweb/avalon/presiden/inaug/cleve1.htm (accessed No-
    vember 5, 2002).
Harrison, Benjamin. *Public Papers and Addresses of Benjamin Harrison,
    Twenty-third President of the United States: March 4, 1889, to March
    4, 1893.* Washington, D.C.: Government Printing Office, 1893.
Harvey, William H. "Coin's Financial School." In George Brown Tindall,
    ed. *A Populist Reader: Selections from the Works of American Populist
    Leaders,* pp. 129–147. New York: Harper & Row, 1966.
Hayes, Rutherford B. *Hayes: The Diary of a President, 1875–1881.* T. Harry
    Williams, ed. New York: David McKay Company, Inc., 1964.
Hoogenbloom, Ari. *The Presidency of Rutherford B. Hayes.* Lawrence: Uni-
    versity Press of Kansas, 1988.
Israel, Fred L., ed. *Major Presidential Decisions.* New York: Chelsea House,
    1980.
"James A. Garfield's Inaugural Address." *Inaugural Addresses of the Pres-
    idents.* The Avalon Project at Yale Law School. www.yale.edu/
    lawweb/avalon/presiden/inaug/garfield.htm (accessed Novem-
    ber 5, 2002).
Macune, C. W. "Report of the Committee on the Monetary System." In
    George Brown Tindall, ed. *A Populist Reader: Selections from the
    Works of American Populist Leaders,* pp. 80–87. New York: Harper
    & Row, 1966.
McKinley, William. *Speeches and Addresses of William McKinley: From
    March 1, 1897 to May 30, 1900.* New York: Doubleday & McClure
    Co., 1900.
Noce, Jamie E., and Matthew Miskelly, eds. *Political Theories for Students.*
    Detroit: The Gale Group, Inc., 2002.
"President Cleveland's Message." The Hawaiian Sovereignty Movement.
    www.hookele.com/non-hawaiians/cleveland.html (accessed No-
    vember 22, 2002).
Richardson, James D., ed. *A Compilation of the Messages and Papers of the
    Presidents.* Volumes X, XI, XIII. New York: Bureau of National
    Literature, Inc., 1897.
"Rutherford B. Hayes' Inaugural Address." *Inaugural Addresses of the
    Presidents.* The Avalon Project at Yale Law School. www.yale.

edu/lawweb/avalon/presiden/inaug/hayes.htm (accessed November 5, 2002).

Socolofsky, Homer E., and Allan B. Spetter. *The Presidency of Benjamin
  Harrison.* Lawrence: University Press of Kansas, 1987.

Spooner, Lysander. "Gold and Silver as Standards of Value: The Flagrant
  Cheat in Regard to Them." www.lysanderspooner.org/
  goldandsilver.htm (accessed November 22, 2002).

———. "A Letter to Grover Cleveland on His False Inaugural Address,
  the Usurpations and Crimes of Lawmakers and Judges, and the
  Consequent Poverty, Ignorance, and Servitude of the People."
  www.lysanderspooner.org/bib_new.htm (accessed November 4,
  2002).

"Statement of Queen Lili'uokalani." The Hawaiian Sovereignty Movement. www.hookele.com/non-hawaiians/chapter3.html (accessed
  November 22, 2002).

Sumner, William Graham. "The Conquest of the United States by Spain."
  The Future of Freedom Foundation. www.fff.org/freedom/1101i.
  asp (accessed November 4, 2002).

———. "On Empire and the Philippines." Addison Wesley Longman.
  http://occawlonline.pearsoned.com/bookbind/pubbooks/nash5e
  _awl/medialib/timeline/docs/sources/theme (accessed Novem-
  ber 4, 2002).

Watts, J. F., and Fred L. Israel, eds. *Presidential Documents: The Speeches,
  Proclamations, and Policies That Have Shaped the Nation from Washington to Clinton.* New York: Routledge, 2000.

Welch, Richard E., Jr. *The Presidencies of Grover Cleveland.* Lawrence: University Press of Kansas, 1988.

"William Jennings Bryan's 'Cross of Gold' Speech." Douglass: Archives
  of American Public Address, http://douglass.speech.nwu.edu/
  brya_a26.htm (accessed November 4, 2002).

INDEX